Oliver Spencer Halsted

The Book Called Job

From the Hebrew with Foot Notes

Oliver Spencer Halsted

The Book Called Job
From the Hebrew with Foot Notes

ISBN/EAN: 9783337417352

Printed in Europe, USA, Canada, Australia, Japan

Cover: Foto ©Thomas Meinert / pixelio.de

More available books at **www.hansebooks.com**

THE BOOK CALLED JOB.

FROM THE HEBREW.

WITH FOOT NOTES.

BY

OLIVER S. HALSTED,

EX-CHANCELLOR OF THE STATE OF NEW JERSEY.

PUBLISHED BY THE AUTHOR, LYON'S FARMS, NEW JERSEY,
SEPTEMBER, 1875.

PRINTED BY JENNINGS & HARDHAM,
NEWARK, N. J.

Entered according to Act of Congress, in the year 1875, by
OLIVER S. HALSTED,
in the office of the Librarian of Congress at Washington.

PREFACE.

Of late years a new translation of the Scriptures from the Originals has been loudly called for: that is, a translation irrespective of our present English versions—the Douay, and Rheims Roman Catholic English versions, and of our authorized English version called the King James version. No such work has yet appeared.

Having been engaged near twenty years, since I left office, in the study of the Scriptures in the languages in which they were written, and published a work a result of such study, I have prepared a translation of the Hebrew of the Book called Job into English.

To show the variant renderings of some passages, the Roman Catholic Douay English of them, and the Diodati Italian of them rendered into English, are given in notes at the foot of the page; also the English of many passages, or parts of verses, as given in Gesenius's Hebrew and English Lexicon, the best beyond comparison; also in some passages, the English of them as given in the version of the Book of Job by George R. Noyes, the title page of which is: "A new translation of the Book of Job, with an Introduction, and notes chiefly explanatory;" also in some passages, the English of them as given in the version of Job published by the "American Bible Union," the title page of which is: "The Book of Job. From the original Hebrew on the basis of the Common and earlier English versions." A copy of which latter work was sent to me by a clergyman.

The design of the writer of the Book of Job is well illustrated in an able Article upon it by "James Anthony Froude, M.A., Late Fellow of Exeter College, Oxford," in his "Short Studies on Great Subjects."

He says: It is the most difficult of all the Hebrew compositions, many words occurring in it, and many thoughts, not to be found elewhere in the Bible. That there are many mythical and physical allusions scattered over the poem, which, in the sixteenth century there were positively no means of understanding, and perhaps, too, says he, there were mental tendencies in the translators themselves, which prevented them from adequately apprehending even the drift and spirit of the composition.

He says: How it found its way into the canon, smiting as it does through and through the most deeply seated Jewish prejudices, is the chief difficulty about it now; to be explained only by a traditional acceptance among the sacred books dated back from the old times of the national greatness.

That its authorship, its date, and its history, are alike a mystery to us. That it existed when the canon was composed; and that this is all we know beyond what we can gather out of the language and contents of the poem itself.

He then says: The earliest phenomenon likely to be observed connected with the moral government of the world is the general one, that on the whole, as things are constituted, good men prosper and are happy; bad men fail and are miserable. That the sun should shine alike on the evil and the good was a creed too high for the early divines, or that the victims of a fallen tower were no greater offenders than their neighbors. The God of this world was just and righteous, and temporal prosperity or wretchedness were dealt out by him immediately, by his own will, to his subjects, according to their behavior. That this theory was and is the central idea of the Jewish polity; and that it lingers among ourselves in our liturgy and in the popular belief.

He says: Utterly different both in character and in the lessons it teaches is the book of Job, the language impregnated with strange idioms and strange allusions, un-Jewish in form, and in fiercest hostility with Judaism, it hovers like a meteor over the old Jewish literature, in it, but not of it, compelling the acknowledgment of itself by its own internal majesty, yet exerting no influence over the minds of the people, never alluded to, and scarcely ever quoted, till at last the light which it had heralded rose up full over the world in Christianity.

That though unquestionably of Hebrew origin, the poem bears no analogy to any of the other books in the Bible; while of its external history nothing is known at all, except that it was received into the canon at the time of the great synagogue.

That, the more it is studied, the more the conclusion forces itself upon us that, let the writer have lived when he would, in his struggle with the central falsehood of his own people's creed, he must have divorced himself from them outwardly, as well as inwardly; that he traveled away into the world, and lived long, perhaps all his matured life, in exile.

That the hero of the poem [i. e., the character called Job in the drama, —Heb. *aiub*—a man persecuted, says Gesenius,] is of a strange land and parentage—a Gentile, certainly, not a Jew.

That the life, the manners, the customs, are of all varieties and places. That there is no mention, or hint of mention, throughout the poem, of Jewish traditions or Jewish certainties.

Again, says Froude: The God of the writer is not the God of Israel, but the Father of mankind. That we hear nothing of a chosen people, nothing of a special revelation, nothing of peculiar privileges; and in the court of heaven, says the writer, there is a Satan, not the prince of this world and the enemy of God, but the angel [i. e., messenger] of judgment, the accuser, whose mission was to walk to and fro over the earth, and carry up to heaven an account of the sins of mankind.

Froude further says: In this, if anywhere, we have the record of some man much traveled, but that the scenes, the names, and the incidents are all contrived to baffle curiosity—as if, in the very form of the poem, to teach us that it is no story of a single thing which happened once, but that it belongs to humanity itself, and is the drama of the trial of man.

That, setting the characteristics of his daily life by the side of his unaffected piety, we have a picture of the best man who could then be conceived, and to whom, that no room might be left for any Calvinistic falsehood, God himself bears the emphatic testimony, that there was none like him upon the earth, a perfect and upright man, who feared God and eschewed evil.

That if such a person as this, therefore, could be made miserable, necessarily the current belief of the Jews was false to the root; and tradition furnished the fact that he had been visited by every worst calamity. How was it then to be accounted for? Out of a thousand possible explanations the poet introduces a single one. He admits us behind the veil which covers the ways of Providence, and we hear the accusing angel [messenger] charging Job with an interested piety: "Job does not serve God for nought."

That his friends see in his misery only a fatal evidence against him. Such calamities could not have befallen a man, the justice [*justness* is the Scripture meaning] of God would not have permitted it unless they had been deserved.

That the burden of the drama is not that we do, but that we do not, and cannot, know the mystery of the government of the world—that it is not for man to seek it, or for God to reveal it.

The poet, indeed, (says Froude,) restores Job in the book; but that in life it need not have been so. He might have died upon his ash-heap.

Such, says Froude, in outline is this wonderful poem. With the material of which it is woven we have not here been concerned, although it is so rich and pregnant that we might with little difficulty construct out of it a complete picture of the world as it then was: its life, knowledge, arts, habits, superstitions, hopes, and fears.

That the subject is the problem of all mankind, and the composition embraces no less wide a range. But what we are here most interested upon is the epoch which it marks in the progress of mankind, as the first recorded struggle of a new experience with an established orthodox belief. True, for hundreds of years, perhaps for a thousand, the superstition against which it was directed continued. That when Christ came it was still in its vitality. Nay, it is alive, or in a sort of mock life, among us at this very day. But that even those who retained their imperfect belief had received into their canon a book which treated it with contumely and scorn; so irresistible was the majesty of truth.

Froude says: If we ask ourselves, what, in all the thousands upon thousands of sermons, and theologies, and philosophies, with which Europe has been deluged, has been gained for mankind beyond what we have found in this Book of Job, it is hard, or rather, (says he,) it is easy to answer.

He further says: While, however, God does not condescend to justify his ways to man, He gives judgment on the controversy [between Job and his friends.] That the self-constituted pleaders for him [God] were all wrong; and Job—the passionate, vehement, scornful Job—he had spoken the truth; he at least had spoken facts, and they had been defending a transient theory as an everlasting truth. He refers to verses 7, 8, of the last chapter, for the reward of Job's constancy in integrity.

This synopsis of Froude's article on Job will, we think, strengthen men's desire to know what the Hebrew of the Book "really does say;" what the system taught in the original of it really is. Froude does not go to the original of it, nor give any particular account of its doctrine. His quotations are from the E. V.

At page 241 he says: Will you quote the weary proverb? Will you say that "God layeth up his iniquity for his children?" He says: Our translators have wholly lost the sense of this passage, and endeavor to make Job acknowledge what he is steadfastly denying.

The passage as he gives it is quoted from the E. V of Job 21:19, and is taken from the Douay of the verse: see the true rendering of it given in its place in this book.

Of the Book of Job Froude says: "a book of which it is to say little to call it unequaled of its kind, and which will one day, perhaps, when it is allowed to stand on its own merits, be seen towering up alone, far away above all the poetry of the world."

I have been asked if there is much difference between a translation of the Hebrew of Job into English and our authorized English version of it. The translation here given, with the notes, will be a satisfactory answer: I suggest a few considerations. The book called Job is the oldest Book of the Scriptures. It existed untold centuries before what is known as, and called, the "Apostasy," (i. e., the departure from the faith,) by which name Protestantism designates the Roman Catholic system.

The early Christians had no Scriptures but Job and the other Old Testament writings. And Christ and his apostles and disciples had no other Scriptures.

The doctrines and faith of the early Christians were the doctrines and faith taught by the Scriptures they had.

"Apostasy," therefore, to be a departure from the faith, was necessarily a departure from the faith of the early Christians,—from primitive Christianity.

And the earliest translations of the originals of the Old and New Testaments into English were publicly burned, and their authors suffered martyrdom at the hands of the "Apostasy"—the power that departed from the faith. And our authorized version—called the King James version, differs materially and fundamentally from the first English translations.

It follows, that the doctrine and faith taught in Job differ from those taught by the "Apostasy" as far as the "Apostasy" is a departure from the faith of the primitive Christians; and differ from those of our authorized version as far as that follows the "Apostasy" in its departure from the faith of the primitive Christians. How far that is, the reader of Job from the Hebrew must be his own judge.

The Roman Catholic English version of the Old Testament was published at Douay, A. D. 1609, three years before our King James version of the Bible was published.

The Roman Catholic English version of the New Testament was published at Rheims, A. D. 1582.

The Latin has no article. The Papacy made the Latin the sacred language. The Douay, and the Rheims took the liberty of using either of our articles or neither of them, as best suited the Papal system, in rendering the Latin into English. And they who gave us our King James version of the Bible often do the same. Many instances of the improper use of *the* occur in the Douay, the Rheims, and our English version.

The reader will observe that I have very seldom used either of our articles in rendering the Hebrew into English. In a very few instances one or the other has been inserted as a help to the sense, as in v. 20, chap. 24, and v. 4, chap. 25, pages 106, 107.

CORRECTIONS.

In line 8, page 22, read 29 for 20.
In the last line of page 22 read, *excuse for him, that neither*.
In note 3, page 24, read, *Donnegan's Greek Lexicon*.
In 4th line of note, page 42, read *shub* instead of *shul*.
Page 48, 9th line from the bottom of the note, read *him* instead of *me*.
Page 53, 2d line of note, read *scorn* instead of *room*.
Page 64, for *soured*, in v. 16, refer to note 5 on that page.
Page 68, for Isaiah 14 : 22 in the note, read 14 : 12.
Page 88, line 7, read *collocation*.
Page 88, line 13, read *brought to light*.
Page 146, line 2, read, *Matt. 25 : 46*.

CHAPTER I.

1 Man was in land Uz, Job name of him, and was that man which he upright and just, and feared God,[1] and turned aside from evil.

2 And were born to him seven sons and three daughters.

3 And was possession[2] of him seven thousand small cattle,[3] and three thousand camels, and five hundred pair of oxen, and five hundred she asses, and household numerous exceedingly; and was that man which he great above all sons of East.

4 And went sons of him and made banquet by house of man,[4] by day of him. And they sent and called to[5] three sisters of them to eat and to drink with them.

5 And it was, when had gone round days of this feasting, that sent Job and consecrated them; and he rose early in morning and offered burnt-offerings according to number of all of them; for said Job, whether not[6] have sinned sons of me, and have cursed *aleim*—(plural)—God in hearts of them. In this manner did Job all those days; Douay ....and have blessed God in their hearts. So did Job all days: Italian....and have spoken evil of God in the hearts of them. Thus did always Job.

6 And it was that day when came sons of that *aleim*

---

1. The Heb. is *aleim*, plural. Gesenius's Heb. Lexicon calls it the plural of majesty.
2. Ges., under *mqnc*, says: "*wealth*, always used of *cattle*, in which alone the riches of nomads consist."
3. That is, sheep and goats, says Ges.
4. ·i. e. of each.
5. i. e., says Ges., invited.
6. i. e. perhaps.

to stand before Jehovah, that came also that *stn*[1] among them. Douay.... before the Lord, Satan was also present among them: Ital.... came to present themselves before the Lord; and Satana came also he in midst of them.

7 And said Jehovah to that *stn*, from where art thou come: and answered that *stn* Jehovah and said, from running up and down in earth and from going along in it.

8 And said Jehovah to that *stn*: whether hast thou set mind of thee upon servant of me Job, that not such as he in earth, man perfect and upright, fearing *aleim* and turned aside from evil.

9 And answered that *stn* Jehovah and said, whether for nothing feareth Job *aleim*[2]:

10 Whether not fencest thou[3] round him, and round house of him, and round all which to him,[4] round about works of hands of him hast blest thou, and possession,—wealth—of him is spread abroad in earth:

11 But indeed, stretch out, I pray thee, hand of thee, and smite on all which to him, whether not to face of thee he will curse thee: Douay.... and see if he blesseth thee not to thy face: Italian..... and thou wilt see if not thee he curse to face.

12 And said Jehovah to that *stn*, Lo, all which to him in hand[5] of thee; only to him not shalt thou stretch out hand of thee; and went out that *stn* from face of Jehovah.

13 And it was that day when sons of him and daughters of him were eating and drinking wine in house of brother of them which first born.

---

1. Defined adversary, enemy, accuser. It is a personification of evil. Personification is the most frequent figure in Scripture. Almost every thing is personified. Even *death* and the grave, are personified.

2. The Hebrew has no interrogation mark.

3. Ges., under *shuk*, citing this v., says, "Metaphor., thou fencest round him," i. e., says he, thou guardest him; and under *la* he gives *ela*, whether not, and says, such a question requires an affirmative answer.

4. The Heb. use *to him* for the possessive.

5. i. e. power.

14. And *mlak*¹ messenger came to Job and said: Those oxen were ploughing, and those she asses pasturing at hands of them²:

15. And fell upon Sabæans and took them, and those servants smote they with mouth³ of sword, and am escaped only I alone to tell to thee.

16 As yet *ze*—this—speaking, and *ze*—that⁴ came and said: Fire of *aleim*⁵ fell from these heavens and burned up sheep and servants, and consumed them, and am escaped only I alone to tell to thee:

17 As yet this speaking and that came and said: Chaldeans set three bands of soldiers, and they rushed upon those camels and took them, and those servants smote they with mouth of sword; and am escaped only I alone to tell to thee:

18 While this speaking, and that came and said: Sons of thee and daughters of thee were eating and drinking wine in house of brother of them which first born:

19 And lo, *ruh*⁶—*wind*—great came from over that desert, and smote on four faces of that house, and it fell upon those young people and killed them; and am escaped only I alone to tell to thee: Douay....and it fell upon thy children, and they are dead: Italian....upon the young persons, whence they are dead.

20 And arose Job and rent upper garment⁷ of him, and

---

1. *Mlak*, defined *a messenger*, is the Hebrew word for which the Douay, and our authorized version, (which I designate by the letters E. V.,) often give *Angel*. *Angel* is not an English word; it is the Greek *aggelos*, pronounced *angelos*, and defined in the Greek lexicons, messenger.

2. i. e., near them.

3. Ges., under *phie*,—mouth, i. e., says he, *edge* of sword.

4. For *another*.

5. Used of lightning, says Ges., under *ash*, citing this v. and 1 Kings 18: 38; 2 Kings 1: 10, 12, 14.

6. Generally sounded *ruach*: this is the Hebrew word for which the Douay and the E. V. often have, spirit.

7. Amer. Bible Union, "rent his garments."

shaved head of him, and prostrated himself of ground, and adored:

21 And said, Naked came I forth from womb of mother of me, and naked shall I return thither[1]: Jehovah gave and Jehovah hath taken away, let be name of Jehovah (or name Jehovah) blessed:

22 With all this[2] not sinned Job, and not uttered impiety towards *aleim:*

Who can read this very first chapter of Job without seeing that the book is a dramatic poem; and that one of the characters is *evil* personified, called that adversary,—enemy, accuser; which accuses us so often to our own conscience; and that the book is an allegory, a mythical legend, in the extravagant Oriental style. Who will say it is a literal history? I said once to one of our most distinguished Newark lawyers, a communing member of one of our churches, and now a very prominent justice of the Supreme Court of the United States, that the book called Job was a dramatic poem, and he answered promptly, "Certainly it is." The Oriental philosophers taught by fable,—parable, legend; and this book contains the sublimest teachings on the sublimest of all subjects.

To suppose that among the almost countless personifications in the Scriptures, *evil,* the greatest adversary, enemy, accuser, of man, is not personified, is worse than idle.

CHAPTER II.

1 And it was that day when came sons of that *aleim* to stand before Jehovah, and came also that *stn* among them to stand before Jehovah:

2 And said Jehovah to that *stn*, whence art thou come: And answered that *stn* Jehovah and said, from running up and down in earth and from going along in it:

3 And said Jehovah to that *stn:* Whether hast thou

---

1. Ges., under *am*—mother, citing this v., says: "Metaphorically used of the earth as the mother of all men."

2. i. e., says Ges., under the Hebrew letter b, citing this verse, For all this, or, nevertheless.

set mind of thee to servant of me Job, that not such as he in earth, man perfect and upright, fearing *aleim* and turned aside from evil, and hitherto of him holding fast to integrity of him; *u*—and, or but, thou didst incite me against him to devour[1] him without cause: Ital....though thou me hast incited against him to destroy him without cause:

4 And answered that *stn* Jehovah and said: Skin for skin; and all which to man he will give for *nphsh*[2] (sound it *en-phsh*)—breath—of him: Douay....and all that a man hath he will give for his life: Ital....for his life: E. V....for his life: And the Amer. Bible Union gives *life*.

5 But indeed, stretch out I pray thee hand of thee, and touch[3] bone of him and flesh of him, whether not to face of thee he will curse thee: Douay....and then thou shalt see that he will bless thee to thy face: Ital....if not thee he will curse to face: Amer. Bible Union, renounce thee to thy face.

6 And said Jehovah to that *stn*, Lo, he in hand of you, only *nphsh*—breath—of him preserve: Douay....but yet save his life: Ital....only guard thee *from to touch* his life; E. V., but save his life; Amer. Bible Union, only spare his life.

7 And went forth that *stn* from face of Jehovah and smote Job with an inflamed ulcer bad from sole of foot of him even to top of head of him: Douay....with a very grievous ulcer: Ital....an ulcer malignant.

---

1. Metaphorical for consume, destroy, says Ges., under *blo*.

2. This Heb. word *nphsh*—breath—is the word where the Latin and Ital. so often have *anima*, and the Douay and the E. V., so often *soul*. Life is not the signification of *nphsh*: the Heb. for *life* is *hi*, see Ges., under *hi*, citing Gen. 42: 15, 16, *hi—life*—of Pharaoh.

3. Ges., under *ngv*, gives "intensive, to touch heavily, to smite," citing Job 19: 21.

8 And he took to him a potsherd[1] for to scrape (or, scratch) upon him, and *eua*—himself—sat down[2] in the midst of those ashes: Douay....and scraped the corrupt matter, sitting on a dunghill:

9 And said to him wife of him, as yet thou holding fast to integrity of thee, *brk aleim*[3]—bless God—and die: Douay....bless God, and die: Ital....bless God and die: E. V.,....curse God and die.

10 And he said to her: as speaks one of those foolish,[4] speakest thou: Indeed, which good shall we receive from that *aleim*, and which bad not shall we receive: With all this not sinned Job with lips of him:

11 And heard three friends of Job all this evil which had come upon him: and they came, man[5] from place of him, Eliphaz that Timni, and Belded that Shuhi, and Tsuphr that Nomti, and came together at appointed time[6] to go to commisserate with him and to comfort him:

12 And they lifted up eyes of them from afar, and not took knowledge of him; and they lifted up voice of them and bewailed, and rent man[7] upper garment of him, and scattered dust over heads of them heavenward: Douay ....they sprinkled dust upon their heads toward heaven: Ital....and each one of them tore his cloak, and scattered of the dust upon his head *throwing it* toward the heaven.

---

1. A piece of broken pot: Ges., for *grd*, gives, "to scrape oneself," to allay itching, citing this verse.

2. i. e. and sat himself down.

3. *brk*, says Ges., is most often *bless*, but is sometimes used for curse: In this v. he gives, "bless God and die," i. e., says he, however much thou praisest and blessest God, yet thou art about to die; thy piety towards God is therefore vain: the words of a wicked woman, says Ges.

4. There is nothing in the Heb. here for *woman* except that the adjective used is in the feminine.

5. For each one.

6. Or place; Ges., under *iod*, gives, "to come together at an appointed time or place," citing Neh. 6: 2, 10; Job 2: 11; Amos 3: 3.

7. For, *each one*.

13 And they sat down with him on earth[1] seven days and seven nights, and no one spoke to him word, for they saw that great that pain[2] to him exceedingly: Douay.... that his grief was very great; Amer. Bible Union, "that the affliction was very great."

CHAPTER III.

1 After thus opened Job mouth of him and cursed day of him:

2 And began to speak Job; and he said:

3 Let perish day I was born in it, and that night which said, is conceived male:

4 That day which it let be darkness, let not care for it God from above, and not let shine upon it light:

5 Let redeem it darkness and shadow of death; let rest upon it clouds; let frighten it obscurations of day[3]:

6 That night which it, let seize upon it *aphl*—thick darkness; let it not rejoice among days of year; in number of months not let it come:

7 Lo, that night which it let be barren[4]; not let enter shouting for joy in it:

8 Let curse it those who curse day[5]; which skillful (or prompt) to arouse serpent[6]:

9 Let be darkened stars of night of it; let it wait for

---

1. Or ground.
2. Pain of body, says Ges., under *Kab* citing this v.
3. i. e., says Ges., under *kmririm*, citing this v., obscurations of th light of day—of the sun—eclipses, which the ancients believed to portend ills and calamities.
4. Ges., under *glmud*, says: "Poetically of a night in which one is born," citing this v.
5. Ges., under *arr*, citing this v., says: "Those who curse the day," a kind of enchanters, says he, who were supposed to render days unfortunate by their imprecations.
6. Figuratively, to excite strife; see Prov. 10: 12.

light and not there be, and not let it look upon eyelids of dawn[1]: Ital....the eyelids of the dawn of day.

10 Because it not did shut up doors of womb of me, and hide calamity from eyes of me:

11 Why not from womb died I, from belly come forth and *aghuo*—breathed out: Douay....Why did I not die in the womb, why did I not perish (for the Heb. *aghuo*) when I came out of the belly? E. V..... Why died I not from the womb? Why did I not give up the ghost when I came out of the belly? Am. Bible Union, come forth from the womb, and expire. (See note to this at end of chapter.)

12 Wherefore met me knees, and wherefore teats that I should suck:

13 For now I had lain down and had quiet; I had slept; then had been rest to me[2]:

14 With kings and counsellors of earth who have built ruins for themselves[3]:

15 Or with princes with gold to them,[4] who filled houses of them with silver;

16 Or as abortion hidden not should I exist, as unborn babes not see light:

---

1. Used, says Ges., under *ophophim*, citing this v., for the rays of the rising sun.

2. Ges., under *nuh*, citing this v., renders "then I should have rest." Under *shkb*—to lie down, he says: it is often used of the death of Kings, in the phrase, laid down with fathers of him, citing 1 Kings 2: 10; 11: 43; 14: 20, 31; 15: 8, 24; 16: 6, 28; and of the dead, citing Isai. 14: 8, "since thou wast laid down," i. e., had died, says Ges.; and citing Isai. 14: 18; 43: 17; Job 3. 13; 20: 11; 21: 26; and Psal. 88: 6, "those who lie in the grave;" the E. V. is v. 5. And under *ishn*, to fall asleep, he says it is used of dead, citing Jer. 51: 39, 57; Ps. 13: 4,—Ital. and E. V., v. 3; Job 3: 13. In Ps. 13: 4, the Heb. is....lest I should sleep that death: Douay, Chap. 12: 4...."that I never sleep in death:" Ital. ....that sometime I may not sleep *the sleep of* death: E. V....lest I sleep the *sleep of* death.

3. i. e., says Ges., under *hrbe*, citing this v., "splendid edifices, presently however to fall into ruins."

4. i. e., possessing gold.

17 There wicked cease troubling, and there are at rest, exhausted of strength :

18 Together captives they are quiet; not hear they voice of driver :

19 Small and great there, *eua*—himself[1]—and servant of him set free from master of him :

20 Why should he give to wretched, light, and life to bitter of *nphsh*[2]—breath: Douay....and life to them that are in bitterness of soul? Ital....and life to them that are in bitterness of mind ?

21 Which wait for death and not it to them, and dig for it more than for underground treasures:

22 Which rejoice even to exultation : are glad that they can[3] find grave : Douay....And they rejoice exceedingly when they have found *the* grave: Ital....And they rejoice exceedingly, *and* are merry when they have found *the* sepulchre : E. V....Which rejoice exceedingly, *and* are glad, when they can find *the* grave : Amer. Bible Un., When they find the grave.

23 To man who way of him hidden,[4] and hedged of God round about him : Ital.... *Why gave he the light* to the man whose way is hidden, and the which God has enclosed on all sides ? See E. V.

---

1. Neither the Douay, nor the Ital., nor the E. V. of the verse has any thing for *eua* in the verse : The Douay and the E. V. give : "and the servant *is* free from his master."

2. Ges., under *mr*—bitter, says: "Metaphorical, sad, sorrowful ;" Amer. Bible Un., "to the sorrowful in heart."

3. The Heb. has but two tenses, the past and the future ; the past being often used for the present, and the future tense being often used for the subjunctive mood of other languages, and therefore often to be rendered in English by may, can, might, would, should, ought, could : See Wilson's "Easy Introduction to the Hebrew," p. 242. If the E. V. had given *that* for the Heb. *ki*, instead of *when*, it would have avoided the absurdity of the Douay and the Italian.

4. i. e., says Ges., who does not know how to escape from calamities, citing this v. under *str* (we should say, whose way is hidden ?)

24 So that to face of food of me groans of me come, and are poured out like water cries of me:

25 Because a fear feared I,[1] and it has come upon me, and that which I was afraid of is come to me.

26 Not was secure[2] I, and have I not kept myself quiet, and have I not set myself down to be at rest[3]—and yet is come trouble.

---

1. So Ges., under *phhd*, citing this v.

2. i. e. confident (or, careless): Ges., under *shle*, citing this v., says: "specially used of one who securely enjoys prosperity."

3. Ges., under *nuh*, gives, "to be at rest," citing this verse. He says: The original idea lies in respiring, drawing *ruh*, for which he gives, under *shub*, "to draw the breath;" and he gives also, under *shub*, draw *nphsh*, i. e., to draw breath.

The word *ghost*, used in the E. V. of Job 3 : 11, occurs in ten passages of the E. V. of the Old Testament, and in seven passages of the E. V. of the New Testament; in the phrases "gave up the ghost," &c. And in each of these passages in the Old and New Testaments, the E. V. phrase "gave up the ghost," &c., is used of man or woman. No one could ever learn from the Douay Roman Catholic version, or from the Italian version, or from the E. V., that every other animal (i. e. breathing creature) as well as man, has a ghost to give up, (to use the E. V. phrase). This is carefully evaded by the Douay, and by the Ital., and by the E. V. When the reader shall find this startling fact established by irresistible proof, he may determine for himself whether *perversion* or *evasion* be the more proper word to characterize the hiding of such a truth.

The ten passages in the O. T. are, Gen. 25 : 8, 17 ; 35 : 29 ; Job 3 : 11 ; 10 : 18 ; 11 20 ; 13 : 19 ; 14 : 10 ; Jer. 15 : 9 ; Lament. 1 : 19. And the seven passages of the N. T are, Acts 5 : 5, 10 ; 12 : 23 ; Mat. 27 : 50 ; Mark 15 : 37, 39 ; John 19 : 30.

In eight of the ten passages in the O. T., all but Job 11 : 20 : and Jer. 15 : 9, the Heb. has only the single word, the verb *ghuo*, in its proper tense, number and person, where the E. V. has the phrase "gave up the ghost," etc.

This Heb. verb *ghuo* is one of the many Heb. words which express by their sounds the thing signified. Sound *ghu* in one sound outward, *g* hard, and a slight aspirate (i. e. breathing) on the *h*,—*ghu*, and continue the outbreathing on and with the sound of the *o*, without drawing back breath, and you have the exact sounds of breathing wholly out,—exspiring. And accordingly, *ghuo* is defined by Genesius, "to exspire, to breathe out one's life," citing Gen. 6 : 17 ; 7 : 21 ; Numb. 17 : 27 ; (and it occurs in v. 28 also ; the verses in the Douay, Ital. and E. V., of Numb. Chap. 17, are 12, 13); Job 3 : 11; 10 : 18; 13 ; 19; 14 : 10 ; 27 : 5 etc. ;" "Sometimes," says he, "with the addition of *mut*," (to die,) citing Gen. 25 : 8. We thus see from Ges., that what *ghuo* means in Gen. 6 : 17 and 7 : 21, is the same that it means in the other verses cited by him. It was not necessary to add "one's life" to the definition : to breathe out,—exspire, completes the sense of *ghuo*. I have found in the Lexicon more than fifty Heb. words which, like *ghuo*, express by their sounds the thing signified. It was a very natural way of forming words when it could be done. And that *to exspire,—breathe out*, is the meaning of *ghuo* is conclusively shown by the Greek verbs used in the passages before cited from the New Test. in which the Rheims Romish version of the New Test., and the E. V. New Test. give the phrase " gave up the ghost." In the first three of those verses, Acts 5 : 5, 10 ; 12 : 23, the Greek uses but one word, to express what is expressed in the Heb. of the O. T. by the one Heb. word, the verb *ghuo*. The Greek verb is *ekpsucho*, to outbreathe,—exspire; compounded of the Greek preposition *ek* out, wholly out, and *psucho*, to breathe ; from which verb *psucho* is the Greek noun *psuche*, breath; Douay and E. V. so often soul. In each of these three verses the Latin has its single word *exspiravit*—exspired,—outbreathed, from its verb *exspiro*, compounded of *ex*—out, (in composition with a verb, wholly out, says Donnegan's Greek Lexicon), and *spiro*—to breathe, from which Latin verb *spiro* is the Latin noun *spiritus*—breath ; Douay and E. V. so often *spirit*.

And in two other of the verses in the New Test. where the Rheims, and E. V. have " gave up the ghost" namely, Mark 15 : 37, 39, the Greek uses but a single word, its verb *ekpneo*, to out breathe, exspire, compounded of *ek*—wholly out, and *pneo*—to breathe ; from which Greek verb *pneo*—to breathe, is the Greek noun *pneuma*—breath; Douay and E. V., so often spirit.

In the other two of the seven passages of the New Test. in which the Rheims and the E. V. have the phrase " gave up the ghost," the Greek uses other appropriate words to express the same idea. These two other verses are Matt. 27 : 50, and John 19 : 30. In the first, the Greek is, he let go the *pneuma*—breath ; Latin....he let go the *spiritum*—the breath : Ital....*rende lo spirito*, he rendered the breath : Rheims " he yielded up the ghost ;" E. V. the same. In John 19 : 30, the Greek is *paredoke to pneuma*, he delivered the breath; Latin....he delivered *spiritum*—the breath ; Ital., *rende lo spirito*, he rendered the breath ; Rheims, " gave up the ghost ;" E. V. the same.

And in Ezekiel 21 : 12 (Douay and E. V. v. 7) we have in the Heb. ....shall fail every *ruh*—breath ; the Greek there is, *ekpsuchei*—shall breathe out—exspire—every *pneuma*—breath ; (ekpsuchei being from the same Greek verb *ekpsucho*, used in the New Test. as before given) :

The Douay, v. 7, is, every spirit shall faint; Ital. v. 12, every *spirito*—breath—shall faint; E. V. every spirit shall faint.

The two other passages of the Old Test. in which the E. V. uses its phrase are, Job 11 : 20, and Jer. 15 : 19:

In Job 11 : 20, the Heb. uses the two appropriate words *mphh nphsh*—the breathing out of *the* breath, to express what in the other eight passages of the Old Test. it expresses by the single verb *ghuo*—to breathe out,—exspire. We write *expire*, without the *s*; and from the omission of the *s* the meaning of the word is by many not understood. It should be written exspire: It is from the Latin word *exspiro*—to breathe out—exspire. See Ges., under *mphh*.

The Douay in Job 11 : 20 is....and their hope the abomination of the soul; Ital....and their *only* hope *shall be* of *render lo spirito*, to render the breath. Graglia's Ital. Dict., under *spirito*, gives "*render lo spirito*, to die"; literally, it is, to *render the breath:* and under *rendere*, it gives "*render l'anima* to exspire"; literally, it is, to render the breath. The E. V. in Job 11 : 20 is...." and their hope *shall be as* the giving up of the ghost." There is a marginal note in the E. V. which I used, the Brown Bible by the Patersons, thus: " or a puff of breath." The last breath is an exspiration, and it goes out with something of a puff; and no inspiration—inbreathing—following, death immediately ensues. There is no *ruh*, Greek, *pneuma*, Lat. *spiritus*—breath, air, in the lungs of a dead man.

In Jer. 15 : 9, also, the Heb. uses two appropriate words, *nphh nphsh*—breathed out *the* breath ; See Ges., under *nphh*, citing this v. and Job 31 : 39: The Douay there is, her soul hath fainted away ; Ital....her *anima*—breath—(soul is the only definition of *anima* in Graglia's Ital. Dict.)—has *ansato*—panted: The E. V. is,...." she hath given up the ghost." It is thus conclusively shown, that ghost means breath.

Even the Ital. alone furnishes conclusive proof of it. In Job 10 : 18 it is, I should have been *spirato*—breathed out. In Job 13 : 19 it is, I shall breathe out—exspire. In Lament. 1 : 19 it is....are *spirati*—breathed out. See E. V. in each. And I cite here—Job 15 : 30, Heb....and he shall go away by *ruh*—breath of mouth of him ; Douay....by the breath of his own mouth ; Ital....by the *soffio*—breath of the mouth of God; and the Patersons in a marginal note adopt this conceit from the Ital.

We now give the first passage in which the E. V. uses its phrase "gave up the ghost," namely, Gen. 25 : 8: The Heb. there is, *ighuo* (from *ghuo*) breathed out and *imt*—(from *mut*—to die)—died Abraham. Two different words are here used: they mean different things: they don't mean the same thing. The verb *ghuo* signifies, to breathe out—exspire: and the verb *mut* signifies to die, which is the consequence that follows exspiring.

In Gen. 25 : 8, the Douay is, And decaying, (Heb. *ighuo*), he died, E. V. "gave up the ghost and died."

In Gen. 25 : 17, the same is said of Ishmael, *ighuo u imt*—he breathed out and died ; Douay, decaying he died.

In Gen. 35 : 29, the Heb. is the same of Isaac—*ighuo u imt*, breathed out,—exspired—and died; Douay....being spent with age he died.

In all the other passages, the verb *ghuo* is used without the addition of *imt*—died, dying being the necessary and immediate consequence of exspiring,—breathing out.

Ghosts are found in the Rheims Romish version of the New Test., published at Rheims, A. D. 1582, some twenty-seven years before the Douay was published, and some thirty years before the E. V. was published. The Douay repudiated the ghosts of the Rheims; but James's ecclesiastics seem to have thought that as the Rheims has them in the New Test. they might as well have them in the Old, so far as relates to man and woman. The Douay uniformly evades the true meaning of the Heb. verb *ghuo*—to breathe out—exspire,—deliver the breath, give up the ghost. They who gave us the Douay version may have been wise enough to perceive, that to give " gave up the ghost," " give up the ghost," &c., wherever the Heb. verb *ghuo* occured, would show that every other breathing creature, as well as man, has a ghost to give up, and so it would be manifest that *ghost* means *breath*. But they were conscientious enough to feel that if they gave the phrase at all, they must give it wherever the Heb. verb *ghuo* occurred; and so they concluded not to treat their readers to a ghost at all; not to inform them that every breathing creature, man included, has a ghost to give up; that they all die in the same way man dies, that is, in consequence of *ghuoing*—breathing out—exspiring; though there is no promise to them of a resurrection. Now, assuming that the Douay versionists knew what the Heb. word was, their course was a piece of Jesuitism,—a so-called "pious fraud," the end, according to Jesuitical ethics, justifying the means. The course of the ecclesiastics who gave us the E. V. was different. They were equally unwilling to let it appear that every breathing creature has a ghost to give up; and so they use the phrase, " give up the ghost," and " gave up the ghost," &c., where it refers to man or woman, and do not use it where the same Heb. word is used in reference to other animals, as in Gen. 6 : 17; 7 : 21; Job 34 : 15; Psal. 104 : 29. Now James's ecclesiastics either knew or did not know what the Heb. word was. On the assumption that they did know, I ask: Which version, the Douay, or the E. V., is, in this particular, the more pious fraud of the two? The reader is, of course, at liberty to put James's ecclesiastics on the other horn of the dilemma.

It will be sufficient to state here, shortly, that in Gen. 6 : 17, the Heb. is, to destroy every flesh which in it *ruh*—breath—*hiim*—of lives—from under these heavens; every which on land *ighuo* (from *ghuo*) shall breathe out,—exspire. Where the Heb. has *ighuo* in the verse, the Ital. and E. V. have, *shall die*. Why this confusion of words? And in Gen. 7 : 21 the Heb. is: And *ighuo*—breathed out—exspired—every flesh....of fowl, and of cattle, and of beast, and of every creeping thing that creepeth upon this earth, and every man. The Ital. and the E. V. here give *died*, where the Heb. is, *ighuo*. The verse shows, that man and all the other animals mentioned in it alike breathe out.—exspire.' Why did not the E. V. give "shall give up the ghost," and "gave up the ghost," in these two verses ?

And in Job 34 : 15 the Heb. is, *ighuo*—shall breathe out—exspire—every flesh together, and man upon dust shall return : E. V. All flesh shall perish together ; the same that the Douay has here.

And in Psal. 104 : 20 the Heb. is ....thou takest away *ruh*—breath—of them, *ighuo*—breathe out,—exspire they and to dust of them return they; (said of creeping things innumerable in the sea, see v. 25) E. V.....thou takest away their breath, they die, and return to their dust. Why did not the E. V. give "shall give up the ghost," and, "they gave up the ghost," in these two verses ? Why evade, and conceal, the fact that the Bible teaches, conclusively, that every breathing creature has a ghost to give up ?

This exhibition in regard to the word *ghost* gives rise to new and strange reflections. More than 1800 years of the Christian era had elapsed, when a man esteemed learned, and who actually made what is called a standard Dictionary of English words, defined, in that Dict. the word *ghost* to be "the soul of a deceased person ; an apparition." And now, for the first time, (as far as I know), near the end of the nineteenth century, by an appeal to the Hebrew Scriptures, it is demonstrated by Scripture authority, that *ghost* is as much the soul of a deceased horse as it is the soul of a deceased person ; and as much an apparition of a deceased dog as an apparition of a deceased person. By apparition is meant the ghost that a few old people may yet believe in. But they must be very old; for the last two generations have outgrown the superstition of ghosts ; without being aware, however, generally, that in getting rid of Noah Webster's ghost, they got rid also of Orthodox souls and spirits. Is it not one of the wonders of all time, that millions of lives should have been sacrificed by wars and persecution growing out of differences of religious tenets, when an appeal to the original Scriptures would show the true religion, and put an end to bloodshed by giving unity to the Church ? There is but one true faith. There can be but one. All others are false ; and belief in a false system cannot be acceptable to God.

The preface to Noah Webster's Abridged Dict. speaks of " The depth and acumen of its etymological researches" ! When in truth, in reference to the word *ghost*, he plainly did not go beyond our English translation, in which the word *ghost* is confined to man and woman. He did not go even as far back as the Latin *exspiro*—to exspire, or to the Greek *ekpsucho* and *ekpneo*—each meaning, to breathe out,—exspire: The E. V. *ghost* was sufficient authority with him. And in reference to several other words in common use, as spirit, soul, Satan, his definitions show like want of research.

The reader may think it somewhat of an excuse for him that neither the Latin version, which the Pope and he Romanists say is the only authentic version; nor the Douay English version; nor the Ital. version; nor our E. V., shows that other breathing creatures besides man have a ghost to give up. And this is true: all these versions studiously conceal the fact. But how much of an excuse this is for men who assume the office of teacher in matters of religion, every one must be his or her own judge. Thinking persons will probably say: nothing short of the original Scriptures is sufficient authority for any doctrine; and that teachers in religion are not excusable for relying on so-called translations, without comparing them with the originals. I adopt here the language of Charles Wilson, formerly Professor of Hebrew in the University of St. Andrew's, Scotland: "English translations and commentaries are the chief object of attention and praise, while the original is almost totally neglected and unknown. It is not easy to discover a plausible excuse for such conduct."

Noah Webster had never learned, either from the pulpit, or from any so-called translation of the Bible, that other animals, as well as men, have ghosts to give up: and the E. V. gives *ghost* only in reference to man and woman. Hence he concluded that *ghost* must mean what Orthodoxy calls the *soul;* and therefore, that *ghost* must mean, the soul of a deceased person; and by his adding "an apparition" I presume we are to understand him as meaning, that what he calls the *soul* can put on a visible shape, especially at night: very good spiritism. And we shall never get rid of spiritism, (spiritualism is the word generally used,) until we get rid of such definitions of the word *ghost*, and others, as Noah Webster has given.

CHAPTER IV.

1 And answered Aliphz that Timni and said:

2 Whether to venture word with thee: wilt thou be offended: but hold back from word who can:

3 Lo, thou hast admonished many, and hands let down thou hast strengthened[1]:

4 Wavering have built up words of thee, and failing knees thou hast made strong:

5 But now it is come to thee and thou faintest, it reaches unto (or touches) thee and thou art terrified:

---

1. Ges., under *rphe,* says: "hands let down" is used figuratively for "courage gone," citing 2 Sam. 4: 1; Isai. 13: 7; Jer. 6: 24; Ezek. 7: 17; Zeph. 3: 16.

6 Whether not piety of thee confidence of thee; hope of thee, indeed, integrity of ways of thee: Douay.... Where is thy fear, thy fortitude, thy patience, and the perfection of thy ways? Ital....Thy piety, not *is* it *been* thy hope, and the integrity of thy ways thy trust?

7 Remember, I pray thee, who *eua*—himself—pure[1] was lost (or, has perished)[2], and where upright were cut off (or, destroyed)[3]:

8 Like as have seen I; they that plow iniquity and sow wickedness, reap them;

9 By breath[4] of God they are destroyed, yea, by breath[5] of nostrils of him they are consumed:

40 Cry of lion and roar of lion, and teeth of young lions are broken out:

---

1. "Metaphorical, innocent," says G., under *nge*.

2. Ges., under *abd*, the Heb. verb used here, gives "to be lost, to perish, to be destroyed;" used, says he, of men and other living creatures as perishing, citing Psal. 37: 20; Job 4: 11.

3. Ges., under *khd*, the Heb. verb used here, gives, "to cut off, to destroy," equivalent, says he, to the Greek *aphanizien*,—from the Greek verb *aphanire*, defined in Douay and Greek Lexicon, to destroy, to abolish; and in Liddell and Scott's Greek Lexicon, to destroy utterly.

4. The Heb. word here is *nshme*, sometimes written *nshmt*, for which Ges. gives breath, spirit, (showing that spirit means breath.)

5. The Heb. word here is ruh—breath; Ges., under *aph*, nostril, gives *ruh aph* (breath of nostril) "the blowing of breath through the nostrils, as of those who are enraged," citing this v. The Douay here gives *blast* for *nshmt*, and for *ruh aph*, the spirit of his wrath. The Ital. for *nshmt*, gives *breath*, and for *ruh* gives *breath*, of his nostrils. The E. V. for *nshmt* gives *blast*, and for *ruh*, breath, of his nostrils. The Amer. Bible Union, for *nshmt* gives *breath*, and for *ruh* gives *blast*, of his anger. For *ruh*, Ges. gives spirit, breath, showing also under *ruh* that *spirit* means *breath;* and under *aph*—nostril, he gives also, "Anger, which shows itself in hard breathing," citing Prov. 22: 24; where the Heb. is *bol aph*—master of nostril; and the Douay and E. V. have "angry man;" and Prov. 29: 22, where the Heb. is *aish aph*, man of nostril. And under *aph*—nostril, Ges. says further, "very often used of the anger of God," citing Deut. 32: 22, where the Heb. is "fire is kindled in nostril of me," and citing other verses.

11 Lion perishes because not prey, and children of lioness are scattered :

12 And to me word was brought by stealth, and received ear of me transient sound of part.

13 In thoughts of visions of night, in falling of deep sleep on men;[1]

14 Terror met me and trembling, and multitude[2] of bones of me were terrified.

15 And breath of air[3] over face[4] of me glided; stood hair of flesh of me.

16 Stood, but not knew I aspect of it, appearance before eyes of me[5], silence and voice I heard[6].

---

1. Ges., under *shophim*, citing this v., and Job 20 : 2, renders, "In the thoughts of night visions," i. e., says he, "in the nocturnal dreams themselves," compare, says he, Dan. 2 : 29, 30.

2. Ges., under *rb*, multitude, citing this v. says, "poetically multitude is used for *all*," citing also Job 33 : 19.

3. The Heb. word here is *ruh*, defined by Ges., wind, air, breath of air.

4. Douay, And when a spirit passed before me the hair of my flesh stood up....Ital. And a *spirito* is passed before me....Am. Bib. Un., Then a spirit passed before me....In the Heb. *face* sometimes means the whole person, but it is wrong to give it that meaning here, where the Heb. is, "breath of air over face of me."

5. Ges., under *tmune*, citing this v. renders, "a (certain) appearance (passed) before my eyes."

6. Ges., under *mrae*, (which he defines, vision, citing Gen. 46 : 2, "visions of night;" and Ezk. 8 : 3; 40 : 2, visions sent by God,") says, "In the prophetic style, the appearance of any thing is what is like such a thing;" compare, says he, Dan. 10 : 18, "there touched me as the appearance of a man ; [read the preceding verses of Daniel's vision] ; and under *dmme*, which he defines, silence, stillness, i. e., says he, of the winds, a calm, citing Ps. 107 : 29 ; and *qul dmme*, voice of silence," i. e., says he, gentle, still, citing 1 Kings 19 : 12; and so poetically, says he, Job 4 : 16, giving the Heb. and rendering, "I heard silence and a voice," i. e., says he, a gentle whispering voice; unless, says he, it be preferred to take it, "there was silence, and I heard a voice." He adds, "The Septuagint, [the Greek version, admitted to be of high authority], and the Latin version understand it, " soft breeze." It is plain that the verse speaks of a vision. We both see appearances, and hear voices, in dreams ; i. e., we seem to see and hear.

17 Whether man more than God just: whether more than Creator of him pure, man:

18 Lo, in servants of him not he trusteth, and to *mlaki* —messengers—[1] of him he sets folly; Douay....and in his angels he found wickedness; Ital....and he discerneth temerity in his angels. E. V. and Am. Bib. Un. give angels.

19 How much more dwellers of houses of clay, who in dust foundation of them; they are crushed before moth.

20 From morning to evening they are smitten, so that lain down, to eternity they perish; Douay....and because no one understandeth, they shall perish for ever; Ital....they perish for ever, without that any one there put mind; Am. Bib. Un....unheeded they perish forever.

Douay....an image before my eyes, and I heard the voice as it were of a gentle wind; Ital....a resemblance was before my eyes; Amer. Bib. Un.....It stood still, but I could not discern its form, an image was before my eyes; there was silence; and I heard a voice.

1. i. e., the prophets; the Heb. word used here—*mlaki*—is the plural of *mlak*, defined by Ges., a messenger, one sent, citing Job 1 : 14; 1 Sam. 16 : 19; 19 : 11, 14, 20; 1 Kings 19 : 2, 7; Exod. 23 : 20, 23; 33 : 2; 2 Sam. 24 : 16, 17; Job 33 : 23; Zech. 1 : 9, 11, 12, 14, 19; 2 : 2 (Douay, Ital and E. V, v. 3); Zech. 4 : 1, 5; Gen. 16 : 7; 21 : 17; 22 : 11, 15; Numbers, 22 : 22, and other verses in the same chapter; Judges 6 : 11, and other verses in the same chap. He then further defines *mlak*, a prophet, citing Haggai 1 : 13; Malachi 3 : 1; and he further defines *mlak*, a priest, citing Eccles. 5 : 5; (Douay, v. 5; Ital. and E. V. v. 6); Once, says he, of Israel, [i. e. Jacob], as being the messenger of God, and the teacher of the Gentiles, citing Isai. 42 : 19. In all these passages the Heb. word is the same—*mlak*. The same word occurs also in Gen. 48 : 16, thus: That *mlak* which redeemed me from all evil. While transcribing some pages in my manuscript of Job from the Hebrew, to make them plain for the printer, I happened to take up the New York Herald of Dec. 27, 1874, and to find in it a part of a sermon of the Rev. Doct. Mendes, of the 44th Street, New York, Synagogue, in which he quotes these verses, thus: "God, before whom my fathers Abraham and Isaac did walk, the God which fed me all my life long unto this day, the angel which redeemed me from all evil, bless the lads." The Doct. then asked: " Is it not a matter of surprise, that the pious Jacob, who had just acknowledged the Almighty as his benefactor, should invoke an angel to

21 Whether not are plucked out cords¹ of them from them; they die and not in wisdom.

CHAPTER V.

1 Call, I pray thee, whether will be answering thee, and to whom among holies wilt thou turn thyself:

---

bless the lads?" And the Doct. then proceeds to say: "But to understand this phrase, we must look at the Biblical meaning of the word angel. It comes from the Hebrew word *mallah*—to go, one who goes for another, and the English word *minister* has exactly the same significance." "Hence the priests of the Lord are his messengers," quoting passages from scripture. "Angels are simply the ways and manner in which God works in the universe. In the destruction of Sodom and Gomorrah, for instance, the attributes of wisdom and justice personified in fire and brimstone, became his angels." *Gabriel* is simply "God's might; it is, "man of God." *Michael*, "who like God." "Hindrance is embodied in the term *Satan*. You are aware how another faith has taken up this name and woven a web around it to make it man's enemy, as if a man had any other enemy than himself." "How much nobler is this doctrine than to teach that the angels are independent personal characters!" "God's angels are always instruments of working good; and if we seek to work we can be angels also. When doubt encompasses us let us seek the angel of faith, and if in our homes the demon of hate and envy reigns, let us call in the angel of love."

1. Douay....And they that shall be left, shall be taken away from them; they shall die and not in wisdom.

Ital....The excellency that was in them not is departed it? They die but not with wisdom.

Gesenius, under *uso*, citing this v., gives, "to pluck out," used, says he, of the cords of a tent; and under *itr*, a cord, he cites this v. again, and, giving the Heb. words, says: "Metaphorically, their cords are torn away, their tents are removed," i. e., says he, they die: compare, says he, the metaphor of a tent, Isai. 38 : 12. The Heb. there is: age (circuit of years, says Ges., under *dur*) of me is removed, or, departed, and rolled away like tent.

The E. V. in Job 4 : 21 is, Doth not their excellency *which is* in them go away? they die even without wisdom.

The Amer. Bib. Un. is, Is not their excellency taken away with them? they die, and without wisdom.

2 For as to fool, killeth grief, and simple, killeth envy:

3 I, have seen I fool taking root,[1] and I cursed habitation of him in a moment:

4 Are far off children of him from welfare, and they are crushed in gate,[2] and not is there prosperer:

5 Who harvest of them[3] hungry shall eat, and even of thorns[4] take, and breathes hard after,[5] snare, wealth of them:

6 For not goeth forth from dust calamity, and from ground not sprouts forth trouble:

7 For man to labor is born, and sons of lightning,[6] they fly on high:

8 But indeed I, I would seek to God, and to *aleim* would I put cause of me:

9 He doeth greatnesses, and not can be searched out, things wonderful and not of number:[7]

10 Who giveth rain on face of earth, and sendeth water on face of fields:[8]

---

1. "Metaphor., of a man flourishing in prosperity," says Ges., under *shrsh.*

2. Often for in forum, in judgment, says Ges., under *shor*, citing this v., and Deut. 25 : 7, and other passages.

3. We should say, whose harvest.

4. i. e. from thorn hedges enclosing fields, says Ges., under *al.*

5. Douay....and the thirsty shall drink up his riches:
Ital....and the robbers swallow up their riches:
Amer. Bib. Un....and the snare is gaping for their substance.
Ges., under *shaph*, the Heb. verb used here, and defined, to breathe hard after, pant after, says : poetically ascribed to a noose or trap lying in wait, citing this v.; and under *tsmim*, a snare, citing this v., he says : "Metaphor., destruction;" and giving the Heb. of the last clause, he renders, "and destruction pants for their wealth."

6. i. e., ravenous birds, flying with the rapidity of lightning, says Ges., unde *rshph*, citing this v.; and under *gbe*, citing this v. again, he renders, "they fly on high." Douay....Man is born to labour, and the bird to fly: Am. Bib. Union....for man is born to trouble, even as sparks fly upward.

7. i. e., innumerable says Ges., under *msphr.*

8. Ges., under *huts*, suggests that *arts*—earth—here means the tilled earth, and *hutsut* (plural of *huts*) the desert regions.

11 Setting cast down to height; and mourning are set on high of welfare :

12 Making void¹ plots of crafty, so that not can do hands of them counsel :²

13 He snares wise in craftiness of them, and counsel of twisted, headlong it :³

14 Of day they light upon darkness,⁴ and as of night they grope at midday :

15 And he sets free⁵ from sword, from mouth of them, and from hand of strong, needy :

16 And there exists to weak, hope ; but wicked⁶ shut mouth :⁷

17 Lo, happy man correcteth him God, so that correction of Almighty do not thou regret :

18 For he woundeth and bindeth up, he smiteth and hand of him healeth :

19 In six troubles he will deliver thee, yea, in seven not shall touch on thee evil :

20 In famine he will preserve thee from death, and in battle from hand of sword :

21 From scourge of tongue thou shalt be hid, and not shalt thou fear from desolation when it shall come :

---

1. So Ges. under *phrr*, citing this v. and others.

2. " and their hands do not perform *their* counsel," says Ges., under *tushie*, citing this v.

3. Ges., under *phtl*—twisted, citing this v., says : " Metaphor., crafty, deceitful," and renders, " the counsel of the cunning is headlong," i. e. says he, being hastily executed it is frustrated.

4. So Ges., under *phgsh*, citing this v.

5. It may be that there is an ellipsis after " set free," to be filled with *victim*.

6. Ges., under *oule*, renders, "wicked persons," citing this v. and others.

7. So Ges., under *qphts*, and he adds, " be gathered," namely, says he, to one's ancestors, equivalent, says he, to *nasph*, (from *asph*) which he defines, "to be gathered together," i. e. says he, to be dead, citing this v. and Job 24 : 24. The Douay is, but iniquity shall draw in her mouth ; Am. Bib. Un., and iniquity shuts her mouth.

22 At desolation and at hunger thou shalt laugh, and of beasts of this earth¹ not shalt thou be afraid :

23 For with stones of these fields covenant of thee, and beasts of these fields shall be friends to thee :

24 And thou shalt know that healthy² tent of thee, and thou shalt visit pasture³ of thee and not shalt miss :

25 And thou shalt know that multitude seed of thee, and springings forth⁴ of thee as green herb of this earth :

26 Thou shalt go in completion⁵ to grave,⁶ as is taken up heap of sheaves in time of it.

27 Lo, this have searched we out ; so it ; hear it, and know thou for thyself.

NOTE.—Can any one imagine that such a speech of two chapters long, which the writer of this poem puts in the mouth of the character Eliphaz in the drama, was made by a man in an off-hand conversation ? Is it not manifest from the speech itself that it is a labored production, of great study and wisdom ?

CHAPTER VI.

1 And answered Job and said :

2 O that with shekel could be weighed vexation of me, yea, calamity of me in scales be lifted up together.⁷

---

1. Or land.
2. So Ges., under *shlum*, citing this v.
3. " Metonymy for flocks," says Ges. ; and under *htha*, citing this v., he gives, " thou numberest thy flock and missest none. The Douay here is....and visiting thy beauty thou shalt not sin.
4. Metaphor., for descendants, says Ges., citing this v. under *tsatsaim*, and citing other verses ; " fully," says he, those that spring forth from thy bowels, citing Isai. 48 : 19.
5. Poetically used of old age, says Ges., under *klh*, citing this v.
6. The Heb. word used here is *qbr*, defined by Ges., sepulchre, grave.
7. i. e. his vexation, calamity, in one scale and shekels in the other.

3 For now more than sand of sea it would be heavy; therefore words of me hasty:

4 For arrows[1] of Almighty with me, which heat of them[2] drinketh[3] breath of me; terrors of God they set in array against me:[4]

5 Whether will bray wild ass over tender grass; whether will low ox over provender of him:

6 Whether can be eaten insipid without salt: whether there be taste in slime of purslain:[5]

7 Refuseth to touch, breath[6] of me; they as loathsome things of my food.

---

1. Poetically for evils, calamities, says Ges., under *hts*, citing this v. and others.

2. We should say, the heat of which.

3. Metaphor, says Ges., under *shte*. The Heb. word used here is *ruh*, *breath;* and for *ruh* in the v. the Douay gives *spirit;* the Ital. *spirito;* E. V., *spirit:* Am. Bib. Un., *spirit*.

4. Ges., under *ork*, citing this v. gives "they set *the battle* in array against me." Am. Bib. Un....the terrors of God array themselves against me.

5. Ges., under *hlmut*, citing this v., gives, *slime of purslain;* but under *dui*, citing this v. there also, he gives, "can that which is unsavory be eaten without salt, or is there taste in the insipid herb?" The Douay is....or can a man taste that which when tasted bringeth death? Ital. ....or is there relish in the white that is round about the yolk of an egg? Am. Bib. Un....or is there any relish in the white of an egg?

6. The Heb. word here is *nphsh*—breath: Douay....*The things which* before my soul would not touch: Ital....*The things which my anima*—breath—would have refused to touch: Am. Bib. Un....My soul refuses to touch.

Ges., under *nphsh*, says, with suffix *i*, and *k*, etc., *nphshi*, and *nphshk*, it is sometimes, I myself, thou thyself, etc., citing Hos. 9:4, where the Heb. is *nphshm*—breaths of them, i. e. themselves; Ges. there gives *l nphshm*, "for themselves." In Job 6:7, the Heb. is, *nphshi*—breath of me refuseth to touch, i. e. I refuse to touch. Ges. cites also Isai. 46:2, where the Heb. is, *nphshm*—breaths of them; Douay, they themselves; Ital., their persons themselves; E. V., they themselves are gone into captivity; and Job 9:21, where the Heb. is *nphshi*—breath of me, for which Ges. gives "me myself," citing that v.

He further says: It has also been remarked by interpreters, that *nphshi*—(breath of me), and *nphshk* (breath of thee) are often put for the personal

8 Who will give, may come asking of me, and hope of me may give God.

9 And having begun God, that he may crush me; let loose hand of him and cut me off:

10 But will be yet consolation of me, yea I will exult in pain which does not spare, that I have not disowned words of Holy :[1]

11 What, strength of me, that I should hope, and what, end of me, that I should prolong breath[2] of me:

12 Whether strength of stones strength of me; whether flesh of me brass;

13 Whether it be not that not help of me in me, and help be fled from me;[3]

14 To one pining away, friend of him kindness, otherwise fear of Almighty may leave him;

---

pronouns, I and thou. That it is often thus used in sentences in which life is said to be in danger, citing Ps. 3 : 3, E. V. v. 2, where the Heb. is, many say to *nphshi*—breath of me, for, me; and Ps. 11 : 1, Why say ye to *nphshi*—breath of me, for, me; and Isai. 3 : 9, Woe to *nphshm*—breaths of them, i. e. to them; and citing also Ps. 7 : 3, E. V. v. 2, Ps. 35 : 3, 7; 120 : 6; Isai : 51 : 23. He also cites Job 16 : 4, (see it in its place). "Once, says Ges. *nphshi*, and *ruhi* (each, breath of me) come so near to the nature of a pronoun that they are even construed with the first person of verbs," citing Isai. 26 : 9: The Heb. there is, *nphshi*—breath of me has, for, I have, desired thee in night, yea *ruhi*—breath of me, in *qrb i*—intestines of me has sought thee, for, I in intestines of me have sought thee.

1. Ital....of the Holy: Douay, E. V., and Am. Bib. Un., of the Holy One.

2. The Heb. is *nphsh*: Douay....that I should keep patience? Am. Bib. Un....that I should be yet patient? Ital....for to prolong *the hope of* my *anima;* E. V....that I should prolong my life. Of course the Romish Ital. version could not allow the idea of a man's prolonging what the great Apostacy (i. e. departure from the faith, Romanism) inaugurated as the immortal soul, and so it interpolates *the hope of*, before *my anima:* And the Romish Douay version avoids giving anything for *nphsh* —breath—in the verse.

3. Ges., under *tushie*, used here, says, it is a word altogether poetical; he renders "aid fled from me."

15 Friends of me act perfidiously like stream, like channel of streams they pass by;

16 Which turbid from ice, in which hideth itself snow:[1]

17 At time they become narrow,[2] they are extinguished;[3] by heat of them they become extinct from place of them:[4]

18 Turn aside journeyers of way of them;[5] they go up desolation of them and perish:[6]

19 Were put to shame band of travellers of Tema; companies of Sheba waited for them:

20 Ashamed that with trust they came to this, and they blushed:

21 So that now ye are become as if not;[7] ye have seen terror, and are afraid:

22 Whether have said I, give to me; or from wealth of you bestow gifts for me:[8]

23 Or deliver me from hand of adversary,[9] or from hand of violent set me free:

24 Teach me, and I will keep silence, and how have erred I make me understand:

25 How forcible words of straightness;[10] but what proveth reproving of you:[11]

---

1. i. e. the snow water in the spring; so Ges., under *olm*, citing this v.
2. So Ges., under *zrb*, citing this v.
3. So Ges., under *tsmt*, citing this v., and Job 23:17.
4. i. e. they dry up, says Ges., under *dok*, citing this v.
5. i. e. says Ges., citing this v. under *lpht*, those who journey that way.
6. Amer. Bib. Un., "and perish:" the Heb. verb used here is *abd*, defined, to perish, to be lost, to be destroyed: "used of men and other living creatures as perishing," says Ges., citing Psal. 37:20; Job 4:11.
7. Ital....ye are come to nothing: Am. Bib. Un....ye are become nothing.
8. "to bribe a judge," says Ges., under *bod*, citing this v.
9. The Heb. word here is *tsar*, defined, an adversary, enemy, just as the Heb. *stn* (Douay and E. V., satan) is defined; and it means the same.
10. Fig., for "what is right, integrity," says Ges., under *ishr*.
11. "what does your reproving prove," i. e., your censure, says Ges., under *ikh*, citing this v.

26 Whether to reprove words ye purpose, although as breath [1] (or wind) words of one despairing :

27 Even upon orphan ye fall,[2] and ye dig[3] for friend of you :

28 And now look, face on me, and on faces of you, whether I lie :

29 Turn about, I pray you; not let be iniquity; and turn about again; righteous I in this :

30 Whether in tongue of me iniquity; whether palate[4] of me not can discern wickedness :

CHAPTER VII.

1 Whether not warfare to man on earth, and as days of hireling days of him :

2 As servant pants after shade, and as hireling awaits wages of him,

3 So are allotted to me months of calamity; and nights of weariness portions of me :

4 When I lay myself down to sleep [5] then say I, when shall I arise and flight of night; [6] and I am wearied of tossings until morning twilight : [7]

---

1. *ruh*—breath, wind, is the Heb. word *here*: Douay, Ital., E.V., and Am. Bib. Un., wind.

2. "as an enemy," says Ges., under *nphl*, citing Job 1 : 15: Douay, you rush in upon the fatherless : Am. Bib. Un., ye would even cast lots upon the fatherless.

3. Under *krc*, Ges., inserts *pits* after dig : Am. Bib. Un., and dig *a pit* for your friend.

4. Am. Bib. Un., "cannot my taste discern what is perverse." Ital., ...my palate.

5. So Ges., under *shkb*, citing this v. and others.

6. "and *when* shall be the flight of night," poetical for, when shall the night flee, come to an end, says Ges., under *ndd*, citing this v.

7. So Ges., under *nshph*, citing this v.

5 Is clothed flesh of me of worms [1] and clods of dust; skin of me draws together and flows : [2]

6 Days of me swift more than weaver's shuttle, and vanish away without hope :

7 Remember that breath [3] life of me ; not shall return eye of me to see good :

8 Not shall behold me eye ; *not* [4] look eyes of thee upon me because not shall exist I : [5]

9 Wasteth cloud and is gone, so who descends *shaul* [6] may not come up :

10 He may not return to house of him, and not may know him more place of him :

11 So I not will hold in mouth of me ; I will speak in distress of breath [7] of me ; I will speak [8] in bitterness of breath [9] of me :

---

1. "bred by putrefaction," says Ges., under *rme*, citing this v. and others : Douay...."clothed with rottenness;" Amer. Bib. Un., the same.

2. "my skin heals up, and again runs with water," says Ges., under *mas* citing this v.

3. The Heb. word here is *ruh*—breath : Ges., under *zkr*, citing this v., renders, "consider that my life is a breath :" Douay....that my life is but wind ; Ital....is a wind ; Amer. Bib. Un....that my life is a breath.

4. The *not* in the first clause belongs also to the second clause, a very common construction in the Heb.

5. Douay....and I shall be no more ; Ital....I not *shall be* more ; Amer. Bib. Un:....but I shall not be.

6. "those who go down to the grave," says Ges., under *ird*, citing this v., and Job 17 : 16 ; 33 : 24 ; Prov. 1 : 12 : Douay....so he that shall go down to hell shall not come up ; Ital....so who descendeth into the sepulchre ; Am. Bib. Un....so he that goes down to the under-world shall not come up. The verb used here is *iole*, in the future tense of *ole*. The Heb. has no subjunctive mood, and the future tense is used to supply the place of the subjunctive mood, and is frequently to be rendered in English by, may, might, can, could, should, would, ought ; see J. P. Wilson's "Easy Introduction to the Heb.," page 242. The doctrine of this book called Job plainly is, that the just, they who shall be accounted just, will be raised from the grave.

7. The Heb. word here is *ruh*.

8. Properly, utter with mouth, says Ges., under *shih*.

9. The Heb. word here is *nphsh*. For *ruh* in v. 11, the Douay has

12 Whether sea I or sea-monster, that thou shouldst set over me guard:

13 When say I, may comfort me bed of me, may bear couch of me of[1] grief of me:

14 Then thou scarest me with dreams, and by visions thou terrifiest me:

15 And chooses strangling breath[2] of me; death than bones of me:

16 Melt away I; not to hidden time shall I live, cease from me, for breath[3] days of me:

17 What *a* man, that thou makest so much of him,[4] and that thou settest on him mind of thee:[5]

18 And thou visitest him at mornings, at moments[6] thou triest (or provest) him:

19 How long wilt thou not look away from me, not let me alone so long as swallow I spittle of me:[7]

---

spirit, and for *nphsh* in the v. it has *soul*. The Amer. Bib. Un. has spirit ....soul.

1. i. e., part of my grief, says Ges., under *nsha*, citing this v.

2. Strangling is destroying life by stopping the breath—*nphsh*—the word used here: Douay....so that my soul rather chooseth hanging; Ital....so that I in the mind would choose rather to be strangled; Am. Bib. Un.....so that my soul chooseth strangling.

3. Heb. *ebl*, under which Ges. gives "for my days are a breath," citing this v. In this v., the Ital., gives, I not shall live to perpetuity; Douay ....I shall now live no longer; Am. Bib. Un....I shall not always live; the E. V. gives, I would not live always.

4. Douay....What is a man; E. V., and Am. Bib. Un....what is man. The succeeding verses show that our article *a* should be used here before *man*: The Douay is right in inserting it. The Heb. has not the article, and it is to be supplied where the sense requires it, the same as in the Greek. Ges., under *gdl*, says; "that thou makest so much of him," citing this v.

5. Am. Bib. Un., and set thy thoughts upon him.

6. Ges., under *rgo*, citing this v., "every moment;" Ital., at every moment thou examinest him.

7. "i. e., thou givest me no breathing space, not even the least moment wilt thou grant me, that I may rest," says Ges., under *blo*, citing this v.

20 Have sinned I,¹ what shall I do for thee, O thou observer of men; why hast thou set me for blow ² to thee, so that I should be on myself for burden.

21 And why not dost thou pardon fault of me, and not dost thou pass by ³ perversity of me, for in short time in dust I shall lie down; and seekest thou me,⁴ even not shall exist I.

CHAPTER VIII.

1 And answered Belded that Shui, and said:

2 Until when wilt thou utter these, and breath ⁵ of circle ⁶ words of mouth of thee:

3 Whether God will bend ⁷ right; ⁸ and whether Almighty will bend straightness: ⁹

4 Though children of thee have sinned against him,

---

1. i. e., If I have sinned; Douay and Ital., I have sinned; Am. Bib. Un., If I sin.
2. Ges., under *mphgo*, citing this v., gives, blow, hence used, says he, of one on whom it is laid.
3. Metaphor., for forgive, says Ges., under *obr*.
4. i. e., if thou seek me, and so the Douay and Ital. Am. Bib. Un., and thou wilt seek me.
5. Heb. *ruh*—breath.
6. i. e., moving in a circle: We say of one whose talk amounts to nothing, he talks, or argues in a circle: The Douay, for *ruh* in the v., gives, a strong wind; and the Ital., *as* a wind impetuous: Am. Bib. Un., and the words of thy mouth be a strong wind.
7. "Metaphor., for pervert," says Ges., under *out*, citing this v. and others.
8. The Heb. word is *mshphth*; the Douay gives, judgment; Am. Bib. Un., " will God pervert right."
9. Heb. *tsdq*, Ges., straightness, rightness; fig., says he, for, what is right; The Douay here is, that which is just: E. V....will pervert justice: Am. Bib. Un. the same. The true word is *justness*. There is not a passage in all scripture where *justice*, in the sense in which believers n eternal torments understand the word, is found.

and he may have cast them into hands of transgression of them :

5 If thou wouldst seek to God, and to Almighty wouldst make supplication :

6 If pure and straight[1] thou, even now he would watch over[2] thee, and make secure, habitation righteous of thee :

7 And be beginnings of thee small, yet latter state of thee would become great exceedingly :

8 For ask, I pray thee, to generation former, and turn mind to searchings of fathers of thee :

9 For of yesterday we, and do not know by experience, for *a* shadow, days of us on earth :

10 Whether not they will instruct thee, will speak they to thee, and from heart of them will cause to go out words :

11 Whether will grow marsh-rush without marsh ; will become great, bulrushes without water :

12 While yet in greenness of it not should it be plucked off,[3] because before every grass it is dried up :

13 So ways of all who forget God, yea, hope of impious shall perish :[4]

14 Who, is cut off hope[5] of him, yea, house of spider, trust of him :

15 He may lean upon[6] house of him,[7] but not shall it endure ; he may hold fast on it, but not shall it stand :

---

1. "Fig., for righteous," says Ges., under *ishr*, citing this v.

2. So Ges., under *our*, citing this v. Douay....awake unto thee : Am. Bib. Un....awake for thee.

3. Am. Bib Un., While yet in its greenness and they cut it not. Ges., not should it be plucked off, citing this v. and others, under *qthph*.

4. The Heb. verb is *abd*, defined, to be lost, to perish, used, says Ges., of men and other living creatures as perishing, citing Job 4 : 11 ; Ps. 37 : 20.

5. i. e., says Ges., under *quth*, whose hope is cut off, citing this v.

6. "Metaphor., for, repose confidence in," says Ges., under *shon*, citing this v. and others.

7. Fig., for offspring, or wealth ; see Ges., under *bt*—house.

16 Green he¹ in face of sun, and over garden of him shoots shall come forth :

17 Over heaps of stones roots of him entwine ; house of stones he seeth :²

18 Though they should devour him from habitation of him, and disavow as to him, *saying*, not have I seen thee :

19 Lo that man,³ rejoicing of way of him, that from dust *an* after⁴ shall sprout forth of him :

20 Lo, God will not reject upright ; but not will he take hold on hand of evil doers :

21 While he fills of laughter mouth of thee, and lips of thee of rejoicing :

22 They that hate thee shall be clothed with shame ; and habitation of evil doers not shall be to them.⁵

---

1. Heb. *eua*—(demonstrative)—the man who : The Ital is, *But the man perfect* is green to the sun. Am. Bib. Un....He in the face of the sun is green.

2. Used, says Ges., by a bold metaphor, of the roots of plants which perceive or feel stones in the earth, citing this v. under *hze*.

3. Heb. *eua*.

4. Heb. *ahr*. The Am. Bib. Un. gives the v. thus : Lo, that is the joy of his way : and from his dust shall others sprout up.

5. i. e., there shall be no place for them.

REMARK : The Douay, E. V. and Am. Bib. Un., word He, at the beginning of v. 16, makes that v. and the three following verses relate to the same man spoken of in verses 14 and 15. This does not give the proper signification to the Heb. *eua* in verses 16 and 19, and makes their renderings faulty and unintelligible. The Ital. gives a different meaning to v. 16 by inserting "*But the man perfect*," at the beginning of it. The true rendering of that part of this chapter beginning with v. 13, gives us the glorious doctrine—the resurrection of the just, and gives death as a finality to evil doers. This did not suit the Douay, nor the E. V., nor the Am. Bib. Union.

CHAPTER IX.

1 And answered Job and said:

2 Truly I know that so; and how can be just, man with God:

3 If he should desire to contend with him, not could he answer him one of a thousand:

4 Wise in heart, and strong of might, who has hardened against him and been safe:

5 Who taking away mountains and not know they; who overturneth them by nostril of him:[1]

6 Who causing earth to shake from place of it, and pillars of it are broken:[2]

7 Who commands to sun and not scatters he rays, and round about stars seals up:

8 Spreadeth out heavens alone of him, and treads upon heights of sea:[3]

9 Made *osh*,[4] *ksil*,[5] and *kime*,[6] and chambers of south:[7]

---

1. i. e. by breath—spirit—of him: Ges., under *aph*—nostril, says: used for anger, which shows itself in hard breathing, citing Prov. 22 : 24; 29 : 22; Deut. 29 : 19; 32 : 22; Job 36 : 13.

2. So Ges., under *phlts*, citing this v.

3. Ges., under *bme*—height—cites this v., and renders, "upon the fortresses of the sea." He says: The holder of the fortresses of a region has secure possession of it; whence, says he, the poetic phrase, "he walked upon," as, "he walked upon the fortresses of the earth," citing Amos 4 : 13; Mic. 1 ; 3; Deut. 33 : 29; and figuratively, says he, "upon the fortresses of the sea," citing this v. in Job; and "upon the fortresses of the clouds," citing Isai. 14 : 14, used, says he, of God as the Supreme Ruler of the world. He cites also Deut. 32 : 13; Isai. 58 : 14.

4. Ges. says: "a very bright constellation, *Ursa Major*, (Bear greater), which we, in common with the Greeks and Romans, call the wain."

5. Ges. says: "the name of a star or constellation," citing this v. and Job 38:31; Amos 5 : 8; "according to many of the ancient translators, Orion, which the Orientals call *nphila*, i. e., the giant." "They seem to have looked on this constellation as the figure of an impious giant bound to the sky; whence Job 38 : 31, canst thou loose the bands of Orion?"

6. Ges. says: "a heap, cluster, specially of stars, hence the Pleiades."

7. Metaphor., for the most southern region, says Ges.

10 He doeth greatnesses even to not searching out, and wonders even to not of number:

11 Lo, he can pass near me and not I see, and come on against[1] and not I attend to him:

12 Lo, he can ravin, who can hinder him: who shall say to him what doest thou:

13 God, not should he turn away nostril of him, under it sink down helpers of pride:

14 How much less I, should I answer him,[2] could I choose out words of me with him:

15 Whom, though I am righteous,[3] not would I answer; to judge of me would I make supplication:

16 If called I and he answered me, not could confide I that he heard and answered voice of me:

17 Who in tempest falls upon me,[4] and multiplies wounds of me without cause:

18 Not gives he me to draw breath,[5] for he satiates me of bitternesses:

---

1. So Ges., under *hlph*, citing this v. and Job 11 : 10.

2. Ges. "How much less if I should answer him," under *aph*, citing this v., and Job 35 : 14 ; Ezek. 15 : 5.

3. Ges., under *am*, "though I am righteous," citing this v. ; Am. Bib. Un., "though I be righteous."

4. So Ges., under *shuph*, citing this v. ; Am. Bib. Un., "For he dashes me to pieces with a tempest."

5. The Heb. word here is *ruh*—breath : For *ruh* in the v. the Douay gives *spirit*, thus, "He alloweth not my spirit to rest;" The Ital. is: He not me permitteth to take breath ; Am. Bib. Un.... He will not suffer me to recover my breath : Ges., under *ruh*—breath, citing this v., renders, "to draw the breath ;" and under *shub* he cites Ruth 4 : 15, where the Heb. is : And he will be to thee for renewer of *nphsh*—breath : Douay ....to comfort the soul : Ital....for to restore the *anima*—breath : And in Lament. 1 : 11, 16, 19, the Heb. is "draw *nphsh*" breath : Douay....to relieve the soul : Ital....to restore the *anima*—breath : E. V....relieve the soul. And 1 Sam. 30 : 12, the Heb. is, come back *ruh*—breath—of him ; Douay and E. V., *spirit*. And in Judges 15 : 19, the Heb. is, came back *ruh*—breath of him : Ital....he returned to life : Douay....he refreshed his spirit : E. V....his spirit came again, and he revived, (i. e.) lived

19 If as to strength, strong *he*, lo, but if as to right who will cite me : ¹

20 Though should speak what is right mouth of me he would declare me guilty ;² upright I he would pervert me :³

21 Perfect I, not should I get to know breath ⁴ of me, I should despise life ⁵ of me :

22 One it, therefore said I, perfect and wicked he consumes :

23 If scourge kill suddenly, at calamity of innocent he can mock :

24 Earth is given into hand of wicked ; faces of judges ⁵ of it he covers ; if not so, who is it : ⁷

---

again. And in Ps. 19 : 8, E. V., v. 7, the Heb. is, restoring the *nphsh*—breath : Ital....it restores the *anima*—breath : Douay....Ps. 18 : 8, converting souls: E. V....converting the soul. To draw back one's *nphsh* —breath—is a figure for, to refresh him, Ges., under *shub*

1. So Ges., under *iod*, citing this v., or call on me to plead, says he.
2. So Ges., under *oqsh*, citing this v.
3. Ges. says : Metaphor., to pervert any one, in a forensic sense, is equivalent to pervert or wrest his cause, citing this v., and rendering, "*although* I were upright *God* would pervert my cause : Douay....my own mouth shall condemn me....he shall prove me wicked : Ital....my mouth me would condemn, *though* I were perfect, it (i. e. the mouth) me would declare guilty : Am. Bib. Un....Though I were righteous, my own mouth would condemn me, if I were perfect, he would show me perverse. The *he*, in the Douay, and Am. Bib. Un., of the last clause of the v., plainly means God, and shows that "my own mouth would condemn me," in the first clause is wrong ; Ges. is clearly right in not making Job say, his own mouth would condemn him. Many preceding verses show that he would not say that ; he insists continually on his integrity. In the Heb., mouth is said to speak, and tongue is said to speak, &c. It is poetical.
4. The Heb. is, *nphsh*—breath—of me, (i. e. myself) : Ges., under *nphsh*, for *nhpsh* of me—breath of me, gives *myself:* The Ital. here is....I would not know myself: Douay....my soul shall be ignorant of : E. V. ....yet would I not know my soul : Am. Bib. Un....I should take no thought for myself.
5. The Heb. word for life is *hie; life* is often wrongly given in E. V. for *nphsh*—breath. For *nphshi*, see note 1 to Job 6 : 7.
6. Or rulers.
7. Metaphor., says Ges., under *ksut*, "covering of the eyes," equiva-

25 And days of me swift above runner; they are fled away; not have seen good:

26 They have passed by like vessels of reed;[1] as eagle dashes on prey:

27 If say I, I will forget quarrel[2] of me, I will leave off face of me[3] and will be cheerful:

28 I am provoked of all pains of me;[4] I know that not wouldst thou declare me innocent:

29 I, have I an unrighteous cause;[5] why then in vain do I labour:

30 Though I should wash me in water of snow, and cleanse in purity[6] hands of me:

31 After that, in *shht*[7] thou wouldst dip me, and would abhor me garments of me:

---

lent, says he, to a gift of appeasing to any one, that he may shut his eyes to, i. e. says he, connive at something reprehensible; or a present given to obtain pardon, a mulct. He says: "so is to be understood Gen. 20: 16, which has a good deal troubled interpreters." He renders it, "Behold this (the gift of a thousand shekels) is to thee a mulct for all things, which have happened to thee, and before all men." He says the Septuagint gives the meaning correctly, but has either been neglected or misunderstood. He says: several interpreters have taken it to be a vail. The Am. Bib. Un. gives, "the face of its judges he vails."

1. Douay....as ships carrying fruit.
2. So Ges., urder *shih*, citing this v.
3. For sad countenance, says ¦Ges., under *phne*, citing this v. and 1 Sam. 1:18; Douay....I change my face, and am tormented with sorrow; Am. Bib. Un....I will change my aspect, and be joyous.
4. Pains of body, says Ges., under *otsbt*, citing this v.
5. So Ges., under *rsho*, citing this v.
6. The Heb. word here is *br*, purity, and Ges. cites under it this v., and Job 22:30; Ps. 18:21, 25; cleanness of hands being put figuratively for innocency, says he. The Douay is....and my hands shall shine ever so clean; Ital....and clean my hands with soap; Am. Bib. Un....and cleanse my hands with lye.
7. Especially the sepulchre, grave, says Ges., citing this v. and Job 17: 14; 33:18, 24, 28, 30; Ps. 30:10, E. V. v. 9; Ps. 55:24, E. V. v. 23; The Douay is....Yet thou shalt plunge me in filth. Ital....plunge me in a *fossa*, defined, ditch, trench, grave. Am. Bib. Un....then thou wilt plunge me into a pit.

32 For not man as I should answer him, entering with him into what is right : [1]

33 Not exists between us one having power to lay hand on both of us :

34 Let him turn aside from upon me rod of me,[2] so that terror of him not may frighten me :

34 I would speak, and not would fear him, for not so I with myself :[3]

CHAPTER X.

1 Loathes breath[4] of me life of me ; I will let loose upon me complaint[5] of me ; I will speak in bitterness of breath[6] of me :

2 I will say to God, do not thou condemn me, make me to know why thou contendest with me :

3 Whether good to thee that thou shouldst oppress, that thou shouldst despise work of hands of thee, and upon counsel of wicked give light :

4 Whether eyes of flesh to thee, whether as seest man thou seest :

---

1. Ital....For he not *is a* man as *am* I, *that* I him should answer, *and that* we should come together in judgment. Am. Bib. Un....the same. The Douay is....For I shall not answer a man that is like myself; nor one that may be heard equally with me in judgment.

2. Ges., under *shbth*, citing this v., says : rod is metaphorically used of calamities sent by God.

3. Ges., citing this v. under *om*—with, renders, not so am I with myself, i. e. says he, my mind is not such within me, namely, that I should fear ; The Ital. is....in myself : Am. Bib. Un....in myself.

4. Heb. *nphsh ;* sound it with mouth in two syllables—*en-phsh*, drawing in *en* and breathing out *phsh ;* the two sounds express breath : *breath of me* is poetical for *I :* Douay....My soul is weary of my life : Am. Bib. Un....the same.

5. "Metaphor., says Ges., under *ozb*, citing this v., i. e. says he, I will let loose as it were the reins, I will not restrain it.

6. Heb. *nphsh* ; "Metaphor. for, in sadness," says Ges., under *mre*.

5 Whether as days of man days of thee: whether years of thee as days of man:

6 That thou shouldst seek for perversity of me, and for fault of me shouldst search:

7 On knowledge of thee[1] that not am I wicked, and not exists from hand of thee deliverer:

8 Hands of thee fashioned me and made me wholly round about, and wilt thou give me up to destruction:[2]

9 Remember, I pray thee, that as clay thou madest me, and to dust thou wilt return me:[3]

10 Whether not as milk thou pouredst me out, and as cheese thou curdledst me:

11 Skin and flesh hast put on me, and with bones and and sinews hast interwoven me:

12 Life and desire thou hast created with me, and hast charged to care of thee breath[4] of me:

13 And these hast thou hid in heart of thee; I know that this with thee:[5]

14 Have sinned I, then thou wilt keep[6] for me, and and from guilt of me will not absolve me:

---

1. "Although thou knowest," says Ges., citing this v. under *ol*.

2. So Ges. under *blo*, citing this v., and Job 2; 3: Isai. 49 : 19; Hab. 1 : 13; Am. Bib. Un....and yet thou dost destroy me:

3. The Douay, and Ital., rightly so have it; Am. Bib. Un....and wilt thou bring me to dust again?

4. Heb. *ruh:* The Douay, the E. V. and the Am. Bib. Un., give *spirit* for *ruh* here; The Ital. is, and thy care has guarded my *spirito*—(from the Latin *spiritus*—breath): Graglia's Romish Ital. Dict., for *spirito*, gives, spirit, soul, ghost, showing that these three words mean the same thing. And the distinguished Bishop Hobart, since deceased, in a "Dissertation" by him, says, they all mean the same. And so they do: they all mean *breath*. But Hobart says, they each mean, the spirit, soul, ghost, that goes to Episcopacy's intermediate place, both good and bad ghosts. See "The Theology of the Bible" by Halsted, page 117.

5. Ital....I know that this *was* with thee.

6. i. e. "keep (punishment)," says Ges., under *shmr*, citing this v. For "Have sinned I," the Douay and Ital. rightly give, "If I have sinned." Am. Bib. Un....If I sin.

15 If wicked I, woe to me; and righteous I, not can I lift up head of me,[1] filled of shame and of seeing of affliction of me:

16 And should it raise itself up,[2] as lion thou wouldst hunt me, and turning about wouldst show thyself wonderful in strength upon me:

17 Thou wouldst renew testimonies[3] of thee against me, and wouldst increase anger of thee with me; changes and hosts against me.[4]

18 Then why from womb didst thou bring me forth, I should have breathed out,[5] and eye not would have seen me:

19 Like as not had been[6] I, I should have been; from womb to grave I should have been borne.

20 Whether not few, days of me: Let him let alone;[7] let him take[8] from me, that I may be made cheerful a little while:

21 Before that I shall go and not shall return, to land of darkness and shadow of death:[9]

---

1. i. e. be cheerful, says Ges., under *nsha*, citing this v.
2. i. e. his head.
3. Properly says Ges., "what testifies."
4. Ges., under *kliphe*, citing this v., renders, "changes and hosts *are* against me," i. e. says he, hosts fight against me continuously succeeding one another.
5. From the Heb. verb *ghuo*—to breathe out, (the meaning of it is shown by the sounds of it): The Douay is...."O that I had been consumed; Ital....I there should have been *spirato*—breathed out; E. V... "O that I had given up the ghost;" Am. Bib. Un....."I should have died." The Ital. uses the right word here. The Douay does not deal in ghosts at all, it uniformly avoids the word. And the Am. Bib. Un. follows the example of the Douay in never using the word. It was too plain, (and too dangerous to their system), that *ghost* means *breath*. The Am. Bib. Un. here substitutes *died*, for *breathed out;* whereas in the Heb. they are two different words, and mean different things; *mut* is the Heb. verb for *to die;* and *ghuo* is the Heb. verb for *to breathe out*.
6. i. e. not had existed I.
7. So Ges., under *hdl*, citing this v. and Job 7:16; Exod. 14:12.
8. "Ellipsis, *the hand*," says Ges., under *shit*, citing this v.
9. Ges., under *tsl*—shadow, says: compare Latin *umbra*. For *umbra*,

22 Land of darkness such as darkness thick, of shadow of death and not order, and giving light like darkness thick.[1]

Anthon's Latin Dict. gives "a shade, shadow," Plural, says he, "the shades of departed souls in the infernal regions," citing Suetonius; as also, says he, of one departing spirit, citing Ovid. Of course Anthon could not omit to give us the meaning of *the shades* in the Roman mythology, from Roman authors. And the reader will observe that Anthon here gives *soul* and *spirit* as meaning the same, thus, the shades of departed souls, and, the shade of a departed spirit.

1. Douay...."and no order, but everlasting horror dwelleth;" very good Romanism.

NOTE.—For the Latin *umbra*, the Ital. is *ombra:* for which Graglia's Romish Ital. Dict. gives, "shadow, shade, ghost, spirit." We thus see how the Papacy—the Apostacy and its priests—availed themselves of Roman mythology in support of their dogma—the immortal spirit,—soul, ghost, shade; a doctrine condemned by the first reformers. A council of the Lateran, held A. D. 1513, under Pope Leo X, pronounced the immortality of the soul an article of Christian faith. It was denied by the Aristotelian school: but the "Pope came in with his baton of infallibility, and at once decided the controversy by the dictum of spiritual authority." The following is a translation of the canon enacted at that Council: "Whereas, in these our days, some have dared to assert concerning the nature of the reasonable soul, that it is mortal, or one and the same in all men, and some rashly philosophizing, declare this to be true, at least according to philosophy. We, with the approbation of the sacred Council, do condemn and reprobate all those who assert that the intellectual soul is mortal, or one and the same in all men, and those who call these things in question; seeing that the soul is not only truly, and of itself, and essentially the form of the human body, as is expressed in the canon of Pope Clement the Fifth, published in the General Council of Vienna, but likewise immortal, and according to the number of bodies into which it is infused, is singularly multipliable, multiplied, and to be multiplied. And seeing that truth never contradicts truth, we determine every assertion which is contrary to revealed truth, to be false; and we strictly inhibit all from dogmatising otherwise, and we decree that all who adhere to the like erroneous assertions, shall be shunned and punished as heretics."

Luther thus ironically responded to the decree, "I permit the Pope to make articles of faith for himself and his faithful, such as the soul is the substantial form of the human body,—the soul is immortal,—with all those monstrous opinions to be found in the Roman dunghill of decretals." And Tyndale, the fellow reformer with Luther, declares, "that they were heathen and fleshly doctrines;" and he says: "And because the fleshly minded Pope consenteth unto the heathen doctrine, therefore he corrupteth the scripture to establish it." And Tyndale says: "In putting departed souls in heaven, hell, and purgatory, you destroy the the arguments wherewith Christ and Paul prove a resurrection."

How many in Christendom know that the dogma—inherent immortality—was established by a decree composed of such stuff? Well might the Rev. J. Panton Ham, of Bristol, England, say: "Behold, ye asserters of your own inherent immortality, the worthy nursing father of your faith! Worthy patron of a pagan progeny! Let it be registered as the genuine genealogy of a fundamental doctrine of modern British Christendom, that the Pagan Plato was its father, and the profligate Pope Leo its foster-father. Born and bred by the Pagan philosophy, and the protege of popery, this notion of the soul's immortality has become a pet dogma of popular Protestantism, which, with a strange forgetfulness of its low lineage, openly declares it to be the honorable offspring of a true orthodoxy." There is no such language in the Bible as we hear from the pulpits,—immortal soul,—immortal spirit, &c. A purse of 100 guineas is offered in England, to any one who will find any such language in the Bible; and yet 99 of every 100 believe that the Bible is full of such language. The same writer says: "The philosophy of Luther led him to conceive of a human soul as a distinct, but not an immortal subsistence. He embraced and taught the sleep of the soul, and continued in that belief to the close of his life." It is no wonder that having been a papist, he should have some such notion.

The same writer says: "It was during the pontificate of this Leo that Luther visited Rome, and where the licentiousness of the papal court and clergy so astonished and disgusted him, that from that time his reverence for the Pope was completely and for ever destroyed."

CHAPTER XI.

1 And answered Zophar, that Nomti, and said:

2 Whether multitude of words not should be answered, and whether man of lips[1] should be accounted just:

---

1. Heb., plural of *shphe*—lip: Douay...a man full of talk: Am. Bib. Un.....a man of talk.

3 Because of thee should men keep silence; and shalt thou deride and not there be putting to shame:

4 For thou hast said, pure, doctrine of me, and pure I have been in eyes of thee:

5 But indeed who will give,[1] God would speak and open lips [2] of him with thee:[3]

6 And would show to thee hidden things of wisdom; for double folds to wisdom;[4] and know that has forgot for thee, God, of iniquity of thee:

7 Whether secret recesses of God thou canst come to; whether to perfection of Almighty thou canst come:

8 Heights of heavens, what canst thou do; deep more than grave,[5] what canst thou know:

9 Long more than earth, measure of it, and breadth of it more than of sea:

10 If he come on against [6] and shut over [7] and gather together, then who will turn him:

11 For, himself,[8] he knows men of wickedness, and sees iniquity, and should he not regard it:

12 But man hollow,[9] void of understanding, and foal of wild ass man is born:[10]

---

1. For oh that.
2. The same Heb. word as in v. 2; The Douay here has, lips; Am. Bib. Un., lips.
3. Douay....to thee: Ital....with thee: Am. Bib. Un....against thee.
4. Ges., under *kphl*, "for God's wisdom has double folds," i. e., says he, is complicated, inexplicable: Douay....that his law is manifold: Am. Bib. Un....how manifold is understanding.
5. Heb. *shaul*: Douay....deeper than hell: E. V....than hell: Am. Bib. Un....than the under-world.
6. i. e. hostilely, says Ges., under *hlph*, citing this v. and Job 9 : 11.
7. Ges., under *sgr*, gives, shut over, namely, says he, a subterranean prison, citing Job 12 : 14; (by subterranean prison he no doubt means the grave): The Am. Bib. Un. of the v. is, If he pass by, and shall apprehend, and call an assembly, who will answer him?
8. Heb. *eua*.
9. Metaphor., says Ges., empty, foolish, citing this v. under *nbb*; and
10. under *lbb*, citing this v., he gives, and man is born like a wild ass's

13 If thou make straight heart of thee, and spread out to him hands of thee:

14 If wickedness in hand of thee, make it go away far from thee, and not shalt thou let dwell in tents of thee iniquity:

15 So that then thou canst lift up face of thee far off from spot,¹ and thou shalt be *a* casting,² and not shalt thou fear :

16 For thou vexation shalt forget, as waters passed on thou shalt remember:

17 And above midday³ shall arise life; covered with darkness, as dawn⁴ shalt thou be:

---

colt," signifying says he, the imbecility and dullness of the human understanding when compared with the divine wisdom.

1. Figuratively, says Ges., for, without spot.

2. Ges., under *itsq*—to be cast from metal, citing passages: Metaphor., says he, for firm, fearless, citing this v.: Douay....and thou shalt be steadfast, and shalt not fear: Am. Bib. Un....the same. We say, a man of cast iron.

3. Metaphor., for great happiness, says Ges., under *tserim*, citing this v., and Ps. 37 : 6.

4. Heb. *bqr:* Ges., under *ouph* renders, "*although now* covered with darkness," i. e. says he, pressed down by calamity, *soon* shalt thou be as the morning;" unless, says he, it be preferred to read with three manuscripts, *touphe*—darkness shall be as morning." I do not think that three manuscripts out of the great number of manuscripts can take away the beauty and sublimity of the verse: The E. V. is better: thou shalt be as the morning: Ital....thou shalt be like to the morning: Douay....thou shalt rise as the day-star: The Latin word used here is Lucifer, light-bringer—from *lux*—light, genitive *lucis*, and *fero*—to bring: The Heb. word for which the Latin *Lucifer* is given is *eill*, defined by Ges., "bright-star, i. e. Lucifer:" The Greek has two words for it, *phosphoros* and *eosphoros: phosphoros* is defined by the Hederci Lexicon (which renders Greek into Latin,) "*lucifer*—light bringing ; phosphoros ; star of Venus rising before the sun; *phosphoros aster*, light bringing star), Lucifer." Liddell and Scott's Greek Lexicon defines *phosphoros*, "the light bringer, Latin Lucifer, i. e. the morning star." And Donnegan's Greek Lexicon defines *phosphoros*, the morning star, Lucifer. *Phosphoros* is compounded of the Greek *phos*—light, and *phero*—to bring. The Greek *eosphoros* is compounded of *eos*—dawn, and *phero*—to bring : It is defined in Liddell

18 And thou shalt be secure, for there will be hope; yea, ashamed ¹ thou, in tranquility shalt thou lie down :

19 And thou shalt lie down and none making afraid; shall stroke face ² of thee, many :

20 But eyes of wicked shall waste away, and refuge perish from them, and hope of them, breathing out the breath:³

---

and Scott's Greek Lexicon, "the morning star, Latin Lucifer;" in mythology, son of *Astraeus* and *Aurora*—defined by Anthon, morning dawn, break of day : and *eosphoros* is defined in Donnegan's Gr. Lex., the Harbinger of day, Lucifer: And Lucifer is defined in Anthon's Latin Dict., "the Planet Venus, the morning star," citing Cicero : according to fable, says Anthon, a son of Aurora, citing Ovid : Metonymy, says he, the day, *tres luciferos* (three lucifers), citing Ovid.

And now shall I be believed when I tell the reader that Noah Webster, in his Dict., defines Lucifer, "the Planet Venus ; Satan : " thus adopting the Papacy's devil, horns, tail, and hoofs,—Milton's devil that fell "nine days and nights" into the horrid pit. Webster did not get Satan as an additional definition of Lucifer, the planet Venus, from any Dict. He either took it from Popery, or from Milton's Paradise Lost, called by Prof. Draper, a Manichean poem. The Manichees were a sect who believed in the absurd notion of the existence of two supreme principles, one good, and the other evil. Milton's Paradise Lost did untold injury. Fortunately for the world he lived long enough to write his work entitled "A Treatise on Christian Doctrine," which was published after his death, and which took from the Satan of his Paradise Lost his "occupation" (and of course his existence), by proving that there are no such entities, or rather non-entities, as the Papacy's souls, spirits, ghosts, shades. I have lately learned with pleasure, that another edition of that Treatise is about to be published in England.

1. (Note to 11 : 18.)

Ges. under *hphs*, citing this v., renders "*now* thou art ashamed, *afterwards* thou shalt dwell in tranquility."

2. Used of flattering a king or noble, says Ges., under *hle*, citing this v. Douay....and many shall entreat thy face; Am. Bib. Un....yea, many shall make their court to thee.

3. Heb. *mphh nphsh*—breathing out the breath : Douay....and their hope the abomination of the soul ; Ital....their *only* hope *shall be* of to render the *spirito*—breath ; E. V....and their only hope *shall be as* the giving up of the ghost ; Am. Bib. Un....and their hope it is the breathing out of life. Why did the Am. Bib. Un. give *life*, instead of *breath*, for the Heb. *nphsh*—breath—in the v. ? What can be breathed out but

CHAPTER XII.

1 And answered Job and said:

2 It is true that[1] ye *are the* people,[2] and with you will die wisdom:

3 Also to me heart[3] as well as you; not fall I[4] with you, and with whom are not such as these:

4 Derision to companion of him I am become who call to God and he answers him: is laughed at *the* upright perfect:

5 Torch of contempt[5] in thoughts of *the* living at ease, as a weapon aimed at *one* tottering of foot:

---

breath? *Life* and *breath* are two different words. The Heb. word for life is *hi*, and the Heb. word for *breath* (Douay, and E. V., so often soul,) is *nphsh*. In this v., two appropriate words, *mphh nphsh*—breathing out the breath, are used to express what in other passages is expressed by the single Heb. verb *ghuo*—to breathe out: so that the E.V. itself proves that its phrase "give up the ghost" means, give up the breath. And in Jer. 15:9, the Heb. uses two appropriate words, *nphh nphsh*—breathed out *the* breath; and there also the E. V. gives "she hath given up the ghost." But the Am. Bib. Un. never uses the word ghost. I can see no better reason for this than what must have influenced the Douay translators in avoiding the word *ghost*, namely, that if they used it at all they must use it wherever the Heb. verb *ghuo* occurs; and that would prove beyond controversy, that *ghost* means breath, and that the Heb. *nphsh* means *breath*. In Brown's Bible by the Patersons there is a marginal note to "the giving up the ghost" in the E. V. of Job 11:20, thus, "or a puff of breath." The last breath is an exspiration—outbreathing, and it goes out with something of a puff. And Graglia's Ital. Dict. for *spirito*, gives, soul, spirit, ghost. What better proof could be asked, that those words all mean the same thing, namely, breath?

1. So Ges., under *amnm*, citing this v.
2. Under *om* Ges. cites this v. again, and renders, "surely ye are the whole human race;" spoken says he in bitter irony.
3. "The faculty of thinking," "understanding," says Ges., under *lbb*, citing this v., and he renders, "I also have understanding as well as you."
4. i. e. says Ges., under *nphl*, citing this v., I am not inferior to you.
5. "A torch despised," says Ges., under *lphid*, citing this v., i. e., says he, a torch cast aside because of its having ceased to give light, an image, says he, for a man formerly highly esteemed, but now low and despised;

6 Are secure tents of oppressors, and securities¹ to them that provoke to anger God, to who carry God in hand of them:²

7 But indeed ask, I pray thee, beasts, and they will teach thee, and winged of these heavens,³ and they will tell thee:

8 Or speak to earth and it will teach thee, yea, shall recount to thee fishes of the sea:

9 Which not knoweth among all these⁴ that hand of Jehovah wrought this:

10 Who in hand of him breath⁵ of every living thing, and breath⁶ of every flesh of man:

---

compare, says he, Isai. 7 : 4; 14 : 19 : The verse in the Am. Bib. Un., is, There is room for misfortune, in the thought of the secure, ready for those who waver in their steps.

1. "i. e. secure tranquility," says Ges., under *bthhut*, citing this v.

2. "Who carries his God in his hand," says Ges., under *bua*, citing this v. Ital...."into whose hands he makes fall *that which they desire:* Am. Bib. Un...."he into whose hands God bringeth : Douay....substantially the same,—a plain misapprehension wholly unsuited to context.

3. Ital....and the birds of heaven : Douay....and the birds of the air ; E. V....and the fowls of the air; Am. Bib. Un....and the birds of heaven. The Heb. word is *shmim*, (plural)—heavens, and is always in the plural in the Heb. scriptures. It includes the atmosphere—air—in which birds fly, and the starry heavens. No such place is known to scripture as the heaven of Papacy, any more than its hell, and its purgatory. The restored—renewed—earth will be the abode of the "children of the resurrection,"—the risen saints.

4. Ital....Among all these *creatures*, which *is that which* not knoweth that the hand of the Lord did this ? Am. Bib. Un....Who knows not by all these.

5. Heb. *nphsh*.

6. Heb. *ruh:* Douay....*soul* for *nphsh;* and *spirit* for *ruh:* Ital....In whose hand is the *anima* of every *man* living, and the *spirito* of every flesh human : The Ital. was not willing to allow here that any living thing but man can have *anima* (for which *soul* is the only definition given in Graglia's Romish Ital. Dict.,) and therfore it interpolates *man:* E. V....In whose hand is the soul of every living thing, and the breath (Heb. *ruh*) of all mankind : Am. Bib. Un....In whose hand is the breath of all living, and the spirit of all the flesh of man ? In this v. the E. V.

11 Whether not ear words tries, and palate food tastes for itself:

12 In hoaries, wisdom, and length of days understanding:

13 With him wisdom and power; to him counsel and understanding:

14 Lo, he pulleth down, and not shall be rebuilt, he shuts over [1] *a* man and he may not be set free: [2]

---

gives *breath* for *ruh*, and the Am. Bib. Un. gives *breath* for *nphsh*, the Heb. word in the v. for which the Douay, and the E. V. give *soul*. Every flesh of man, in the v., is used for, every man; as is every *nphsh*—breath —of man in other passages: each by the familiar figure synecdoche, by which a part is put for the whole; flesh, and breath, being each an essential part of a living creature. We thus have in this v. Job 12 : 10, the authority of the Am. Bib. Un. that *nphsh* is *breath:* and the authority of the E. V. that *ruh* is *breath;* and that the Ital. *anima* is *breath*. Our word *spirit* is the Latin word *spiritus*, with the Latin termination *us* struck off; and the Ital. *spirito* is the Latin *spiritu*s. And we have only to turn to the Latin classics to find that their testimony is in full concurrence with that of the Heb. scriptures as to the meaning of the Lat. *spiritus*. Under *halitus*—breath—Anthon's Dict. quotes from Cicero, *efflavit extremum halitum*—he breathed out the last breath; and under *efflo*—to breathe out—he cites from Cicero, *efflare animam*—to breathe out the breath, for which Anthon gives, to breathe one's last; and under *spiritus* he cites from Cicero, *excipere extremum spiritum*—to draw out the last breath. And in the English-Latin part of his Dictionary, for *ghost* he gives *"spiritus, anima :" "supremum spiritum efflare"*—the last breath to breathe out; " to give up the ghost," adds Anthon. And of all the numerous passages cited by Anthon in his Dict. from Latin writers in which the Latin *spiritus* occurs, there is not one but shows that *spiritus* means *breath*. And where else shall we go for the meaning of a Latin word but to the Latin writers. What would the English versions, the Douay, and the Ital., and our Spiritists, have done for their spirits if the Latin had not had its word *spiritus ?* The concurrent testimony of two such witnesses as the Hebrew Scriptures and the Latin writers is abundantly sufficient to exorcise them.

1. Ges., under *sgr*, citing this v., renders, " he shuts over *a* man," namely, a subterranean prison, (meaning, no doubt, the grave.)

2. And under *phth*, citing this v. again, he gives, "set free, used," says he, " of a captive;" (meaning, I think, from the bondage of the grave.)

15 Lo, he shall withhold [1] waters, and they dry up; [2] and he shall [3] let go and they will overturn land:

16 With him strength and counsel; to him erring and leading astray: [4]

17 Causing to go captive, leaders; and judges he makes foolish:

18 Discipline of kings he looses, and binds bonds on loins of them:

19 Causing to go captive, priests, and potent he sends headlong: [5]

20 Turning aside lip [6] of trustworthy, and taste [7] of old men he takes away:

21 He pours contempt on princes, and girdle of strong he loosens:

22 Making naked deep things from darkness, and he brings forth to light shadow of death: [8]

23 Making great, peoples, [9] and he causes them to perish; and he spreads out peoples [10] and causes them to be at rest:

24 Turning aside mind of leaders of this land, [11] and he causes them to go astray, in wasteness not path:

---

1. i. e. If he shall; and so the Douay, and Ital.
2. Impersonal, for, it becomes dry.
3. i. e. If he shall; and so the Douay, and Ital.
4. Ges., under *shgg*, citing this v., renders, "erring—led astray, and leading astray," a proverbial phrase, says he, denoting men of every kind; compare, says he, similar phrases, Mal. 2 : 13; Deut. 32 : 36.
5. So Ges., under *slph*, citing this v.
6. Metonymy for speech, says Ges. under *shphe*—lip.
7. Metonymy for discernment, reason, says Ges., under *thom*, citing this v.: The Am. Bib. Un. of the verse is: The trusted he deprives of speech, and takes away wisdom of the aged.
8. Poetical for very thick darkness, says Ges., under *tslmut*, citing Job 13 : 5; 10 : 21; 28 : 3; 34 : 22; 38 : 17.
9. Specially used of the other nations besides Israel, says Ges., under *gui*.
10. i. e. gives them ample territories, says Ges., under *shthh*: Am. Bib. Un....He extends the bounds of nations, and he leads them away.
11. Douay....of the earth.

25 They feel out darkness,[1] and not light, and he causes them to wander as drunk:[2]

CHAPTER XIII.

1 Lo, the whole has seen eye of me, has heard ear of me, and I have turned mind to it:

2 As know you also I; not fall I from you:

3 But indeed I, to Almighty would I speak, yea, to argue to God I would desire:

4 But indeed ye patch lies;[3] comforters vain all of you:[4]

5 Who will give, caused to be deaf ye might be dumb,[5] and it might be to you for wisdom:

6 Hear, I pray you, showing of right of me, and abundance of lip[6] of me attend to:

7 Whether on behalf of God will ye speak iniquity, and for him will ye speak deception:

8 Whether face[7] of him ye will be partial to; whether for God ye will contend:

9 Whether good that he should search you; whether as is deceived man can ye deceive him:

---

1. "Explore with the hands," says Ges., under *mshsh*, citing this v. and others.

2. Ges., under *toe*, says: "Metaphor., to cause a people to wander from virtue and piety to impiety," citing Isai. 3:12; 9:15; "and the worship of idols," citing 2 Kings 21:9; Isai. 63:17: Am. Bib. Un....he makes them reel like a drunken man.

3. Fig. for frame lies, says Ges., under *thphl*, citing this v.

4. So Ges., under *rpha*, citing this v.

5. Ges., for *hrsh* gives, to be deaf, to be dumb; and says: to be dumb is often the result of deafness, and is thus connected with it.

6. Metonymy for speech, says Ges., under *shphe*.

7 For person, often so used in scripture: Douay....person: Am. Bib. Un....person.

10 Reproving he will reprove you if secretly faces ¹ ye be partial to:

11 Whether not majesty of him will make you afraid, and fear of him fall upon you:

12 Memorial sentences of you, similitudes of ashes ; as fortresses of clay, fortresses of you: ²

13 Keep silence from me and will speak I, and let pass over me whatever: ³

14 Wherefore carry I flesh of me in teeth of me, and breath ⁴ of me put I in hand of me:

15 Lo, should he kill me, to him will I hope,⁵ but ways of me to face of him I will argue : ⁶

---

1. For persons : Am. Bib. Un., persons.
2. Douay....and your necks shall be brought to clay.
3. Ges., under *me*, citing this v., renders, "and let happen to me whatever will."
4. Heb. *nphsh:* Douay....and carry my soul in my hands? Ital.... and *why* hold my *anima* in the palm of my hand? Am. Bib. Un....and put my life in my hand? Ges., for "a similar proverbial phrase," cites, under *kph*, Judges 12 : 3 ; 1 Sam. 19 : 5 ; 28 : 21 ; Ps. 119 : 109 : in each of these verses the Heb. word used is *nphsh*—breath. In the first three, Douay, tor *nphsh*, gives life : In the last it gives, " My soul is continually in my hand." And the E. V. gives *life* in the first three, and in Ps. 119 : 109 gives, " My soul *is* continually in my hand." In Job 13 : 14 the the Am. Bib. Un. gives, and put my life, (Heb. *nphsh*—breath) in my hand ? Why this confusion of words ? *hi* and *hie* are the Heb. words for life. The two clauses of the v. form what is called a parallelism, (of which there are many in the Scriptures ;) to carry one's flesh (for which Ges. here gives *life*) in his teeth, being equivalent to, to put one's *nphsh*—breath— in his hand ; each meaning to expose one's life to the greatest danger.
5. Douay....Although he should kill me, I will trust in him : Ital.... Though he kill me, yet will I hope in him : Am. Bib. Un....Behold, he will slay me ; I may not hope. My copy of the Heb. has *la* in this v., making "not may I hope," as the Am. Bib. Un. has it. Gesenius, in a note to *la*, says : By a certain neglect in orthography *la* is sometimes written for *lu*—to him ; according to the Masorah fifteen times, citing the passages, among which this v. and Job 41 : 4. In this v., Job 13 : 15, the Douay and Ital. have not been misled, and the E. V. is right. The Am. Bib. Un. has been misled by the misprint *la*.
6. Ges., yet my ways I will argue before him.

16 And he to me for deliverance, when not to face of him unpious shall come:[1]

17 Hearing hear words of me, and declarations of me in ears of you:

18 Lo, now, have set in order cause,[2] I know that I shall be declared just:[3]

19 Who he will contend with me, for now should I keep silence I should even breathe out:[4]

20 Only two do not with me, then from face of thee not will I hide myself:

21 Hand of thee from upon me remove, and terror of thee let not terrify me:

22 And call and I will answer, or I will speak, and answer thou me:

23 How many to me iniquities and sins; transgression of me and sins of me cause me to know:

24 Why face of thee dost thou hide, and take me for adversary[5] of thee:

25 Whether leaf driven wilt thou terrify, and chaff dry pursue:

26 That thou writest against me bitternesses[6] and makest me to possess the sins of my youth:[7]

---

1. Douay....And he *shall be* my saviour: for no hypocrite shall come before his presence: Ital....And he himself to me *shall be* to salvation: Am. Bib. Un....And he too will be my deliverance; for the impure shall not come before him.

2. i. e., I suppose, when I shall have set in order: The Heb. word is *mshphth*—cause.

3. Ital....*when* I shall have expounded in order my reason, I know that I shall be found just.

4. The Heb. verb used here is *ghuo*—to breathe out: Douay....why am I consumed holding my peace? The Ital. here is *spirero*—I shall breathe out, *exspire:* E. V....I shall give up the ghost: Am. Bib. Un... For then would I be silent, and die.

5. Heb., *auib*—adversary, enemy, the same definitions given of the Heb. *stn*, Douay, and E. V. satan.

6. Metaphor., for, That thou layest on me such heavy punishment, says Ges., under *mrre,* citing this v.: Ital....That thou writest: Douay ....For thou writest: Am. Bib. Un....the same.

7. i. e., that thou now imputest them to me, says Ges., under *irsh*, citing this v.

27 And puttest in stocks feet of me, and watchest all paths of me; around roots of feet of me thou hast dug up:[1]

28 And this man[2] as rotten wood is brought to nothing, as garment eaten of moth:

CHAPTER XIV.

1 Man born of woman, short of days and full of commotion:

2 Like flower he goeth forth and is cut off, yea, he fleeth away as shadow and not endureth:

3 And on this openest thou eyes of thee; and me dost thou bring into question of right with thee:

4 Who can make pure out of impure, not one:

5 If are determined days of him, *if* number of months of him with thee; *if* bound of him thou hast made and not can he go beyond:[3]

---

1. Ges., under *hqe*, "around the roots of my feet thou hast dug up *the ground*," or, says he, made a trench so that I cannot go on; i. e., says he, thou hast stopped up my way; compare, says he, Job 19 : 8; Lam. 3 : 7. He says: It is commonly interpreted, around the roots of my feet thou hast delineated, i. e. marked out to my feet how far they should go: The Am. Bib. Un. is, thou settest a bound to the soles of my feet.

2. The Heb. is *eua*—this man,—I : Douay.... Who am to be consumed as rottenness, and as a garment that is moth eaten : Ital.... Whence *costui*—this man—is unmade, as wood worm eaten, as a garment gnawed of the moth: Am. Bib. Un.... thou settest a bound to the soles of my feet. And he, (necessarily meaning I, agreeing with *my*) as rottenness, shall waste away : See E. V., *my feet*. And he, &c.

Ges., citing this v. under *eua*, says: *eua* is for the pronoun of the first person, I, as in Lat., *hic homo*—this man. And the editors of the Brown Bible by the Patersons, in a marginal note to the word *he* in the E. V., gives, "this man," a form of expression, say they, common in both Greek and Hebrew for *I*. The same form of expression is used in Job 19 : 25, where *he* in the E. V. should be *I*.

3. The *if* before the first clause extends to the clauses following : a common construction.

6 Look away from upon him that he may rest until he receive graciously as a hireling the fatal day of him: [1]

7 While there is for tree hope, if it be cut off, that again it may revive, and suckers of it not may cease:

8 Though be old in ground root of it, and in dust be dead trunk of it:

9 Through scent [2] of water it may put forth buds, and make branches like a plant: [3]

10 But man dies and wastes away, yea, breathes out [4] man, and where he: [5]

11 Go away [6] waters from sea, and river is dried up and is dry: [7]

12 Even so man lies down and will not arise so long as heavens [8] not shall they be awakened, yea, not shall they be aroused from sleep of them: [9]

---

1. Ges., under *ium*—day, gives, fatal day, the day of one's destruction, referring to Job 18 : 20.

2. Heb. *rih*, for which Ges. refers to *ruh*—as being of the same meaning, namely breath,—smell, which is done, says he, by drawing air in and out through the nostrils : used figuratively in Job 14 : 9.

3. Newly planted, adds Ges., under *ntho*, citing this v., and referring to the Greek, for which Liddell and Scott's Greek Lex. gives "newly planted : " Am. Bib. Un....like a sapling.

4. Heb. *ighuo*, from the Heb. verb *ghuo*—to breathe out: E. V....yea man giveth up the ghost: Am. Bib. Un....yea man expires, (it should be written exspires ;) It is not the Heb. word ; the Heb. word is, breathes out; and the sounds of *ghuo* express its meaning ; exspires is a Latin derived word, and means outbreathes. The verse shows that *breathes out*, expires, and, 'gives up the ghost, all mean the same thing, namely, gives up the breath.

5. "And where he," is a form of question in the Heb. for, he is no where.

6. Metaphor., fail, says Ges., under *azl*, citing this v.

7. Heb. *ibsh*, an intensive form, says Ges. The Ital gives, and the rivers are dried up and are dry: Am. Bib. Un....and the stream decays and dries up.

8. So Ges., under *blti*, citing this v. : Douay....till the heavens be broken; Am. Bib. Un....till the heavens are no more, they will not awake: The Douay rightly gives, he shall not awake. The Heb. *they* in the verse, is impersonal, no one will be awakened, &c., as the next verses show: See chap. 15 : 29 for a like construction.

9. Douay....nor rise up out of his sleep: Am. Bib. Un....from their sleep, as in the Ital.

13 Who will give,¹ in grave ² thou wouldst hide me ; that thou wouldst hide me until turn away nostril of thee ; mayest set for me appointed time and mayest remember me:

14 Though die *a* man, he may live again ;³ all days of warfare⁴ of me I shall wait till my exchanging come:

---

1. For, oh that.
2. Heb. *shaul:* Douay, *hell:* Ital. *sotterra*—under ground: E. V., in the grave: Am. Bib. Un., in the under-world; if it had said, the under-ground-world, it would have been nearer the Ital., and more correct. This word *sotterra* is the Ital. word in the only place in the E. V. of the five books of Moses where it has the word hell, namely, Deut. 32 : 22. The same Heb. word occurs seven times in the Pentateuch, namely, Gen. 37 : 35 ; 42 : 38 ; 44 : 29 ; 44 : 31 ; Numb. 16 : 30 ; 16 : 33 ; Deut. 32 : 22 ; and the Greek word is the same in all of them, namely, hades. The Douay has its word *hell* in all the seven places. In four of them the E. V. gives *grave;* and in two of them, pit. But our translators seem to have thought they had better have *hell* somewhere in the Pentateuch,—the law. They chose a very unfortunate place for it. Do not the Heb. and Greek words mean the same in the seventh place as in the six places where they before occur ?
3. This was Job's hope,—the hope of a resurrection from the grave. In Job 17 : 15, 16, he says, beautifully : It (his hope) shall go down into grave when together upon dust at rest. The Douay of Job 17 : 15, 16, is: v. 15, Where is now then my expectation, and who considereth my patience ? v. 16, All that I have shall go down into the deepest pit: thinkest thou that there at least I shall have rest? (A perversion.) Ital. v. 15, And where *is* now my hope ? yes, my hope ? Who it can see ? v. 16, *my hope* shall go down to the bottom of the sepulchre ; since the rest *of all* equally *may be* in the dust : E. V., v. 15, And where *is* now my hope? as for my hope, who shall see it? v. 16, They shall go down to the bars of the pit, when *our* rest together *is* in the dust : Am. Bib. Un., v. 15, And where then is my hope ? yea my hope, who shall see it ! v. 16, It will go down to the bars of the under-world, so soon as there is rest in the dust.
4. Douay....shall man that is dead, thinkest thou, live again? Am. Bib. Un....If a man die, will he live again? For *tsba* in the v. Ges. gives, warfare, and says it is almost always used figuratively of a wretched and miserable condition, citing Job 7 : 1 ; 10 : 17 ; Isai. 40 : 2 ; and under *hliphe* used in Job 14 : 14 ; he says, specially used of soldiers keeping guard ; whence, says he, metaphorically, Job 14 : 14, all the days of my warfare I will wait till others take my place ; literally, says he, till my exchanging come ; the miserable condition in Orcus being

15 Thou wilt call, and I shall answer thee, towards work of hands of thee thou wilt have desire:

16 For now steps of me thou numberest; dost thou not watch narrowly misstep of me:

17 Sealed up in bundle transgression of me, and thou patchest upon perversity of me:[1]

---

compared to the hardships of a soldier on watch. Orcus is defined in Ainsworth's Latin Dict., the house or receptacle of the dead: (The grave is called in Scripture a house, and we say, the narrow house.) The Greek of Job 14 : 14 is, For though die *a* man, he may live again ; I shall await until again I exist,—plainly the sense of the Hebrew. Fry renders the Greek thus: He gives the last two words of v. 13, and the 14th v. thus: "and remember when there shall die a man that shall live again ; all my set time will I patiently wait, till the period of my reviving (i. e. living again) shall come. And Charles Thomson, Secretary of Congress during our Revolution, in a work published by him, renders the Greek of the v. thus: He puts a semicolon after "remember me" in v. 13, and renders v. 14 thus: For though a man die he may be revived (i. e. caused to live again) after finishing the days of this life of his. And that the Greek *zesetai*—the word used here—means live again, see Ezek. 37 : 9 ; Habak 2 : 4, where the Heb. is, the just by or on account of faith of him shall live again, or, be called back to life : the Greek there is *zesetai*—shall live again. The Latin is....but the just by reason of his faith shall have life. The Douay in Hab. 2 : 4 is,....but the just shall live in his faith: Ital... but the just shall live by his faith : E. V....but the just shall live by his faith. And the Rheims Romish version of the New Test. and the Ital. give the same senseless phrase in Rom. 1 : 17 ; Gal. 3 : 11 ; Heb. 10 : 38 ; and the E. V. follows the Ital. in each of those verses : whereas the true rendering is : the just by faith, (they who by faith of them shall be accounted just) shall live again : but this didn't suit the Papacy, nor James's ecclesiastics. The Ital. in Job 14 : 14 is, If a man die, can he return to life : Am. Bib. Un....If a man die, will he live again ? all the days of my warfare would I wait, until my change come : See E. V. l have asked several persons, members of different churches, one of them of my own profession, more than forty, and a Sunday school teacher, what they understood by the E. V. words, *till my change come*, and they all answered, *till my death*. But the Heb. and Greek of the v. teach, that Job—the character in this poem which represents the just man—will await in the grave a resurrection to life again. As to what will become of the wicked, I will refer here only to a single v. in the E. V. Prov. 21 : 16.

1. Figuratively for, framest lies, says Ges., under *thphl*, citing Job 13 : 4 ; Ps. 119 : 69 : elliptically, says he, Job 14 : 17, "thou devisest *false*

18 But indeed mountain falling lies prostrate,[1] and rock is removed from place of it:

19 Stones, wear away waters; sweeps away flood dust of earth, and hope of man thou causest to perish:

20 Thou destroyest him for ever,[2] and he vanishes; thou changest face of him and causest him to be cast forth:

21 May come to honor sons of him and not he know, and they may become small[3] and not he perceive as to them:

22 Surely flesh of him[4] on account of[5] him shall have pain, and breath[6] of him on account of him shall mourn:

CHAPTER XV.

1 And answered Eliphaz that Timni and said:

2 Whether *a* wise should answer knowledge of breath,[7] or wind, and fill of east wind belly of him:

---

things upon my iniquity," i. e., says he, thou increasest my sins with false charges: Douay....thou hast cured my iniquity: Ital....thou hast sewed upon my iniquity: Am. Bib. Un....and thou sewest up my iniquity.

1. Ges., under *nbl*, citing this v., says: Figuratively applied to men; he renders, " the mountain that falls lies prostrate," i. e., says he, is like a dead man, it cannot get up: Fig. used of idols, citing Jer. 16 : 18.

2. Douay....that he may pass away forever: Am. Bib. Un....Thou assailest him continually.

3. Metaphor., for mean and despised, says Ges., under *tsor*, citing this v. and Jer. 30 : 19.

4. Poetical for *he*.

5. Heb. *oliu*, Fig., says Ges., for, on account of him.

6. Heb. *nphsh*—breath of him—poetical for he—on account of him shall mourn : (mourning and sorrow affect the breath, and are shown by it:) The Douay of the v. is....But yet his flesh, while he shall live, shall have pain, and his soul shall mourn over him: Am. Bib. Un....Only, his flesh for itself shall have pain, and his soul for itself shall mourn.

7. Heb. *ruh:* Am. Bib. Un....with windy knowledge, and fill his breast with the east-wind.

3 Whether reprove with speech not doing kindness and words not having profit in them:

4 Yea, thou castest off reverence, and withholdest meditation before God:

5 For teacheth perversity of thee mouth of thee, although thou choosest tongue of crafty:

6 Condemns thee mouth of thee, and not I, yea, lips of thee testify against thee:

7 Whether first man thou wast born, and before hills wast thou brought forth:

8 Whether in council of God thou hast listened, and hast taken in to thee knowledge:

9 What canst thou know and not we know: canst understand thou, and not with us this:[1]

10 Also aged, also hoary, among us, great, above father of thee, of days:

11 Whether small with thee consolations of God, and word muffled with thee:

12 Wherefore doth seize upon thee heart of thee, and why wink eyes of thee:[2]

13 That thou turnest against God breath[3] of thee, and utterest from mouth of thee words:

14 What, man, that he should be pure, and that should be just, one born of woman:

15 Lo, in holy of him[4] not trusteth he, and heavens not pure in eyes of him:

16 How much less *the* abominable and soured[5] man drinking like water iniquity:

---

1. Heb. *eua*—this.

2. Ges., under *rzm*—to wink with the eyes, citing this v., says: as done in insolence and pride.

3. Heb. *ruh*—breath: For *ruh* here the Douay has spirit: Ital., *soffio*—breath: E. V., spirit: Am. Bib. Un., spirit. How can mouth utter words without breath: Orthodoxy's fear and avoidance of the word *breath* is truly pitiable.

4. Douay and Ital., in his saints.

5. Metaphor., says Ges., for corrupted in a moral sense, citing under *alh*, this v., and Ps. 14 : 3 ; 53 : 4 ; E. V. v. 3.

17 I will breathe out [1] to thee; hearken to me, and this have seen I, and I will recount it:

18 Which wise have told and not have disowned from fathers of them:

19 To whom alone was given this land, and not passed adversary [2] among them:

20 All days of wicked he in pain, and number of years[3] destined to violent:

21 Sound of fears in ears of him; in peace destroyer comes upon him:

22 He trusteth not to return out of darkness,[4] and is destined he to sword:[5]

23 Wanders this man[6] for bread where;[7] he knows that ready at hand of him day of darkness:

24 Terrify him adversary[8] and distress; they overpower him as king ready for military tumult:[9]

25 For he has stretched out against God hand of him, and against Almighty he has strengthened himself:

26 He rushes upon him with neck,[10] with thick bosses of shields upon him:[11]

---

1. The Heb. verb here is *hue*—to breathe out, hence says Ges., to declare, to show: He says it is a word used in poetry.

2. Heb. *tsr*—adversary, enemy, the same defininition as the Heb. *stn*.

3. i. e. says Ges., under *msphr*, years that can be numbered, for few years, citing many passages.

4. Darkness here and elsewhere, is used for the grave: Ges., under *hshk*—darkness, cites this v., and renders, "he does not hope to return out of darkness or destruction."

5. The sword is used in Scripture figuratively for destruction.

6. Heb., *eua*—this man: Latin, *hic homo*—this man, says Ges., under *eua*, citing Job 13 : 28.

7. Where *it may be*, says Ges., under *aie*, citing this v.

8. Heb. *tsr*.

9. So Ges., under *kidur*, citing this v.

10. Namely, proudly lifted up, says Ges., under *tsuar*.

11. Ges., citing this v., says: It is said proverbially, he rushes upon him....with thick bosses of shields, a metaphor, says he, taken from soldiers, who join their shields together like a tortoise, and so make an onset.

27 For he has covered face of him with fatness of him,[1] and made fat upon loin:

28 And he dwelleth in cities destroyed, houses not dwellers in them, which destined for heaps of stones:

29 Not shall he prosper, and not shall continue wealth of him, and not shall stretch out in land possession of him:[2]

30 Not shall he depart out of darkness; suckers of him shall make dry, *a* flame; and he shall pass away by breath[3] of mouth of him:

31 Not let him trust in evil; he wanders;[4] for evil will be retribution of him:

32 Before time of him it will be fulfilled, and branch of him not shall put forth leaves:

33 He shall shake off from himself, as vine, unripe grapes of him, and shall cast away as olive tree flowers of him:

34 For family of impious, lean, and fire shall consume tents of gifts:

35 He has conceived mischief, and will bring forth falsehood, and womb of him prepares fraud:

---

1. i. e. says Ges., under *hlb*, the best of any kind.
2. Ges. prefers, their fold, poetical, says he for their flocks.
3. Heb. *ruh*—breath: Douay....he shall be taken away by the breath of his own mouth: Ital....he shall be taken away by the *soffio*—breath—of mouth of God. The Patersons, editors of the Brown Bible, do, in a marginal note to this v., what King James's ecclesiastics were not bold enough to do. They adopt the absurd perversion of the Romish Ital., which even the Douay pointedly condemns. The orthodoxy of the Patersons could not endure the idea that a man dies by breathing out his breath. And the Am. Bib. Un. is, and by the breath of His mouth shall he pass away. I have seen *His* (capital H,) used in poetry for God's. And there can be no doubt that the Am. Bib. Un., by His means God's mouth, thus adopting the Italian absurdity.
4. Metaphor., for he is deceived, errs in a moral sense, says Ges., under *tve*, citing this v.

CHAPTER XVI.

1 And answered Job and said:

2 Have heard I like these, myriads; comforters wearisome all of you:

3 Whether end to word of breath,[1] or what irritateth thee that thou shouldst answer:

4 Also I like you could speak if were breath[2] of you in place of breath[3] of me; I could make a league against you with words and could shake against you with head of me:

5 I would strengthen you with mouth of me, and solace of lips of me[4] would I restrain:

6 If I speak, not is restrained pain of me; and if I forbear, what from me goeth:[5]

7 Surely he has wearied me with these desolations of all family of me:

8 And thou hast seized me for witness to be, and rising up against me, leanness of me to face of me bears witness:

9 Nostril of him tears in pieces, and he lays snares for me; he gnashes upon me with teeth of him; adversary[6] of me, he sharpens his eyes against me:[7]

10 They gape[8] upon me with mouth of them; in scorn they smite cheek of me; together against me they unite:

---

1. Heb. *ruh:* Am. Bib. Un....to words of wind.
2. Heb. *nphsh*—breath.
3. Heb. *nphsh*—breath: Am. Bib. Un....were your soul in place of mine. If breath of you were in place of breath of me, is the Heb. way of saying, if you were in my place: The Douay is....would God your soul were for my soul: Noyes....if ye were now in my place.
4. i. e., says Ges., empty solace, citing this v. under *nid:* Am. Bib. Un...and the comfort of my lips should uphold.
5. i. e., says Ges., citing this v. under *me*, nothing of my sorrow goeth from me.
6. Heb. *tsr*—equivalent to *stn*—adversary.
7. So Ges., under *lthsh*, citing this v. i. e., says he, he watches me with stern and threatening eyes.
8. Impersonal, for, people.

11 Has shut up me God to evil,[1] and into hands of wicked he has cast me:

12 Securely lived I, and he has agitated me; and he has taken hold on neck of me and has broken *bones* of me, and has set me up to him for mark:

13 Have surrounded upon me powerful of him; he has pierced reins of me and not has spared; he has poured out to ground bile of me:

---

1. The Heb. word here is *ouil*, a noun—evil, so defined by Ges., citing this v. The Heb. *u* is written *v*; so that *ouil* is *ovil*—evil. We thus see how easily the great Apostasy, which made the Latin the sacred language of Scripture, with its preposition *de*—of, could make devil; thcs *deovil*—of evil; and striking out *o* one of the two vowels, as is done where two vowels come together, we have devil; and by supplying the article *the*, which is so often supplied, we have *the devil*: and by personifying *evil* we get the Devil. But not long since, in a conversation with a devoted Rom. Cath. lady, she said to me that the word *devil* only meant the principle of evil. I was greatly surprised, and told her she was right: and I thought she had got rid of his Satanic majesty. But before the conversation ended I found she had got the Orthodox Satan from where Noah Webster got it, namely, from *Lucifer*—the morning star, or more probably from her priest; whence, no doubt, she had the information that *devil* meant the principle of evil : and in that her priest was right. There must have been a liability to err in our first parents, or their condition would not have been a state of trial; and that liability to err may well be called the *of evil*—the principle of evil. And as to the Orthodox Satan, her priest, no doubt, got it from the foot note of the Douay Rom. Cath. version to Isai. 14 : 12—"How art thou fallen from heaven, O Lucifer, who didst rise in the morning: How art thou fallen to the earth that didst wound the nations?" That v. is a part of the similitude in Isai. chap. 14, comparing the fall of the King of Babylon from his high estate to the fall of Lucifer—the morning star—from heaven—the heavens. The Douay, in v. 4, properly calls it *parable*. The E. V., for a purpose, wrongly calls it proverb. The foot note in the Douay to v. 12 is, " O Lucifer—O day star: All this, according to the letter, is spoken of the King of Babylon : It may also be applied, in a spiritual sense, to Lucifer the prince of devils, who was created a bright angel, but fell by pride and rebellion against God." And this foot note of the Romish priesthood, is the authority on which has been imposed on human credulity for long centuries the enormous cheat of a personal devil! Strange that so wise a book as Job didn't give the information contained in the foot note to the Douay v. 12.

14 He breaks forth upon me breach on face of breach; he rushes upon me like *a* mighty:

15 Sackcloth have I sewed together over skin of me, and have put in dust horn of me:[1]

16 Face of me is made to boil[2] with weeping, and upon eyelids of me shadow of death:

17 Although not violence in hands of me, and prayer of me pure:

18 Earth, cover not thou blood of me, and not let there be place[3] to outcry of me:

19 Truly already, lo, in heavens what testifies of me, yea, eye witness of me in lofty places:

20 Mockers of me friends of me; to God sheds tears eyes of me:

21 And shall altercate[4] *a* man with God, as son of man[5] with companion of him: .

22 For years of number shall come to him,[6] and way not shall I return I shall go:

CHAPTER XVII.

1 Breath[7] of me is destroyed; days of me are extinguished; graves for me:

---

1. So Ges., under *qrn*, citing this v., and he says: "where we, in the usage of our language, would say *my head*, on which is the highest honor and glory.

2. Ges., under *hmr*—passive—to be made to boil, citing this v., says: used of the face as inflamed with weeping.

3. Ges., under *mqum*, citing this v., renders, "let there be no place, or abiding to my outcry," i. e., says he, let it never delay, but let my cry come without tarrying to God.

4. So Ges. under "*ikh*, followed by *l;*" Am. Bib. Un....that he would do justice to a man with God.

5. Son of man, poetical for man, says Ges., citing this v. and others.

6. i. e. few years.

7. Heb. *ruh:* Douay....spirit: Ital....*spirito:* E. V....my breath is corrupt: Am. Bib. Un....my breath is consumed.

2 Whether not mockings with me, and on these bitternesses of them rests eye of me:

3 Put I pray thee, surety; be surety for me with thee; who he into hand of me will strike:[1]

4 For heart (or mind) of them thou hast restrained from wisdom, wherefore thou wilt not exalt them:

5 To spoiler, *who* betrays friends of him, even eyes of children of him shall pine away:

6 And he set me for song of derision, and spittle to face of them I am become:[2]

7 And is blasted from vexation eye of me, and members of me like shadow all of them:

8 Will be astonished upright at this, and pure[3] against impious will be helpless:[4]

9 But shall hold just way of him, and clean of hands shall add strength:

10 But indeed all of you may return;[5] come on, I pray you, and not shall I find among you *a* wise:

11 Days of me have passed away; purposes of me are broken off; possessions of heart of me:[6]

---

1. Ges., under, *tqo*, citing this v., renders, "who is there that will strike hands with me," i. e. says he, who will give his right hand to be surety for me: Am. Bib. Un.... Who is there that will give his hand for mine?

2. Ges., under *tpht*, citing this v., renders, "I am become as one in whose face they spit," i. e., says he, the most base and despised of mortals: Am. Bib. Un.... I am become one to be spit upon in the face: Ital. ....And I am publicly led about upon drum: E. V....and aforetime I was as a tabret.

3. Metaphor., for innocent, says, Ges., under *nqe*.

4. Will be helpless, see Ges., under *orr:* Douay....and the innocent shall be raised up against the hypocrite: Am. Bib. Un....and the innocent will be roused against the impure.

5. i. e., says Ges., under *shub*, do again, i. e., what they had done before.

6. i. e., says Ges., under *mursh;* my delights, my dearest counsels, citing this v.

12 Night for day they put; light near from face of darkness:[1]

13 Lo, I await grave [2] house of me; in darkness spread out I bed of me:

14 To pit [3] have called I, father of me thou; mother of me and sister of me, to worm:

15 And where then hope of me, yea, hope of me who will care for it:

16 To bars of grave [4] shall go down it when together upon dust laid down:[5]

CHAPTER XVIII.

1 And answered Belded that Shhi, and said:

2 When will ye put end to words;[6] understand; and afterwards we will speak:

3 Why are we taken to be like beast, are unclean [7] in eyes of you:

---

1. i. e., says Ges., under *qrub*, citing this v., will presently be changed into darkness: Am. Bib. Un....light is just before darkness.

2. Heb. *shaul:* Douay....hell: Ital....the sepulchre: E. V....the grave: Am. Bib. Un....the under-world.

3. Heb. *shht*, especially the sepulchre, says Ges., citing this v. and others: Douay....I have said to rottenness: Ital....to the *fossa*—grave: Am. Bib. Un....I have said to corruption.

4. Heb. *shaul:* Douay....deepest pit: Ital....into the bottom of the sepulchre: Am. Bib. Un....to the bars of the under-world.

5. The hope of the just man is here beautifully said to be laid down with him in the grave, i. e., the hope of being raised to life from it. Ges., under *ol* gives *ol ophr*—upon dust, not only used, says he, of the surface of the ground, but also in the grave, where the dead both lie upon dust and under it, citing Job 20 : 11 ; 21 : 26.

6. Ges., under *qts*, citing this v., "when will ye make an end of words:" Am. Bib. Un....How long will ye hunt for words.

7. i. e., impious, says Ges., under *thme*, citing this v.

4 Tearing in pieces breath[1] of him in nostrils (for in anger) of him: whether for your sake shall be forsaken earth, and be removed rock from place of it:

5 Truly light of wicked shall be put out, and not shall be made to shine flame of fire of him:[2]

6 Light darkens in tent of him, and lamp of him over him shall be put out:

7 Are straitened steps of strength of him, and shall cast him down counsel of him:

8 For he is thrown into net by feet of him, and on net he walks:

9 Will seize by heel net; will take hold upon him snare:

10 Hid in ground cord of it, and snare of it on pathway:

11 From every side frighten him terrors, and open at footsteps of him:

12 Becomes stricken with famine strength of him, and destruction is ready at side of him:

13 Will devour *the* parts of skin of him, will devour members of him *the* first born of death:[3]

14 Is torn away from tent of him security of him, and he is caused to hasten steps of him to king of terrors:[4]

---

1. Heb. *nphsh* of him: A similar phrase is put into the mouth of Hamlet: "O, it offends me to the soul to hear a robustious periwig pated fellow tear a passion to tatters, to very rags:" The Douay is....Thou that destroyest thy soul in thy fury: Ital....*O thou* that tearest thy *anima* in thy passion: E. V....He teareth himself in his anger: Am. Bib. Un....One that teareth himself in his rage: *himself* being given for *breath of him*.

2. Ital....and no spark of fire to them shall be relighted.

3. Ges., under *bkur*, citing this v., "the first born of death," i. e., says he, the greatest of deadly maladies: for, says he, disease may fitly be called by a Hebraism, the son of death, as procursor and attendant; as Arabic, daughters of fate, or of death, used of fatal fevers; and the most terrible death is here figuratively called the first born of brethren. He cites Isai. 14:30, the first born of the poor, i. e., the poorest.

4. Am. Bib. Un....and he led them away to the king of terrors.

15 Terror dwells in tent of him, so that no more to him;¹ shall be scattered over habitation of him brimstone:

16 Beneath, roots of him shall become dry, and above shall be cut off branch of him:

17 Remembrance of him perishes from earth, and not name of him on face of street:²

18 They shall thrust him³ from light into darkness, and from inhabited earth they shall cast him out:

19 Not offspring to him, and not progeny among people of him, and not survivor in abodes of him:

20 At day of him are astonished they that come after; and they who went before took hold of horror:⁴

21 Surely these *the* dwelling places of evil,⁵ and this *he* place not knows God:

CHAPTER XIX.

1 And answered Job and said:

2 Until when will ye make sad breath⁶ of me and break me in pieces with words:

3 Already ten treads have ye reproached me; not are ye ashamed; ye stun me:⁷

---

1. There shall dwell in his tent they that are not his.
2. Am. Bib. Un....on the face of the fields.
3. Impersonal for, he shall be thrust: Am. Bib. Un., the same.
4. For, horror took hold of them, says Ges., under *ahz*, citing this v.: Am. Bib. Un....are terror-stricken.
5. Heb. *oul*—a noun—Ges., evil, citing this v., and Job 27:7; 29:17; and under the noun *ouil* citing Job 16:11: The Douay gives....of the wicked, and this place of him that knoweth not God: Am. Bib. Un.... the same.
6. Heb. *nphsh*—breath: Douay....soul: Ital....*anima:* E. V., and Am. Bib. Un....soul.
7. So Ges., under *ekr*, citing this v.

4 And even if indeed I have erred, with me continues error of me:

5 If indeed over me you would become great, then prove against me my reproach:

6 Know that God has bent[1] cause of me, and has thrown net of him over me surrounding:[2]

7 Lo, I cry out oppression, and not am answered, I cry for help, and not there is right:[3]

8 Path of me he has hedged and not can I pass over; and over footpaths, or by-ways,[4] of me darkness he has put:

9 Glory of me from upon me he has stripped off, and has taken away crown of head of me:

10 He has broken me down from every side, and I shall vanish;[5] and he has plucked up as tree hope of me:

11 And has breathed hard[6] against me nostril of him; and he has taken me to be to him as adversary[7] of him:

---

1. Metaphor., for perverted, says Ges., under *out*, citing this v.

2. A pregnant construction, says Ges., under *nqph*, citing this v., he has cast me into his net and has surrounded me with it.

3. Heb. *mshphth*—defined by Ges., right, that which is just: Douay... and there is none to judge: Ital.... and not *to me is done* reason, or justness: E. V....I cry aloud but *there is* no judgment: Am. Bib. Un.... "and there is no justice," meaning justness; and justice in E. V. always means justness: The Greek word is *dikaiosune*, defined in Liddell and Scott's Greek Lex., uprightness, righteous dealing; and in Donnegan's Gr. Lex., equity, the practice of rectitude.

4. Heb. *ntibut*, plural of *ntib*, a poetic word, says Ges.

5. i. e., die, says Ges., under *elk*, citing this v. and others: Am. Bib. Un....and I perish.

6. Ges., under *nhr*, " to breathe hard through the nose;" and under *aph*—nostril, he gives, "anger, which shows itself in hard breathing," citing Prov. 22: 24; 29: 22: Am. Bib. Un....he makes his anger burn against me.

7. Heb. *tsr*, adversary; sound it *tsar*.

12 Together have come troops[1] of him, and they cast up[2] to me way of them ; and encamp around tent of me:

13 Brethren of me, from near me he has moved far off, and they that knew me *are* altogether estranged from me:

14 Have forsaken kinsmen of me, and those knowing me have forgotten me:

15 Sojourners of house of me, and hand-maidens of me for stranger take me ; foreigner I am become in eyes of them:

16 To servant of me call I and not answers he, with mouth[3] though I entreat him:

17 Breath[4] of me loathsome to wife of me, and entreaties of me to sons of womb of me:[5]

18 Indeed children despise me, and rise I up, they even talk at me:

19 Abhor me all familiar acquaintances of me, and those I breathed after[6] are turned against me:

20 On skin of me and on flesh of me cleaves bone of me, and I have escaped with the skin of my teeth:[7]

---

1. Used of ills sent by God, says Ges., under *gdud*, citing this v.

2. i. e., prepare, says Ges., under *sll*, citing this v., he renders, "and they cast up their way to me."

3. Ges. under *phe*—mouth, citing this v., renders, "with *all* my mouth," i. e., says he with the loudest voice I can.

4. Heb. *ruh*—breath: Douay, breath: Ital....breath: E. V.... breath: Am. Bib. Un....breath. Here we have the concurrent authority of the Heb., the Douay, the Ital., the E. V., and the Am. Bib. Un., that the Heb. *ruh* is breath: *ruh* is the Heb. word for which the Douay, and the E. V., so often have *spirit;* the Latin, is *spiritus*, for which in the Latin writers *breath* is always the meaning, (as before shown.) The Heb. noun *ruh* is from the Heb. verb *ruh*, defined by Ges., to breathe, to blow, an onomatopoietic, says he, that is, expressing by its sounds the thing signified; sound it *ruach :* it take *ach* to spell *h :* as in *Rachel*, for which the Heb. has three letters, *r h l*—i. e. rachel, it taking *el* to spell *l*.

5. i. e., to my brethren, says Ges.

6. i. e., loved, says Ges., under *aeb*—defined to breathe after: Douay ....I loved: Ital....I loved: E. V....I loved: Am. Bib. Un....I love.

7. So. Ges., under *mlth*, citing this v., proverbial, says he.

21 Be gracious to me, be gracious to me, you friends of me, for hand of God has touched on me:

22 Why persecute you me as God, and with flesh of me not are you satisfied:

23 Who will give, altogether were written down words of me ; who will give, in book they were engraved:

24 With style of iron, and lead, to perpetuity of time in stone they were graven:

25 But I, know I Redeemer of me lives,
    And at last upon dust shall be raised ;

26 Yea, after skin of me they destroy, this,[1]—
    That in flesh of me I shall see God:

27 Whom I, I shall behold for myself;
    Yea, eyes of me shall see and not stranger ;
    Reins of me spent[2] in bosom of me.

(See note to this passage, verses 25, 26, 27, at the end of the chapter.)

28 So that you should say, why should we persecute him ; and yet root of words[3] is found in me :

29 Turn aside for yourselves from face of sword, for, anger, crimes of sword ;[4] for you know there is right,[5]— that which is right.

---

1. Ges....this, namely, says he, shall come to pass.

2. i. e., says Ges., under *kle*, citing this v., I myself pine or languish.

3. i. e., root of controversy, says Ges., under *shrsh*, citing this v.

4. Ges., under *oun* citing this v., gives, crimes to be punished by the sword ; and he cites Ezk. 21 : 30, "crime of end," i. e., says he, which brings an end or destruction.

5. Heb. *din*—right,—that which is right, equivalent to *mshphth* in v. 7: Douay....and know ye that there is a judgment: Am. Bib. Un....that ye may know there is a judgment. Ges. defines *din*, secondly, right, justice, (i. e. justness,) citing Dan. 4 : 34.

NOTE.

Latin :

25 For I know that my Redeemer lives, and that at last *day* out of earth I shall be raised ;

26 And again I shall be compassed about with my skin, and in my flesh discern my God :

27 Whom I myself shall discern ;
Yea, my eyes shall look towards, and not another:
Is laid by, or, laid up, this my hope in my bosom.
The Douay is:
25 For I know that my Redeemer liveth, and in the last *day* I shall rise out of the earth.
26 And I shall be clothed again with my skin, and in my flesh I shall see God:
27 Whom I myself shall see, and my eyes shall behold, and not another: this my hope is laid up in my bosom.
The Italian is:
25 Now as to me, I know that my Redeemer lives, and that in the last *day* egli—he—will be raised upon the dust:
26 And *though*, after my skin this *body* be gnawed, yet I shall see with my flesh God:
27 Whom I shall see, my eyes shall see, and not another ; my reins *si consumano*—(Ital. passive)—are consumed—in bosom.
The E. V. is:
26 For I know *that* my Redeemer liveth, and *that* he shall stand at the latter *day* upon the earth:
26 And *though* after my skin *worms* destroy this *body*, yet in my flesh shall I see God:
27 Whom I shall see for myself, and mine eyes shall behold, and not another ; *though* my reins be consumed within me.
The Amer. Bible Union version is:
25 But I, I know my Redeemer lives, and in after time will stand up on the earth, or, on the dust ; (so given in foot note.)
26 And after this my skin is destroyed, and without my flesh (in foot note "and from my flesh") shall I see God.
27 Whom I, for myself shall see, and not another, when my reins are consumed within me.

The Latin is in the future tense passive, I shall be raised ; and the Ital. is in the future tense passive—*si levera*—shall be raised : and this is necessarily the true rendering, for Job could not raise himself.

And Mr. Charles Wilson, Professor of Hebrew in the University of St. Andrews, Scotland, on page 133 of his Hebrew Grammar, informs us, "that several persons in the future tense passive coincide with corresponding persons in the same tense active." So that the Heb. *iqum* in v. 25, may be rendered in the future tense passive ; and the subject matter of the verse requires that it be so rendered. An instance of this is found in Isai. 9 : 5, E. V., v. 6. where the Heb *iqra*—future active, is rendered by the Douay, the Ital., and the E. V. "shall be called"—the future passive.

We now give the version of the passage by John Eadie, D.D., LL. D., "Professor of Biblical Literature and Exegesis to the United Presbyterian Church," in his Biblical Cyclopædia," under the head, Job. He says:

"The Book of Job exhibits a complete picture of the Patriarchal religion, a religion one in spirit with Christianity, as the fundamental doctrines of both are the same."

We agree with the Professor that the doctrines taught in Job became, and are now, fundamental doctrines of Christianity; and they have always been fundamental doctrines of the true Scriptures from beginning to end.

The question, then, is, What are the doctrines of the Book of Job and of Christianity?

One of the "fundamental doctrines" which the Professor says is taught in the Book of Job is: "The immortality of the soul, and the resurrection of the dead;" and for this he cites this passage—Job 19 : 25, 26, 27, giving his own version of the verses as herein after given.

By his words "immortality of the soul, and resurrection of the dead" we are of course to understand, *inherent immortality in man*, and the resurrection of all the dead,—the tenet of the Papacy, and, in general, of so-called Protestantism.

Before giving his version of the passage we will see what the Professor understands by the word "soul."

Under "soul" he cites Gen. 2 : 7, and says : "The Scriptures evidently distinguish between the spirit and the soul," citing 1 Thes. 5 : 23 ; Heb. 4 : 12. "The word which we call soul is used to denote mere animal life or the seat of the sensations, appetites and passions," citing Gen. 1 : 20; "here the word translated *life* is the same which is elsewhere translated soul." [The Heb. word there is *nphsh*—breath.] "Hence," (says the Professor) "it may be inferred, that as we have our bodies and animal life in common with brutes, it must be spirit which was created in the likeness or image of God, and which raised man above the brutes that perish, and makes him a rational and accountable being. The spirit, in contrast with the soul, is the higher portion of our nature—the seat of the reason, conscience and the loftier affections—the holy of holies in that temple which God has constructed for himself within us." [The Professor has never discovered any use of a brain.] And see what the Hebrew is where so-called translations use the words *within* us in note to Job 32:18. at end of that chapter.

John Milton, in his work entitled "A treatise on Christian Doctrine," published after his death, and which, I am glad to learn is being republished in England, says: (see pages 249, 250, 252, of the first vol.,) "Man is a living being, intrinsically and properly one and individual, not compounded or separable, not, according to the common opinion, made up and formed of two distinct and different natures as of soul and body,—but that the whole man is soul, and the soul man, a body, or substance individual, animated, sensitive, and rational." And on page 252 of the first vol., after citing Luke 1 : 46, 47, where the E. V. has *soul* in v. 46, and *spirit* in v. 47, he cites the two verses—1 Thes. 5 : 23; Heb. 4 : 12; cited by Professor Eadie, and says : "But that the spirit of man should be separate from the body, so as to have an intelligent existence independently of it, (*without* it, as Professor Eadie would have it,) is no where said in Scripture, and the doctrine is evidently at variance both with nature and reason." In his chap. 13, page 363, vol. 1, Milton says; "I will show that in death, first the whole man, and secondly, each component part, suffers privation of life." As to the whole man, he says : " It is evident that the saints and believers of old, the patriarchs, prophets and apostles, without exception, held this doctrine," citing Gen. 37 : 35 ; 42 : 36 ; Job 3 : 13, 14, 16; 10 : 21 ; 14 : 10, 13 ; 17 : 13, 15, 16 ; Ps. 6 : 5; 88 : 11 ; ; 115 : 17 ; 39 : 13 ; 146 : 2. Milton, then, at page 367, vol. 1, proceeds : " But lest recourse should be had to the sophistical distinction, that though the whole man dies, it does not follow that the whole *of* man should die, I proceed to give similar proof with regard to each of the parts, the body, the spirit, the soul." We need not give what he says as to the body, or the soul. As to the *spirit*, he says : " The Preacher himself, (Solomon,) the wisest of men, expressly denies that the *spirit* is exempt from death," citing Eccl. 3 : 19, 20 ; and in v. 21, Milton renders, "who knoweth the *spirit* of man whether it goeth upward ; " the rest of verse is, and *spirit* of beast, whether goeth down it to earth ? The same Heb. word *ruh*, for which the E. V., in v. 19 gives *breath*, is the word used twice in v. 21, where the E. V. gives, *spirit*. He cites also, Ps. 146 : 4. Milton uses *spirit* and *breath* as meaning the same ; and has the authority of the Latin, the Douay, the Ital. and the E. V. for it ; they all give *breath* for the Heb. word *ruh*,—Greek, *pneuma* in v. 19.

We have given all that the Professor gives under the word "soul." He means that his readers should understand him to affirm that the passage in Job teaches the doctrine—the immortality of the spirit,—inherent immortality in man. He assumes that there is something inherent in man which is immortal ; and having shown plainly and rightly, that what is called *soul* is not it, he says, "it must be spirit."

We will now see what the Professor gives for *spirit*. He gives "Spirit, Gen. 6 : 3." " This term (says he,) is often employed figuratively by the sacred writers, and its import may be generally determined by its connection." And without giving any other citation he then goes to ''The third person of the Trinity."—" Holy Spirit,"—"Holy Ghost." The Heb. in Gen. 6 : 3, is : And said Jehovah, not shall remain *ruh*—breath—of me in man for ever, because he flesh, but may be days of him 120 years: The Douay gives *spirit* (small s) for *ruh* in the verse: The Ital. *Spirito* (capital S): E. V., *Spirit* (capital S). The—*ruh*—breath—spirit—here spoken of is *ruh alue*—breath of God, "as being breathed into man by God, and returning to him," says Ges., under *ruh*, citing Job 27 : 3 ; Gen. 2 : 7 ; Eccles. 12 : 7 ; Ps. 104 : 29, in which last the Heb. has the same word *ruh*—breath, and the Douay, Ital., and E. V., have *breath*. How Eadie gets "immortal spirit,—inherent immortality in man, from Gen. 6 : 3, we leave for the reader to imagine. But under *Angel* he gives, " He maketh his angels spirits," i. e., says he, they are not corporeal—have not an animal organism like man. He cites no passage for his phrase. The Douay, in Ps. 103 : 4, has, " Who makest his angels spirits ; and the Rheims, in Heb. 1 : 7, has, " He that maketh his angels, spirits (with a comma after angels.) The E. V., Ps. 104 : 4, is, " Who maketh his angels spirits ; " and in Hebrews 1 : 7, " Who maketh his angels spirits : The Ital. in Ps. 104 : 4 is " He maketh the *venti*—winds his *Angeli*—messengers ; and in the Hebrews 1 : 7, "Who maketh the *venti* —winds—his *angeli*—messengers. And that the Ital. is right is shown in a note at the end of Chapter XXXIII.

And in the New Testament the Greek word used is this same *aggelos*. In Mat. 1 : 10, the Greek word is *aggelos*—(sounded *angelos:*) the Latin given there is *angelus*, (there is no such Latin word, and Anthon's Latin Dict. does not give *angelus ;* it is the Greek *angelos* with the Latin termination *us*, instead of the Greek termination *os:*) The Ital. word there is *angelo :* The Rheims, angel : The E. V. messenger. So that John the Baptist was an angel, i. e., messenger—one sent.

We will now see how Professor Eadie proposes to read the passage in Job, the only passage in the book on which he rests his assertion that the Book of Job teaches " the immortality of the soul, and the resurrection of all the dead." He renders the passage thus :

25 "Yet I know my Redeemer, he liveth,
And the last (citing Rev. 1 : 11) will he arise on the dust," ("ashes of the grave," says he in parenthesis.)
26 And after this my skin has been decomposed by disease,
Even from (without) my flesh I shall see God,
27 Whom I shall see to me (propitious,)
And mine eyes shall behold him and not estranged,
Thus the ardent longings of my heart (will be) completed."
The parentheses are his.

We thus get from Prof. Eadie where the word "without," used by the Am. Bib Un. in v. 26, instead of the word " from," which it gives in a note, and used by the Professor in the same verse, in parenthesis after the word "from" used by him in that verse, comes from. The Professor uses "without" as a substitute for the English preposition "from," which he gives for the Hebrew preposition *m*. So that by his own showing the Heb. would read, "from flesh of me I shall see God." But he saw, that "from" would not get him any nearer his conclusion that the Book of Job teaches "the immortality of the soul, or spirit," than the preposition *in*, or the Ital. preposition *with ;* and therefore for "from" he substitutes in parenthesis, "without," the exact opposite to the Ital. *with*.

The Professor cites but this single passage in the Book, yet he gravely offers to our understandings the proposition, that from a single Heb. letter,—the preposition *m*, which he takes to be used in the verse for *from*, we must understand Job as teaching the "immortality of the soul" ! ! Words in answer to such a proposition would be thrown away.

But further, the Professor claims that the Book of Job teaches "the resurrection of the dead," by which he means we shall understand, of all the dead. Now Job, "the hero of the poem," is a just man. The writer of the Book makes God a witness to his innocence. And as a just man the writer represents him as hoping, and even confidently expecting to be raised from the dead. But how does this prove "the immortality of the soul," i. e., inherent immortality in man? How is it that men can become so wedded to a system as to attempt to support it by such feeble efforts! It is said that with the Hindoos, he who refuses instruction, and will not be convinced, is told to ask the cattle.

And who does the Professor understand by the Redeemer, in v. 25, who, he says, "will arise on the dust,—ashes of the grave?" The Deity is the Redeemer spoken of in the verse. One reference will be sufficient to show this: Ps. 49:16, E. V. v. 15: David there says: But God will redeem breath of me (poetical for *me*) from hand of *shaul* when he shall fetch me: The Douay is Ps. 48:16; and is: But God will redeem my soul from the hand of hell, when he shall receive me: The Ital. is, 49:16, But God will redeem my *anima* from the sepulchre, for he me will receive *to him:* E. V. But God will redeem my soul (poetical for *me*) from the power of the grave, for he shall receive me.

This 49th Psalm, with the correction of a single verse in the Ital. and E. V. gives the true Bible teaching as to the destiny of the wicked, and of them who shall be accounted just: and it is the uniform teaching of all scripture from beginning to end, including the Book of Job. The Heb. of Ps. 49:12, E. V. v. 11, is: Graves of them (the wicked) houses of them for ever, habitations of them to circle and circle: The Septuagint—the Greek version—is: The graves of them houses of them for ever, covers of them to generation and generation: Latin —sepulchres of them houses of them for ever, tents of them to progeny and progeny: Douay, v. 12, And their sepulchres shall be their houses for ever; their dwelling places to all generations: The E. V. is, v. 11: Their inward thought *is that* their houses *shall continue* for ever, *and* their dwelling places to all generations, (interpolating five words.) And now we will see where this E. V. rendering came from. The Ital. is, v. 12: Their inward *thought is that* their houses *shall continue* for ever, *and that* their habitations *shall continue* through every age (interpolating nine words:) and the Ital. puts the word *thought* in italics as not being in the Hebrew, but the E. V. puts it in the Roman letter, thereby affirming that the word *thought* is in the Hebrew. The Heb. of v. 15, E. V. 14, is: Like sheep in *shaul* they place them, death shall pasture them (figuratively for guard them, says Ges., under *roe.*) It will suffice to read in the E. V. verses 14, 15, 19, 20, with the knowledge that the Heb. word *shaul* is used twice in v. 14, and once in v. 15, and that the Douay uses its word *hell* in each of those three places: and that the Ital. in v. 14, uses first *sotterra*—under ground, and secondly the sepulchre: and in v. 15 gives, But God will redeem my *anima* from the sepulchre: The E. V. using *grave* in each of these three places.

And here, perhaps, is as good a place as I shall find to give the meaning of the two Heb. words *nphsh hie*, for which our E. V., in Gen. 2 : 7 gives "living soul."

I have heard these two English words *living soul* in Gen. 2 : 7 cited as proving the tenet,—inherent immortality; and Commentator Scott, in a note to that verse makes those words teach that tenet. The two Heb. words in that v. are *nphsh hie*. Now these two Heb. words, used together, occur twelve times in the Pentateuch—the five books of Moses—and in eleven of them, all except Gen. 2 : 7, are used of the lower orders of animals of every grade; and in the two passages cited from Leviticus are used of fishes.

The twelve places in the Pentateuch are: Gen. 1 : 20; 1 : 21; 1 : 24; 1 : 30; Gen. 2 : 7; 2 : 19; 9 : 10; 9 : 12, 15, 16; Levit. 11 : 10, 46. In five of these places, namely Gen. 2 : 7; 9 : 10, 12, 15, 16, the Douay gives *living soul*, all except Gen. 2 : 7, being used of other living creatures besides man. The E. V. gives *living soul*, only in Gen. 2 : 7. In Ezek. 47 : 9, the Heb. has the same two words *nphsh hie*, used of fishes : The Douay there is, every living creature; E. V., every thing that liveth.

The two Greek words used in the Greek version of the Old Testament for the two Heb. words *nphsh hie* are *psuché zosa*—breath living ; and in Rev. 8 : 9 and 16 : 3, we find that all aquatic living creatures have *psuche* —breath—soul, equivalent to the Heb. *nphsh*. The Greek of Rev. 8 : 9 is, And died the third part of those creatures in the sea having *psuchas* (accusative plural of *psuche*)—breaths—souls : For *psuchas* in the v. the Rheims Rom. Cath. version gives *life:* Ital.... of the creatures in the sea which had *anima*—breath—soul—died : (We see unequivocally from this verse in the Ital., and from the Ital. of Gen. 1 : 30, that *anima*, the Latin and Ital. word, means breath : the only definition given of it in Graglia's Ital. Dict. is, *soul:* The E. V. of Rev. 8 : 9 is, And the third part of the creatures which were in the sea, and had life, died. And in Rev. 16 : 3 the Greek is, and every *psuche zosa*—breath living--died in the sea: Rheims....and every living soul died in the sea : E. V....the same.

Adding these two verses, Ezek. 47 : 9 and Rev. 16 : 3, we have fourteen passages in the Hebrew and Greek Scriptures in which the two Heb. words *nphsh hie*, and their Greek equivalents *psuche zoza* are used together; and in thirteen of these fourteen passages, (every one except Gen. 2 : 7, where the Douay and E. V. give *living soul*,) they are used of the lower orders of animals of every grade : *animal* means a breathing creature, from the Latin *anima*—breath.

The Hebrew, after having often used its two words *nphsh hie* together, uses most often its one word *nphsh* to express what its two words *nphsh hie* signify. The first instance of its use of the one word *nphsh* is in Levit. 11 : 46 before cited. In that v. it gives first, and of every *nphsh hie* which creepeth in waters, and then gives, and every *nphsh*—breath—soul—which crawleth on this earth: The Douay gives no word for the single word *nphsh* in the verse: The Ital. gives, first, every animal living, and then gives every animal: The E. V. gives, first, every living creature, and then, every creature.

And so, our ecclesiastics, after using their words *immortal soul* sufficiently, use their word *soul* alone, leaving their word *immortal* to be understood.

In Prov. 12:10, we have, Heb., careth for *a* just, *nphsh*—breath—soul—of beast of him: Douay....The just regardeth the lives of his beasts: Ital....the life of his beast: E. V....A righteous *man* regardeth the life of his beast.

Under *nphsh*, Ges. says: specially *nphsh* is, a man, a person: "if any soul—*nphsh*, i. e. says he, if any one sin," citing Levit. 5 : 1, 2, 4, 15, 17: "seventy *nphsh*—souls—came out of the loins of Jacob," citing Exod. 1 : 5; and citing Exod. 16 : 16, where the Heb. has its word *nphsh*, for which the Douay there gives, souls: the Ital. persons; and the E. V. persons.

Gesenius takes *hie* (in *nphsh hie*) to be the genitive (by position) of the noun *hie*—life; and for *nphsh hie*—breath of life, gives, animal of life, i. e. says he, endued with life, "living creature," citing under *nphsh*, Gen. 1 : 21, 24; 2:7; 2 : 19, and other passages; and in Gen. 1:24 and 2:19, the Douay gives, *living creature:* and the E. V. *living creature.* Why not give living creature for the same two Heb. words in Gen. 2 : 7?

We will now dispose of Prof. Eadie's word "without." In the Hebrew of the passage in Job, I is used five times, thus: In the first clause, "And I, know I." In the second clause, "I shall see God." In the third clause, "whom I, I shall behold for myself." It is clear that "And I," and "know I," in the first clause, each means the living man Job in his flesh.

But the Professor asks us to believe, that when Job is made to say, in the second clause of the same passage, "*in*, or *with*, or *from* my flesh *I* shall see God," *I* means "without" my flesh. And that when Job is made to say in the third clause of the same passage, "Whom I, I shall behold for myself," I means "without" my flesh! It would be sufficient to say here, that "without" is not at all given as a definition of the Heb. preposition *m*. It is defined by Gesenius, by, with, out of—a clean thing *out of* an unclean, citing Job 14 : 4. Noyes there gives, *from* an unclean. Am. Bib. Un., out of the unclean. And Ges. gives, "to conceive *m* any one," citing Gen. 19 : 36. I suppose the Professor would agree that *m* in that v. had better be translated *from.* To translate *m*—"without" there would certainly be a miraculous conception; quite as much so as the Professor's "without" for the same Heb. preposition *m*, in Job 19 : 26, is.

To hang upon the single preposition *from*, given for the Heb. preposition *m*, in a single verse in Job, the proposition that the Book of Job teaches "the immortality of the soul,"—inherent immortality in man, without a pretense that there is any other language or word in the Book to sustain that tenet, is as absurd as the tenet itself. And strange to say, Eadie himself says, that the word Soul "is used to denote mere animal life," as before given.

In Job 12 : 4, Job is made to use *him* for *me*. The Heb. is *u*—him; Douay, Ital., E. V. and Am. Bib. Un., *him :* Mr. Noyes gives *me :* It is analagous to *he* for I, in Job 13 : 28, and to Job 19 : 25, if the Ital. is right in using *egli*—*he*—in that verse.

The writer of the Book makes Job say, in v. 25 : "And I, know I Redeemer of me lives." Is that all he meant Job to say of himself? We think he plainly meant that Job should say further of himself: "And I at last upon dust shall be raised."

The title page for Mr. Noyes's Job is :

"A new translation of the Book of Job, with an Introduction, and Notes chiefly explanatory. By George R. Noyes. Second edition. With corrections and additions. 1838."

In the Introduction he says : "of the alterations in the last translation some have been made for the sake of more literal exactness, of the importance of which I have a deeper impression than when I began to translate. In other words, I have yielded less to the besetting sin of a translator, a disposition to paraphrase." " In a few cases my judgment is somewhat different from what it was ten years ago, and in others I have received new light from the later researches of the German Hebraists."

We thus find that Mr. Noyes began to "translate" (or rather to "paraphrase") in 1823,—forty seven years ago. How much less he yielded to that " sin of a translator" in 1838, the reader will form his own opinion from what will be given from the second edition of his so-called Translation.

Mr. Noyes must have been quite young when he "began to translate." The world had not begun then, or even in 1838, to complain much that I know of, of the license of paraphrasing the revealed word, so freely indulged in the Roman Cath. English versions, and in our authorized E. V. The Christian world of our language has moved since 1838, and within a few years past has called so loudly for a translation of the Bible from the originals, without paraphrase, that the clergy have felt obliged to do something in answer to the call. But what they have done is no compliance with it. See the preface to this book.

I extract another remark, a very just one, from Mr. Noyes's Introduction : " That the sentiments of Job, and of the different disputants, as well as those which are represented as proceeding from the lips of the Creator, must all be regarded as the effusions of the poet's own mind, is also too plain to need argument. The whole structure and arrangement, thoughts and language, form and substance of the work must all have proceeded from one and the same mind."

I now give Mr. Noyes's rendering of the passage, Job 19 : 25, 26, 27 :—

25 Yet I know that my Vindicator liveth,
   And will stand up at length on the earth ;
26 And though with my skin this body be wasted away,
   Yet in my flesh I shall see God.
27 Yea, I shall see him my friend ;
   My eyes shall behold him no longer an adversary :
   For this my soul panteth within me.

Job 14 : 19, Noyes renders, so thou destroyest the hope of man, i. e. says he in a note, the hope of living again after death.

We will now see Mr. Noyes's interpretation of the passage Job 19 : 25, 26, 27, in a note. He thinks the object of the writer was, to make Job express the firm persuasion that God will be the vindicator of his integrity from the charges of his friends ; that he "will stand upon the earth," as a judge, and decide the cause in his favor ; that " though his body be wasted away to a mere skeleton, yet in his flesh, restored to soundness, or before he dies, he shall see God—interposing in his favor, and taking his side in the controversy."

Noyes then goes into a course of reasoning from which he concludes that "it is probable that the main, if not sole, object of Job's confident expectation was, "the vindication of his character by the Deity.

Noyes then says: that the supposition that Job here expresses his expectation of a resurrection to a life of happiness is unfounded ; and he gives his reasons for this opinion : Though he says under his first reason, "The belief in *a future state of retribution* would have in some measure solved the difficulty respecting the afflictions of the good, and the prosperity of the wicked. He says, "that there is no allusion to Christ in the term Redeemer, nor to the *resurrection to a life of happiness* in the three verses. That this has been the opinion of the most judicious and learned critics for 300 years, such as Calvin, Mercier, Grotius, LeClerc, Patrick, Warburton, Durell, Heath, Kennicott, Doederlein, Dathe, Eichhorn, Jahn, DeWette, and many others."

We agree that there is no allusion to Christ in the word Redeemer, used in v. 25. And we agree, too, that there is no allusion in the three verses to a resurrection *to a life of happiness*. This phrase, "resurrection *to a life of happiness*," has been introduced by papists and others who have taught *resurrection to a life of misery*. Strike out that blasphemous tenet and there is no need of or sense in the words, *to a life of happiness*, added to resurrection—living again—from the grave. There is no such language in Scripture as "resurrection *to a life of happiness*." Job, and all other Scripture, teaches the resurrection of the just—of them who shall be accounted just, and the life of the resurrected just will certainly be a happy life.

Noyes says: " Dr. Stock supposes that Job expected to die, and to be raised again to life in this world, to see his innocence vindicated, and his calumniators punished." [Of course to die again, Doctor.] And Noyes adds: If we even suppose him to have had his death in view, there is not the slightest reason to believe that he referred to "a general resurrection," but only that he should be restored by the power of God to this world, [of course to die again.]

Again we agree with Mr. Noyes, that there is no reference in the passage to "*a general resurrection.*" This is another phrase introduced by those who have taught the tenet that all are to be raised from the dead, the just and the wicked; the latter to an eternity of woe.

Noyes says, at foot of page 122 of his Job, that chap. 14 renders it highly probable, either that Job had no belief in the resurrection of the dead, or in a future state of existence equally desirable with the present life; or that the author of the poem excluded from it all regard to a future state, as inconsistent with its plan and design. That it contains several assertions of man's utter annihilation. It is true, says Mr. Noyes, that if we make some allowance for his language of strong emotion, we may suppose that he had some vague notions of the existence " of the disembodied spirit," [another of orthodoxy's invented phrases,] in a half conscious, inactive state, in the interior of the earth, [a disembodied—immaterial spirit—confined in the interior of the earth! How about that, Mr. Noyes? That wouldn't do for Modern Spiritism,] such, for instance, as prevailed among the ancient Greeks, but more gloomy and less definite; an existence wholly undesirable, and offering no equivalent for the loss of present enjoyments and of the present life: Here he refers us to chap. 10 : 21, 22 : Read them in the E. V. "These verses," says Noyes, "contain a description of sheol, or hades, the under-world, the place of all the dead." He proceeds to say, "It is almost impossible for the human soul to conceive that its consciousness will be wholly lost;" for which he refers us to ch. 14 : 22, and his note thereon. But before we give that we ask Mr. Noyes whether he ever had such a concussion of his brain as stopped the circulation of blood in it; and if so, whether his consciousness was not lost. Chap. 14 : 22, in the E. V. is, But his flesh upon him shall have pain, and his soul within him shall mourn. (See the verse in this book.) Noyes's note upon it is at page 133. He says : "By a bold but not unnatural personification, the dead man in his grave is represented as conscious of his own miserable condition, and of that alone." [And is the dead man conscious of anything because by personification he is represented as conscious of his own miserable condition?]

Noyes then proceeds to say: "The separate existence of the soul seems to be implied in the distinction which is made between *sheol* and *the grave;* the former being represented as a vast subterranean cavern, where all the spirits of the dead dwell together." Now the reader of this work will see, that *shaul—sheol*, wherever it occurs in Job and in all other Hebrew Scripture, and the Greek *hades* in the Old and New Testaments, means *the grave.* There is no such distinction as Mr. Noyes suggests. His language, "a subterranean cavern where all the spirits of the dead dwell together," shows that he is absolutely possessed by Orthodoxy's *spirits*, or by some *spirit* escaped from the cavern, and not yet successfully materialized by any spiritist medium.

His own renderings of *shaul* prove that there is no such distinction. *Shaul* occurs seven times in Job, as follows: We give Noyes' rendering in each place, and the rendering of the Am. Bib. Un. in each. Job 7 : 9, Noyes, *grave;* Am. Bib. Un., *under-world.* Job 11 : 8, Noyes, *hell:* Am. Bib. Un., the *under-world.* Job 14 : 13, Noyes, *under-world:* Am. Bib. Un. the same. Job 17 : 13, Noyes, *grave:* Am. Bib. Un., underworld. Job 21 : 13, Noyes, *grave:* Am. Bib. Un., under-world. Job 24 : 19, Noyes, *grave:* Am. Bib. Un., underworld. Job 26 : 6, Noyes, *under-world:* Am. Bib. Un. the same. What has become of Mr. Noyes's "distinction between shaul—(he writes it sheol)—and the grave." He must have forgotten himself.

Mr. Noyes then proceeds to say : "The belief in some sort of existence of the soul after death seems also to be implied in the credit which the ancient Hebrews gave to the art of necromancy," citing 1 Sam. 28 : 3 to 10. This is too much. In that chapter a cunning female ventriloquist necromancer, called a witch, pretends to communicate with the dead, and has the power to support her pretensions by making her ventriloquist voice appear to come from the ground. And the witch herself tells Saul, (she pretending not to know him, though in 1 Sam. 9 : 2 we are told, in the E. V., "from his shoulders and upwards *he was* higher than any of the people,") that he had cut off all those that have familiar spirits, and the wizards out of the land ; and asks him, "wherefore then layest thou a snare for my life, to cause me to die ?" And in v. 10, "Saul sware to her by the Lord, saying, *As* the Lord liveth, there shall no punishment happen to thee for this thing." Saul himself had condemned the consulting of witches and wizards and necromancers as a superstition. And yet Mr. Noyes thinks that "the separate existence of the soul" may be "implied" from such a superstition. This matter of the Witch of Endor is more fully exposed in "The Theology of the Bible," page 412 and following. Mr. Noyes then says: "But the language of this chapter" (ch. 14) "appears to be wholly inconsistent with the supposition that Job had any expectation of a *desirable* existence after death. "It was reserved for the Prince of Life, the author and finisher of our faith, to bring the glad tidings of great joy to the aching hearts of men,—to bring life and immortality to light." Here we see that Mr. Noyes adopts the faulty rendering by the E. V., and by Albert Barnes, D. D., of Philadelphia, since deceased, of 2 Tim. 1 : 10; (see page 326 of the work just cited.) Mr. Barnes says: "I have seen no evidence, I now see none, of the immortality of the soul as derived from human reasoning which would be satisfactory to my mind; and my belief that the soul will exist for ever is founded on the fact that 'life and immortality are brought to light through the Gospel.' "The reasoning of Plato on the subject, in the Phædo, has done nothing to convince me on that point, nor have I met with any reasoning, apart from the statements of the Bible, which would convince me, or which would give support or consolation to my aching mind when I think on this great subject." The immortality of the soul spoken of by Mr. Barnes is, inherent immortality in man; and for his belief in this he puts himself on Paul's language to Timothy, as he would have us understand that language, in 2 Tim. 1 : 10 ; thus discarding, as well he might, all the numerous other efforts to find "the immortal soul" in the Bible. Mr. Barnes's collocation of the words in that v. is : " life and immortlity are brought to light through the gospel," making the verse to mean, that through the gospel life and immortality of all is brought to light : The E. V. is, " hath brought life and immortality to light through the gospel." Now the Greek—the original—is, " having brought to light a life and incorruptibility (equivalent to immortality) through the gospel." What is that the Greek says is brought to light? It is, a life and immortality through the gospel, i. e., through belief in the gospel, and of course to those only who believe in the gospel—good tidings—of the Christ come : the phrase here being equivalent to the language of the same Apostle,—Paul, in Rom. 6 : 23, a life eternal through Jesus Christ. And Mr. Noyes proceeds to say, further: " some critics have endeavored to lessen the force of Job's express denials of a future life, in this chap. (chap. 14) by the remark that he only meant that he could not hope to live again *in the present world;* but that he might still have believed that he should exist hereafter in a better world." "I admit," says Mr. Noyes, " that a second life in this world was what he intended to deny ; but I think it was because the idea of a desirable existence in any other place had never entered his mind." "If, as he asserts, the hope of living again in this world would have afforded him consolation and comfort under his afflictions," (where does Mr. Noyes get this from), then surely the hope of a happier state of being than the present life might have afforded him still greater comfort and consolation. How can it possibly be accounted for, says Mr. Noyes, that he should sink in despair because he could not hope to enjoy the doubtful good of living again in this world of sin and misery, whilst (i. e. if) at the same time he believed in the existence of a world of happiness and purity, to which the righteous were to be admitted ?" He says: see note upon ch. 19 : 25, [we have given that.] He says: " In chap. 10 : 21, 22, we have a description of the place where Job expected to be after death ; see the E. V. We have given five different English versions of the passage in Job 19 : 25, 26, 27, namely, the Douay, Professor Eadie's, Mr. Noyes's, the E. V. and the Am. Bib. Union. The last named is the only one that gives the peculiar construction of the Hebrew verse : thus : " But I, I know my Redeemer lives, and in after time will stand upon the earth, or, on the dust." It does not insert *he.* Who will stand up on the earth, or dust ? I, certainly, (Job). It is the nominative to will stand up. And the Latin gives, I shall be raised up : The Douay ....I shall rise out of the earth : Ital....*si levera*—(the Ital. passive)— shall be raised up upon the dust: the Ital. inserts *egli*—he, which the construction of the verse shows means Job himself, just as the Ital. *costui*—this man, in Job 13 : 28 means, where the margin tells us that he means I. The marginal note to the E. V. word *he*, in that v. is: "This man, a form of expression both in Greek and Hebrew for *I*." The Heb. in that verse is: And *eua* he (i. e. Job himself;) and Ges. cites several passages in which *eua* is used for *himself*: The Greek in Job 13 : 28 is, " Who (i. e. Job himself) is," &c. Latin....Who am to be consumed, &c. : Douay....Who am to be consumed as rottenness : Ital....*costui*—this man : E. V....*he*, as a rotten thing consumeth.

Mr. Noyes makes no pretension that the passage in Job 19 : 25, 26, 27, or any other passage in the book teaches "The immortality of the soul." If he had thoroughly repented of the sin of paraphrasing, and given his talents to a literal translation of scripture, he would, we think, have become willing to accept the doctrine which the Book clearly teaches, namely, the resurrection of the just—of them who shall be accounted just, and of them only, to a life eternal: the same doctrine that Paul, centuries after, taught in Rom. 2 : 7, " To them who by patient continuance in well doing seek for glory and honour and immortality," a life eternal, (i. e. immortality.)

One more version of the passage remains to be given, namely, that of the Septuagint—the Greek version of the Old Testament, " so-called because it was the work of seventy, or rather seventy-two interpreters." It was made in the third century before the Christian era."

We now give a translation of the Greek of the passage,—Job 19 : 25, 26, 27 :

25 I know, but, that eternal is he who deliver me is to upon earth,

26 To make stand up again the skin of me which going patiently through these ; for, but, of the Lord these with me are to be brought to an end :

27 Which I in myself know, which the eye of me has seen, and not another ; all, but, with me brought about together in bosom :

In a work I have but lately seen, the title page of which is: " The Septuagint version of the Old Testament with an English translation : and with various readings and critical notes ;" (It is not said by whom ;) Published in London ; the passage in the Greek is rendered in English thus :

25 For I know that he is eternal who is about to deliver me,

26 *And* to raise up upon the earth my skin that endures these *sufferings:* for these things have been accomplished to me of the Lord ;

27 Which I am conscious of in myself, which mine eye has seen, and not another, but all have been fulfilled to me in my bosom.

There is nothing in the Greek of the passage giving the least countenance to the idea that "the Deity" is to stand up on the earth : or to the idea that the passage teaches " the immortality of the soul," as Professor Eadie tries to make it teach by his substituted word " without."

Professor Eadie says: "The Scriptures evidently distinguish between the spirit and soul," and cites 1 Thes. 5 : 23 ; Hebrews 4 : 12. He then says : "The word which we call soul is used to denote mere animal life, or the seat of sensations, appetites and passions," citing Gen. 1 : 20, and saying: "There the word translated *life* is the same with that which is elsewhere translated soul." [The Heb. word there is *nphsh*, one of the definitions of which is, *life*.] The Greek word uniformly used for the Heb. *nphsh* is *psuche*, and *life* is one of the definitions given of *psuche*.

Our E. V. of 1 Thes. 5 : 23 is : "And the very God of peace sanctify you wholly ; and *I pray God* your whole spirit and soul and body be preserved blameless unto the coming of our Lord Jesus Christ." That coming was then expected soon, as we learn from other parts of the New Testament also.

It is plain that "your whole spirit and soul and body," in the second clause, make up the "you,"—the living man, in the first clause.

The Professor says, that, as "soul is used to denote mere animal life which we have in common with brutes," "it may be inferred that it must be spirit which was created in the likeness or image of God, and which raised man above the brutes that perish, and makes him a rational and accountable being."

And does the Professor gravely ask us to infer that the word *spirit* used in the E.V. of this verse must mean " immortal spirit," " immortal soul ?" that the E. V. word *spirit* in the verse teaches the immortality of the soul," which Pope Leo tenth, in A. D. 1513, decreed to be an article of Christian faith ? " Can it be possible, Professor, that there is no better ground in all scripture for a tenet on which your entire system of religious teaching rests ? It is even so. And if there was any better ground in Scripture for the tenet " immortal spirit," surely the Professor would not have been content to infer it from the E. V. word *spirit* in 1 Thes. 5 : 23, used in connection with its words *soul* and *body*, as he evidently intends, though he does not say so in words.

The Professor says : " We cannot comprehend the exact connection and relation of the various parts of our being ; " (alluding to the words, " spirit and soul and body," in 1 Thes. 5 : 23 ;) " but that they exist is the declaration of Scripture." And he has before said : " The Scriptures evidently distinguish between the spirit and soul." And certainly they do when the words *spirit* and *soul* are used in such connection as in 1 Thes. 5 : 23, and Heb. 4 : 12, the only verses in all Scripture where they are so used. But does that prove that the word *spirit* used in these verses means " immortal spirit,"—teaches the tenet—inherent immortality in man ?

The Professor himself has told us that in Gen. 1 : 20, the word elsewhere translated *soul* is translated *life :* so that we have only to read in 1 Thes. 5 : 23, the spirit and life and body, to show the distinction there made between spirit (the Latin *spiritus*—breath) and *life*. The substitution of his own word *life*, for the Douay word soul, the Ital. and Latin word *anima*, and the E.V. word *soul*, makes plain both the verses he cites.

The Greek words in 1 Thes. 5 : 23 are *pneuma* and *psuche* and *soma*. *Pneuma* is defined by the Greek Lexicons *breath*, from the Greek verb *pneo*—to breathe : *psuche* is the Greek word for the Heb. *nphsh :* and *anima* is the Latin and Ital. word for the Heb. *nphsh*. The Heb. word *hie* is defined by Gesenius, first, life ; "then, equivalent to *nphsh* No. 2, vital power:" and for *nphsh* No. 2, he gives "life, vital principle," and for *ruh*, he gives, first, spirit, breath ; and second, "equivalent to *nphsh* No. 2, *psuche*, *anima*, the vital principle ;" and Luther gives, the life principle ; and Anthon's Latin Dict. for *anima*, gives, "animal principle of life." And the Greek word *soma* in the verse is defined, "body, living body, person, man." And the two other Greek words in Hebrews 4 : 12, are *psnche* and *pneuma*, life, or, vital power, and breath.

Now I think that but for a certain " mental tendency" the Professor might have got the idea, that there is in the breathing and thereby living creature a vital principle back of the act of breathing which impels breathing, without volition—act of will ; else the first sleep would be the last. In sleep the breathing creature would forget to do the act of will. He might have got the idea, that the internal organism,—the lungs, heart, liver, blood, and its circulation—is such that when set in motion by the inbreathed breath of lives, it continues to work of itself without the act of will. And having got this idea he would have been able "to comprehend the connection and relation of the various parts of our being," spoken of in the two verses cited by him, without imagining that they gave any support to the tenet —"the immortal spirit." He might have been content to read the verse in 1 Thes. 5 : 23, "And the very God of peace sanctify you wholly ; and your breath (by which you live,) and the vital principle (which impels it,) and your living body (which lives by both) may be preserved until the coming of our Lord Jesus Christ :" And to read correspondingly the verse he cites from Hebrews.

How is it that men will attempt such frail support of a tenet which, if true, we might expect to find plainly taught on almost every page of the Bible ? Who is answerable for the astounding fact, that almost without exception all believe that the Bible abounds with the language—"immortal soul,"—"immortal spirit,"—when no such language is to be found in it, or in any translation of it ? It has been so long the language of the pulpit, that it has been taken for granted that it is the language of the Bible. There is another far-reaching question that may well be put here : By what potency was brought about the amazing fact, that the languages in which the revealed word of God is written became dead languages, and are classed even by so-called orthodox writers as dead "languages." Think of it, reader : The languages in which the revealed word of God is written, dead languages ! ! By what potency ? ! The great Apostasy,—departure from the faith of the primitive Christians,—Romanism, is that potency. By its system of proscription translation from the originals was denounced as heresy, and punished with death. Professor Draper of the city of New York in his work on the Intellectual Development of Europe, pages 469, 470, says: that in 1470, when the Greek and Hebrew threatened to take from the Latin language the sacred character with which Romanism had clothed it, the ecclesiastic, with a quick and jealous suspicion, soon learned to detect a heretic from his knowledge of the Greek and Hebrew. That the Romish clergy could not conceal their dread at the incoming of the Greek: and could not speak without horror of the influence of the Hebrew." And page 484, he says, "the study of the Greek and Hebrew was recognized by all parties to be dangerous to the Latin system." And the attempt about that time made to revive the Hebrew and the Greek seems to have been crushed.

The first translation of the Greek (the original) of the New Testament into English was made by William Tyndal, "who had studied both at Oxford and at Cambridge, and was, for a time, a preacher at St. Dunstan's church near Temple Bar, London." "He soon became an object of suspicion as a favorer of the reformation." "He retired to Flanders, where he could pursue his purpose of translating the Bible, and avow his opinions on points of religion with greater personal safety." What! It is even so, reader. For long centuries a man could not even in England translate the Bible from the originals into English with personal safety.

At Antwerp, A. D., 1526, Tyndal published his translation of the New Testament; but all the copies were rapidly bought up by Bishop Tonstal and burned at Paul's cross before a year had elapsed.

Tyndal published a translation of the Hebrew of the Pentateuch into English in A. D. 1530. In translating the remainder of the Old Testament he was assisted by Miles Coverdale, afterwards Bishop of Exeter, but seems himself to have advanced only to the end of Nehemiah at the time of his imprisonment. The Tyndal and Coverdale complete translation of the Bible into English was printed in A. D. 1535, at Zurich. "Coverdale, assisted by John Rogers, who corrected the press, revised the whole of Tyndal's work before they reprinted it."

Tyndal died a martyr, October 7, 1536. "He was first strangled and afterwards burned at Tylford Castle in Flanders, at which place he had previously suffered a cruel and tedious imprisonment."

"The second complete Protestant Bible in English was that of John Rogers, who had assisted Coverdale. It was printed at Hamburgh, as is supposed, though it bears date, London, A. D. 1537." This John Rogers was "the first martyr in the reign of the Papist Queen Mary of England."

"Coverdale prudently remained abroad till the accession of Queen Elizabeth."

I suppose there are thousands in this country who have never read this horrid tale; and it would not be at all surprising that by many such it should be thought to be a baseless fiction. But perhaps they may come to believe in its reality when they recollect, that even at this late day in the nineteenth century ecclesiastics decline to give or direct to be made, a version from the original scriptures except "on the basis of the common and earlier English versions." How early the American Bible Union meant by the word "earlier" (earlier English versions) on the title page of their Job, we are not told. They certainly did not mean the earliest translations of Scripture into English, for those translations repudiated the dogma "immortal soul,—spirit," and the authors of them were put to death as heretics. The language of the rule prescribed by the Am. Bib. Un. as a guide for the revisers employed by them is more definite,—"The common English version must be the basis of revision."

CHAPTER XX.

1 And answered tsuphr that nomti and said :

2 Nevertheless thoughts of me lead me to answer, and because of hasting of me within me : [1]

3 Admonition of reproach of me I have heard, and breath [2] from understanding of me shall answer for me:

4 Whether this knowest thou from perpetuity of time, from to put man upon earth:

5 That shouting for joy of wicked short, yea joy of impious so long as to wink:

6 Though go up to heavens height of him, and head of him to cloud reach:

7 As dung [3] of him to eternity he shall perish; they who had seen him shall say: where he:

8 As dream he shall fly away and not shall they find him, yea, he shall flee away as vision of night:

9 Eye has seen him but not shall it add, and not again shall behold him place of him:

---

1. i. e., says Ges., under *hush*, citing this v., on account of the emotion by which I am moved.

2. Heb. *ruh*—breath : Douay....spirit; Ital....*spirito;* E. V....spirit; Am. Bib. Un....spirit; Noyes....and my understanding enableth me to answer.

3. So Ges., under *gll*—dung ; and he adds : "as to this comparison, by which ignominious destruction is denoted, see 1 Kings 14 : 10. The same Heb. word is used there; and the Douay, the Ital., and the E. V. there is dung: The Am. Bib. Un. in Job 20 : 7 is, "according to his greatness so shall he perish for ever."

10 Children of him shall seek favour of weak, and hands of them shall restore substance of them: [1]

11 Bones of him are full of youth of him,[2] and with him upon dust it shall lie down: [3]

12 Though be sweet in mouth of him evil, *though* he hide it under tongue of him:

13 *Though* he use it sparingly and not let loose it; keep back it in middle of palate of him:

14 Food of him in intestines of him is perverted, gall of asps in entrails of him: [4]

15 Riches he swallowed down and he shall vomit up them; from belly of him will drive out them God:

16 Poison of asps he sucked; shall kill him tongue of viper:

17 Not shall he look upon streams, streams of rivers of milk and honey:

18 Caused to restore fruit of labor, and not shall he swallow down; as wealth of exchange of him, and not shall he rejoice:

19 For he broke in pieces poor; of weak, house he plucked away and not rebuilt:

---

1. Ges., under *rtse*, citing this v., renders, "his children shall seek the favor of the poor, i. e., says he, conciliate the poor, by restoring the goods taken from them; Douay....His children shall be oppressed with want; Ital....His children shall endeavour after the favour of the poor, and their hand shall restore that which he shall have ravished from them: Am. Bib. Un....His sons the weak shall oppress.

2. Ges., under *olumim*, says: It is used poetically for juvenile strength; and he cites this v. and renders, "*Although* his bones are full of juvenile strength," as well rendered, says he, by the Septuagint, Chaldee and Syriac.

3. i. e., says Ges., under *ol*, citing this v., "in the grave, where the dead both lie upon the dust and under it;" Am. Bib. Un....it shall lie down with him in the dust; Noyes....but they (his bones) shall sink with him into the dust.

4. Douay....within him; Ital....in entrails of him; E. V....within him; Am. Bib. Un....within him.

20 So that not knew he tranquility in belly of him ;[1] in things desirable of him not shall he be smooth:[2]

21 Not was there survivor[3] to devouring of him; therefore not shall he possess welfare of him:

22 In fullness of redundance of him, it shall be narrow to him ; every hand of wretched comes upon him:[4]

23 It shall be at filling belly of him *God* shall send out upon him heat of nostril of him, and shall pour down upon him with food of him:[5]

24 Should he flee from weapon of iron, would pierce through him bow of brass:

25 Draw he out, and goeth it forth from middle, and lightning[6] from gall of him: shall fall upon him terrors:

26 Every darkness[7] is laid up for treasures of him ; shall devour him fire not blown; it shall feed upon survivors in tent of him:[8]

27 Shall disclose heavens depravity of him, and earth shall stand up against him:

28 Shall go away produce of house of him, wealth scraped together,[9] in day of nostril of him:

---

1. Douay, Ital. and E. V., belly ; Am. Bib. Un., in his bosom.

2. i. e., at ease; Am. Bib. Un....of all his delights he shall save nothing.

3. Used of things, says Ges. under *shrid*, citing this v. Am. Bib. Un. His greedy appetite nothing escaped.

4. Ges., uder *id*, citing this v., renders, "every stroke of the wretched comes upon him," i. e., says he, whatever usually falls upon the wretched ; Douay....every sorrow shall fall upon him.

5. Ges., under *lhum*, citing this v., renders, " and he shall rain upon them with their food." Am. Bib. Un....and shall rain his food upon them ; Noyes....and shall rain it (his anger) down upon him for his food.

6. Poetically, says Ges., for the glittering sword itself, citing this v., under *brq*.

7. Ges., under *tsphn*, gives, "every misfortune," citing this v.

8. See v. 7. and note to it.

9. So Ges., under *grr*, citing this v.

29 This, portion of man wicked from God, and lot said of him from God:

CHAPTER XXI.

1 And answered Job and said:
2 Hearing hear words of me, and let be these,¹ consolations of you :
3 Bear with me and I will speak, and after have spoken I, mock you:
4 Whether I with man quarrel of me, and whether not should be short breath ² of me:
5 Turn eyes to me and be astonished and put hand upon mouth:
6 Even when remember I, also am terrified I, and taketh hold of flesh of me horror:
7 Wherefore wicked, live they, be old they, even be strong they of wealth:
8 Seed of them set up to faces of them, and they which spring forth from them to eyes of them:
9 Houses of them secure from fear, and not rod of God upon them:
10 Cow of him lets pass,³ and not casts away; delivereth ⁴ heifer of him and not maketh abortion:

---

1. The Heb. is *zat*, feminine of *ze*—this : Ges., under *ze*, says *zat* stands also for the plural : Am. Bib. Un....and let your consolations be this.
2. Heb. *ruh*—breath. In the Hebrew, to be of short *ruh*—breath, and to be of short *nphsh*—breath, is to be impatient. Ges., under *qtsr*, cites Numb. 21 : 4, where the Heb. is, was of short *nphsh*—breath—that people: and Judges 10 : 16, where it is said of Jehovah, was short *nphsh*—breath—of him. The Douay of Job in 21 : 4 is, that I should not have just reason to be troubled. Ital....Why should not I be pressed in my *spirito*. E. V....Why should not my spirit be troubled. Am. Bib. Un....Wherefore should I not be impatient? And Ges. cites Prov. 14 : 29, where the Heb. is, of short *ruh*—breath ; and the Douay is....he that is impatient : E. V....hasty of spirit.
3. Ges., under *obr*, citing this v., says : a female is said to let pass, to conceive seed. [The Heb. "lets pass" gives the true idea.]
4. The young from the womb, says Ges., under *phlth*, citing this v.

11 They cast forth like small cattle¹ sucklings of them, and brought forth of them dance:

12 They lift up² with timbrel and harp, and rejoice to sound of pipe:

13 They spend in good, days of them, and in wink grave³ they go down:

14 And they say to God : Depart from us, for knowledge of ways of thee not desire we:

15 What, Almighty, that we should serve him, and what should we be profited, that we should assail him: (with prayers, says Ges., under *phgb*.)

16 Lo, not in hand of them welfare of them : counsel of wicked let be far off from me:

17 How often⁴ is lamp of wicked put out, and cometh upon them heavy misfortune of them ; pains of them allotted in anger of him:

18 How often are they as straw to face of wind,⁵ and as chaff driven away of whirlwind:

19 God, will he lay up for children of him wickedness of him : Let him requite to him that he may know:

20 Let see eye of him calamity of him ; and of wrath of Almighty let him drink:

21 For what matter to him about house of him after him, when number of new moons of him are cut off:⁶

---

1. i. e., says Ges., under *tsan*, sheep and goats.

2. Ges. under *nsha*, citing this v., renders, "they lift up the voice," i. e., says he, they sing, "to the sound of timbrel and harp."]

3. Heb. *shaul:* Douay....they go down to hell : Ital....into the sepulchre : E. V....to the grave : Noyes....to the grave : Am. Bib. Un.,... to the underworld.

4. i. e., seldom, says Ges., under *kme*, citing this verse. Under *nr*—lamp, he says : It is figuratively applied in various ways, as, to happiness, and to glory, citing passages. The verse is an interrogation : the Heb. has no interrogation mark.

5. Heb. *ruh*—wind. The Ital. and Noyes, and the Am. Bib. Un., righlty put an interrogation mark at the end of this verse also.

6. i. e., finished, ended, says Ges., under *htsts*, citing this v., spoken, says he, of the months of one's life.

22 Whether to God would *one* teach knowledge, seeing that he the exalted judges:

23 This¹ dies in bone of integrity of him, wholly tranquil and secure:

24 Resting places of cattle of him full of milk,² and marrow of bones of him watered:³

25 And that⁴ dies in breath⁵ bitter, and not has eaten that which is good:

26 Alike⁶ upon dust they lie down, and worm covers over upon them:

27 Lo, I know projects of you, and counsels upon me you would oppress:⁷

28 For you say: where house of tyrant⁸ and where tent of dwelling places of wicked:

29 Whether not should you ask them that go by the the way, and signs of them you will not be ignorant of:⁹

30 Though in day of calamity¹⁰ may be spared wicked, in day of outpourings¹¹ they shall be borne:¹²

---

1. Ital., *costui*—this man: see the Ital. in Job 13 : 28.

2. Douay....His bowels are full of fat: Ital....His pails are full of milk: E. V....His breasts are full of milk: Noyes....His sides are full of fat: Am. Bib. Un....the same: Ges., under *othin*, citing this v., renders, "The resting places of his cattle abound with milk."

3. i. e., says Ges., under *shqe*, is fresh vigorous: Douay....his bones are watered with marrow: See E. V., Noyes....And his bones are moistened with marrow: Am. Bib. Un....and the marrow of his bones is moistened.

4. i. e., another.

5. Heb. *nphsh*—breath—bitter: Douay....in bitterness of soul: Ital. ....in bitterness of mind: See E.V.: Am. Bib. Un....in bitterness of soul.

6. The two spoken of in verses 23 and 25.

7. i. e., says Ges., under *hms*, citing this v., counsels with which you wish to oppress me.

8. So Ges., under *ndib*, citing this v. and Isai. 13 : 2.

9. i. e., says Ges., under *nkr*, citing this v., you will readily know who it is they point out as if with the finger.

10. So Ges., under *aid*, citing this v. and Ps. 18 : 19.

11. Heb. *obrut* (plural of *obre*)—outpourings, i. e., says Ges., of anger; hence, says he, used of wrath itself as poured out, citing Isa. 14 : 6; 10 : 6.

12. Heb. *iublu*, passive of the Heb. verb *ibl*—to bear, carry,—they shall

31 Who will tell to face of him way of him, and *what* he has done who will requite to him:

32 And he to graves is borne,[1] and in sepulchral heap shall watch:[2]

33 Sweet to him clods of valley, and after him all men will draw, as before him not number:[3]

34 And how can you cause me to draw breath:[4] and answers of you remain perfidy:

---

be borne—carried; and Ges., under *ibl*, renders, " be borne," as to the the grave, says he, citing this v. and v. 32, where the same verb *ibl* is used: The Douay of the v. is: Because the wicked man is reserved to the day of destruction and he shall be brought to the day of wrath: the E. V. is, That the wicked is reserved to the day of destruction? They shall be brought forth to the day of wrath: [Better Romanism than even the Douay gives:] Noyes....That the wicked is spared in the day of destruction, and that he is gone to his grave in the day of wrath? Am. Bib. Un....That the wicked is kept unto the day of destruction; they are brought on to the day of wrath.

1. The Heb. here is the same verb *ibl, iubl*—is borne: Douay, he shall be brought to the graves: Ital....Then afterwards he is carried to the sepulchre: E. V....yet he shall be brought to the grave: Am. Bib. Un....And he, to the graves is he borne away.

2. So Ges., under *gdish* and *shqd*, citing this v. under each: Figurative says he under *shqd*, citing this v., and Jer. 31 : 28; 44 : 27; Dan. 9 : 14: Douay....and shall watch in the heap of the dead: Ital....and not waits more to other than to the grave: The E. V. of the v. is, yet he shall be brought to the grave, and shall remain in the tomb: Am. Bib. Un.... and watch is held over the tomb: Noyes renders the v., " Even this man is borne with honor to the grave; yea, he still survives upon his tomb."

3. i. e., innumerable: the Douay of this v. is, He hath been acceptable to the gravel of Cocytus, and he shall draw every man after him, and there are innumerable before him. Anthon's Latin Dict. defines Cocytus, " In Mythology, a river in the infernal (lower) regions," citing Cicero and Virgil. It is the Greek *kokutos*. Liddell and Scott's Greek Lexicon gives for it Cocytus, and defines it, one of the rivers of hell, citing Odyssey 10, 54. The Roman priesthood, in their apostasy, adopted the system of the Pagan priesthood, by which they subjected the Pagan masses to their rule. That the Romish priesthood thereby acquired like rule history conclusively teaches.

4. i. e., be comforted.

CHAPTER XXII.

1 And answered Aliphaz that tmni and said:

2 Whether to God can profit man when he profits himself acting prudently:

3 Whether delight to Almighty that thou shouldst be righteous; and whether gain, that upright, ways of thee:

4 Whether from fear of thee will he altercate with thee; will enter he with thee into right:[1]

5 Whether not wickedness of thee great, and no end to perversities of thee:

6 For thou hast taken pledge from brother of thee for nothing; and garment of ragged thou hast stripped off:

7 Not water languishing hast thou given to drink, and from hungry thou hast kept back bread:

8 But man of arm, to him this land; and lifted up of face[2] sat down in it:

9 Widows hast thou sent away empty-handed, and arms of orphans were broken:

10 Therefore round about thee snares, and terrifieth thee terror sudden:

11 Or darkness, not canst thou see, and great multitude of waters covers thee:

12 Whether not God of height of heavens, and behold head[3] of stars, that high:

13 And thou sayest: How knows God: Whether behind thick clouds he can judge:

14 Clouds *a* vail to him and not sees he, and vault of heavens[4] he walks upon:

---

1. The Heb. word is *mshphth*, defined, right—that which is just: Douay, E. V., and Am. Bib. Un., into judgment.

2. i. e., I think, the proud: Am. Bib. Un., the honored one.

3. Figuratively for highest, says Ges., under *rash*—head; Am. Bib. Un....in the height of heaven.

4. Douay....about the poles of heaven: Am. Bib. Un.. .upon the vault of heaven.

15 Whether pathway of time long past wilt thou keep, which have trodden men of wickedness:

16 Who were seized and not time;[1] river flowed out, foundation of them:[2]

17 Which said to God: Depart from us, and what could do Almighty to them:

18 And yet he filled houses of them of good : therefore, counsel of wicked let be far from me:

19 Shall behold just and rejoice, and pure shall mock at them:

20 Whether not are cut off adversaries of us,[3] and that which is left of them consumeth fire:

[See note to fire at end of chapter.]

21 Form acquaintance, I pray thee, with him and be safe: by these shall come upon thee welfare:

22 Receive, I pray thee, from mouth of him instruction, and put words of him in heart of thee:

23 If thou wilt turn thyself to Almighty thou wilt be built,[4] thou wouldst thrust away iniquity from tents of thee:

24 And thou shalt lay on ground ore of gold and silver,[4] yea ore of streams of Ophir:

---

1. i. e., before the time, prematurely, says Ges., under *ot*, citing this verse.

2. i. e., they have no foundation.

3. Ges., our adversaries, citing this v. under *qim:* Am. Bib. Un.... Truly our adversary is cut off.

4. Ges., under *bne*, citing this v., says: men are said to be built when set in a fixed abode and in prosperity ; and a woman is said to be built if her house is built, that is, says he, when she has offspring. In Gen. 16 : 2, he renders, "perhaps I may be built by her," i. e., says he, I may have children by the aid of this handmaid. He cites also Gen. 30 : 3.

4. As it is dug out, or cut out from mines, or broken off, says Ges., under *btsr*, citing this v. ; and he there gives, lay precious metals on the dust ; and under *ophr*, citing this v. again, he gives, "on the ground." The idea is, bring precious metals from the mines to the surface of the ground. Am. Bib. Un....And cast to the dust the precious ore, and the gold of Ophir to the stones of the brooks.

25 And will be Almighty precious ores to thee, and money of treasures to thee:[1]

26 So that then in Almighty thou mayst delight thyself.

27 Thou canst pray to him and he will hear thee, and vows of thee thou canst pay:

28 And thou canst decree thing and it will come forth to thee; and on ways of thee will shine forth light:[2]

29 When they act humbly[3] then thou commandest lifting up;[4] and cast down of eyes he will save:

30 Will he deliver not pure:[5] nay, to be delivered by cleanness of hands of thee:

---

1. i. e., great plenty of money, says Ges. under *tuophut*, citing this v. Am. Bib. Un....and silver sought with toil for thee.

2. Metaphor., says Ges., under *aur;* light, says he, furnishes an image of good fortune, prosperity, citing this v., and Job 30 : 26; and others.

3. Impersonal, for, when men act humbly.

4. i. e., says Ges., under *gue*, citing this v., thou liftest up the modest, meek, man.

5. Metaphor., for innocent, says Ges., under *nqe*: Douay....The innocent shall be saved; and he shall be saved by the cleanness of his hands: See E. V. Am. Bib. Un....He will deliver one that is not guiltless and he shall be saved by the pureness of thy hands. (The first part of the verse is plainly an interrogation.)

NOTE TO FIRE, IN V. 20.

Ges., under *ash*—fire, says: Fire and burning are used in the Heb. to denote any destruction, whether of men or things, citing Job 15 : 34; 20 : 26; 22 : 20; 31 : 12; Isai. 30 : 30; 33 : 11, 14. (Fire is the destroying element, as well as the purifying element.) Ges. further says: "the fire of God," often used of lightnings, says he, citing 1 Kings 18 : 38; 2 Kings 1 : 10, 12, 14; Job 1 : 16; compare, says he, Exod. 9 : 23. Also figuratively used says he, of the anger and wrath of God, citing Deut. 32 : 22, "a fire kindled in mine anger:" Jer. 4 : 4; 15 : 14; 21 : 12; Lament. 2 : 4; Ezek. 22 : 21; and by a similar figure, says he, fire, when speaking of men, is also applied to internal ardour of mind; Jer. 20 : 9; Ps. 39 : 3. Poetically, says he, "fire is used of war, so that to be consumed with fire is equivalent to to be destroyed in war," Numb. 21 : 28; Jer. 48 : 45; Judges 9 : 15, 20; Isai. 10 : 16; 26 : 11; Ps. 21 : 10, E. V.

v. 9: "to kindle *a* fire," metaphor., says he, for, to excite the tumult of war, citing Isai. 50 : 11. The same figure, says he, is very familiar to the Arabian poets; compare, says he, on Isai. 7 : 4. [There is, also, the fire, —combustion—of the grave.—The decay in the grave is combustion.]

CHAPTER XXIII.

1 And answered Job and said:

2 Truly this day, bitter, quarrel[1] of me; hand of Jehovah[2] heavy more than groaning of me:

3 Who will give might know I and might find I him, might enter even to place[3] of him.

4 I would put in order to face of him cause,[4] and mouth would fill of arguments:

5 I would know words he would answer me, and hear what he would say to me:

6 Whether with vast power he would plead cause with me: No; only himself would he put against me:[5]

7 There *an* upright over against him, and I could slip away altogether[6] according to right[7] of me:

8 Lo, East I may go, and not there he; and West and not might I discern him:

9 North, *the* work of him, and not might I see: cover he himself over South,[8] then not could I behold:

---

1. Am. Bib. Un....my complaint is frowardness: Noyes....still is my complaint bitter.

2. Ges. under *id*—hand, cites this v. and says: *idi* in the v. is for *id ieue*—hand of Jehovah: [This makes v. 3 plain :] The Am. Bib. Un. is....The hand upon me is heavier than my groaning.

3. So. Ges., under *tkune*, citing this v.: Am. Bib. Un....seat.

4. Heb. *mshphth*: Douay....judgment: Am. Bib. Un...."cause."

5. Douay....the weight of his greatness: E. V....No, but he would put *strength* in me: Am. Bib. Un....No, he surely would give heed to me.

6. So Ges., under *phlth*, citing this v.

7. Heb. *mshphth*—right: Douay....judgment: Ital....and I should be for ever delivered from my judge: Am. Bib. Un....the same. See E.V.

8 Ges., under *othph*, citing this v. says, "i. e., if he hide himself in the South."

10 When he knows way with me let him try me; I shall go forth like gold:

11 On step of him has taken hold foot of me; path of him have kept I, and not have turned aside:

12 Command of lips of him, also, not have I turned aside from; more than appointed portion [1] of me have I turned myself to words of mouth of him:

13 But he in one only [2] and who can turn him; breath [3] of him, that even he doeth:

14 So that he will complete that which is appointed for me,[4] and like these, many with him:

15 Therefore because of face (presence) of him I am confounded; I discern and tremble because of him:

16 And God has broken [5] heart of me; and Almighty confounds me:

17 That not have been extinguished I [6] from face of darkness,[7] and *not* from face of me he has covered thick darkness:

---

1. Ges. under *hq*, citing this v., gives, "that which is appointed for me:" Ital....more *tenderly* than my provision ordinary: E. V....more than my necessary food: Noyes....the words of his mouth I have treasured up in my bosom: Am. Bib. Un....above my own law I prized the words of his mouth.

2. So Ges., under *ahd*—one, citing this v.

3. Heb. *nphsh*—breath, for desire, "breath of him," is poetical for he: Douay....his soul: Ital....his *anima*: Noyes...."and what he desireth that he doeth:" Am. Bib. Un...."and what his soul desires he will do.

4. So Ges., under *hq*, citing this v.

5. So Ges., under *rkk*, citing this v.: Douay....hath softened my heart....Am. Bib. Un....makes my heart soft.

6. So Ges., under *tsmt*, citing this v., and Job 6:17.

7. Metaphor., says Ges., for misery, adversity, citing this v. under *hshk*—darkness; and citing this v. again under *kse*, he renders, "and (because) he hath (not) covered the darkness from my sight," i. e., says he, has not set me free from calamities. The *not* at the beginning of the v. applies also to the second clause, a construction which occurs frequently in the Hebrew: The Ital. is....Because not am I been cut off for not to see darkness; and *because* hath he hid darkness from before

CHAPTER XXIV.

1 Why from Almighty not are hid times, and they that know him not see days of him:

2 Boundaries they remove; flock they pluck and depasture:¹

3 Ass of orphans they drive away; they take in pawn ox of widow:

4 They push needy from way; together are forced to hide themselves afflicted of earth:

5 Lo, wild asses at pasture, they go forth to work of them of seeking for food; desert to them bread for young of them:

6 In fields provender of them they reap, and vineyard of wicked they glean :

7 Ragged, they lodge without clothing, and not there is covering from cold:

8 From storm of mountains they are wet; and because of not refuge they embrace rock:²

9 They pluck from teat orphan, and on poor they take in pledge:³

10 Ragged, go without clothing, and hungry they that carry sheaf:

11 Within walls of them they that squeeze out winepress of them trample and thirst:⁴

---

me: [The Ital. should have inserted *not* in the last clause:] Noyes renders, "Because I was not taken away before darkness came, and he hath not hidden darkness from mine eyes: Am. Bib. Un....For I should not be dumb because of darkness, because thick darkness covers me. The E. V. is better; "Because I was not cut off before the darkness, *neither* hath he covered the darkness from my face."

1. Figurative for consume, says Ges., under *roe*. Am. Bib. Un.... flocks they seize upon and feed.

2. i. e., says Ges., under *hbq*, make their bed on it.

3. i. e., says Ges., what is on the poor, their garments, citing this v. under *ol*. Am. Bib. Un....and on the sufferer is imposed a pledge: Noyes....the garment of the needy is taken in pledge.

4. Metaphor., says Ges., for, desire eagerly, citing this v. under *tsma*.

12 From heat of mind men groan, and breath¹ of pierced through² cries out,³ and God not attributeth folly:⁴

13 These be rebellious to light,⁵ not are they ignorant of ways of it, but not return they into paths of it:

14 At dawn of day rises homicide; he slays afflicted and needy; and at night will be as thief:

15 And eye of adulterer watches darkness, saying: not will lie in wait for me eye, and vail of face he puts:

16 He breaks through⁶ in darkness into houses; of day they shut up themselves; not know they light:

17 For at once morning to them shadow of death; when can discern, terrors of shadow of death:

18 Swift he on face of waters; cursed, allotments of them in land; not let him turn face way of gardens and orchards:⁷

19 Drought and heat take away waters of snow; the grave⁸ them that have sinned:⁹

20 Will forget him womb; will feed sweetly on him worm; more not will *any* remember; and shall perish¹⁰ like tree *the* wicked:¹¹

---

1. Heb. *nphsh*.
2. i. e., says Ges., mortally wounded, citing this v. uhder *hll*.
3. For vengence, says Ges., under *nphsh*, citing this v.
4. So Ges., under *tphle*, citing this v. With what can one cry out but with breath? Douay....the soul of the wounded hath cried out, and God doth not suffer it to pass unrevenged: Ital....the *anima* of the wounded to death crieth, and yet not God imputeth to them any fault: Am. Bib. Un....And the soul of the wounded cries out; and God heeds not the prayer: Noyes....and the wounded cry aloud.
5. So Ges., under *mrd* citing this v.
6. i. e., the thief, says Ges., under *htr*, citing this v.
7. i. e., to a cultivated country inhabited by men, as opposed to a desert, says Ges., citing this v. under *krm*.
8. Heb. *shaul*.
9. i. e., that is as a finality, as the sense of the v. and the verses following prove. For *shaul* in the verse the Douay gives, hell; the Ital., the sepulchre: the E. V., the grave; the Am. Bib. Un., the under-world: Noyes, the grave.
10. The Heb. verb used here is *shbr*, for which Ges. gives, thirdly, "to be destroyed, to perish," as a kingdom, a city, a people, says he, citing Isai. 8 : 15; 24 : 10: 28 : 13; Jer. 48 : 4; Dan. 8 : 25; Ezek 30 : 8.
11. The Heb. word here is *oule*, which says Ges. is used for wicked per-

21 He oppressed barren not beareth, and to widow not doeth he good:

22 And he takes away powerful by power of him; he rises up and not can *any* trust in life:

23 He gives to them to be secure, and they lean upon,[1] and eyes of him on ways of them:

24 Lifted up a little while, and not there is of them; and they perish;[2] as whoever; they are gathered,[3] and as top of ears of corn[4] they vanish:

25 And if not so, who will convict me of falsehood, and put to nothing words of me:

CHAPTER XXV.

1 And answered *bldd* that *shhi* and said:

2 Dominion and fear with him; he doeth welfare in heights of him:

3 Whether is number to troops of him, and on whom not rises light of him:

4 And how can be just *a* man with God;[5] and how can be pure *a* born of woman:

---

sons, citing this v. and Ps. 107 : 42: the Douay gives....let him be broken; the Ital. here gives....the perverse; E. V....and wickedness shall be broken: Am. Bib. Un....and iniquity will be broken as a tree: Noyes....the unrighteous man shall be broken like a tree.

The verses in the Heb. beginning at v. 19 show plainly that to the wicked death is a finality. This plain doctrine is evaded in the E. V. by its substitution of the word *wickedness* instead of *wicked* in v. 20; and the evasion is followed in the Am. Bib. Un. by its substitution of the word *iniquity* in v. 20 in place of "the wicked."

1. Metaphorical., for repose confidence, says Ges., under *shon*.
2. So Ges., under *mkk*, citing this v.
3. Namely, says Ges., to their ancestors, i. e., says he, are dead, citing this v. under *qphts*.
4. The silk I suppose.
5. i. e., in the judgment of God, says Ges. under *om*.

5 Behold even to moon, and not it shineth,[1] and stars not clean in eyes of him:

6 How much less man, a worm, and son of man, a worm:

CHAPTER XXVI.

1 And answered Job and said:

2 How hast helped thou to not strength; whether hast aided thou arm not strong:

3 How much hast thou counselled to not wise; and counsel how much hast thou caused to know:

4 To whom hast thou brought to light words and breath[2] of whom has gone forth from thee:

5 Those dead,[3] *ihullu* under water and dwellers of it:

---

1. i. e., says Ges., it is not pure in sight of God, citing this v. under *ael*.

2. Heb. *nshme*, defined by Ges., breath, spirit, (as synonyms.) Douay ....was it not him that made life: Ital....the *spirito* of whom is gone out from thee? E. V....whose spirit came from thee? Am. Bib. Un... whose breath has come forth from thee? Noyes....And whose spirit spake through thee?

3. The Douay of this v. is, Behold the giants groan under the waters, and they that dwell with them: The Ital. is, The giants are been formed *by God*, and *the animals* that exist in the waters *are been formed* under them: The E. V. is, Dead *things* are formed under the waters, and the inhabitants thereof: Noyes gives the v. thus: Before Him the shades tremble; the waters and their inhabitants. [There is no Hebrew in the v. for "Before Him."] The Am. Bib. Un. of the v. is, "The shades tremble, beneath the waters and their inhabitants!" The reader now no longer wonders that we left the Heb. *ihullu* untranslated in the text. We may say something about it in this note. But first we will give the Heb. word we have rendered "dead," in the text. The Heb. word is *rphaim*, for which the Douay, and the Ital. give "giants;" the E. V., Dead (*things*, inserted;) Noyes, and Am. Bib. Un., "shades."

Ges., under *rphai*, "only in used the plural, Rephaites," says: "a very ancient nation of the Canaanites beyond Jordan, famous on account of their gigantic stature," citing several passages: "the remains of which continued to the age of David," citing 2 Sam. 21 : 16, 18.

But "giants" is not the meaning of the word *rphaim* here. The worp means here, "dead." Ges., under *rpha*, plural *rphaim*, not under *rphai*, cites Isai. 14 : 9 : Psal. 88 : 11, E. V. v. 10 ; Prov. 2 : 18 ; 9 : 18 ; 21 : 16 : Isai. 26 : 14, 19. In every one of these our E. V. gives, "*the* dead," where the Heb. word is *rphaim*. In Isai. 14 : 9, the Douay and the Ital. give, "*the* giants." In Ps. 88 : 11, E.V. v. 10, for the second "*the* dead" in the verse, in the Ital. and the E. V., the Heb. word is, *rphaim*—dead. The Douay there for *rphaim*, gives physicians ; the v. in the Douay is Ps. 87 : 11. In Prov. 2 : 18, for to *rphaim*, the Douay gives "to hell :" Ital. "to *the* giants :" E. V., "to *the* dead." In Prov. 9 : 18, for *rphaim*, the Douay, and Ital. give, "*the* giants :" E. V., "*the* dead." In Prov. 21 : 16, for *rphaim*, the Douay, and the Ital. give, " *the* giants :" E. V., "*the* dead." I think it proper to give here the whole of this verse : The Heb. of it is : Man going astray from way of understanding, in congregation of *rphaim*—dead—will be left : The Douay is....shall abide in the company of *the* giants : Ital....in the company of *the* giants : E. V...."shall remain in the congregation of the dead." In Isai. 26 : 14, the Heb. is : Dead, not shall they live, *rphaim*—dead, not shall they be raised : for *rphaim* in this v. the Douay gives, "*the* giants," thus....let not *the* giants rise again : The Ital. for *rphaim* in the v. gives, "*they are* dead :" The E. V. is, they are deceased. In Isai. 26 : 19, the Heb. is...."and earth *rphaim*—dead—(without article) shall bring forth :" So Ges., under *nphl*, citing this v. : The Douay is : " and the land of *the* giants thou shalt pull down into ruin :" Ital....and the earth shall cast forth *the* dead : E. V....shall cast out *the* dead.

Noyes, by "shades beneath," in Job 26 : 5, means the same that he means by his "spirits of the dead," which he has before said, " dwell together in *shaul* as a vast subterranean cavern : " he having said in that connection that, " The separate existence of the soul seems to be implied in the distinction which is made between *sheol* and the grave. We have before shown that even by his own definitions of *sheol* there is no distinction between *sheol* and the grave. But he having before got "separate souls,"—"spirits of the dead " in the lower " regions in Grecian and Roman mythology," (language used by him in another place,) it was natural that he should in this verse use another word,—"shades," familiar in that mythology.

The Heb. word *ihullu* in Job. 26 : 5, may be from the Heb. verb *hll*, (under which *hull* is given,) defined, " to be pierced through," i. e., says Ges., mortally wounded, citing Job 24 : 12, where the Heb. word is *hllim;* or, " slain," in battle, says he, citing Deut. 21 : 1, 2, 3, 6, where the Heb. is *hll:* and *hll* is also defined, to cast down : so that the verse might be rendered, " Those dead are cast down under water and dwellers of it. (The Heb. *mi*—water—is not used in the singular,—water, see Ges., under *mi*.) Or *ihullu* may be from the verb *hul*, defined, to writhe, be in pain, whence, I suppose, the Douay got its word "groan" in the v. ; and *hul* is also defined, to create, to form, whence, I suppose, the Ital. got its

6 Naked, grave,[1] in sight of him, and not is there covering to place of destruction:[2]

7 He stretched out North[3] upon emptiness, and hanged up earth on nothing:

8 He binds up water in clouds of him, and not is rent cloud under it:

9 Shutting face of seat he spreads out around him clouds of him:

10 Bound of circle he drew on face of waters to extremity of light with darkness:

11 Pillars of heavens[4] are shaken, and are smitten with fear and terror[5] at rebuke of him:

---

word "formed" in the verse. And *hul* is also defined by Ges., to "tremble," citing this v. If this be the true meaning of the Heb. verb used in the v., then " dead,"—E. V., "*the* dead," are here figuratively represented as trembling, as they are figuratively represented as speaking, in Isai. 14 : 9, 10.

The attempt made by Noyes and by the Am. Bib. Un., to get from this v.—Job 26 : 5, by the word "shades" (familiar in mythology) support for what the Rev. J. Panton Ham, of Bristol, England, calls " the notion of the soul's immortality, the protege of Popery and a pet dogma of popular Protestantism," is about equal in futility to what I saw yesterday in the New York Observer of May 27, 1875. That thoroughly orthodox (so called) paper gives a notice of a volume entitled, " The Unseen Universe, or Physical Speculations on a Future State." The notice of it is : " The anonymous author of this volume contends, that the analogies of Science, and especially ' the principle of continuity' tend to confirm the proof of the soul's immortality.

All such attempts to support the dogma are so many proofs that there is no such doctrine.

1. Heb. *shaul:* Douay....hell; Ital....the *inferno*: E. V....hell; Am. Bib. Un....the under-world ; Noyes....the same.

2. Heb. *abdun*, defined by Ges., " place of destruction," nearly synonymous with *shaul*, says he, citing this v. and Job 28 : 22; and Prov. 15 : 11: The Douay in the v. is....and there is no covering to destruction : Am. Bib. Un....and destruction has no covering.

3. Heb. *tsphun*, poetical, says Ges., for the Northern heavens, which, says he, is almost the same as the heaven generally, as the greater part of the Southern hemisphere is hidden, citing this v.

4. Pillars of heavens are *shaken:* so Ges., under *ruph*, citing this v.: see E. V.; Douay....the pillars of heaven tremble.

5. So Ges. under *tme*, citing this v.

111

12 By power of him he rebukes that sea, and by wisdom of him he smiteth pride of it:

13 By breath [1] of him heavens, brightness; set free hand of him serpent fleeing: [2]

14 Lo these, extremities [3] of deeds of him; and what transient sound of word is heard concerning him; and thunder [4] of power of him who perceives:

CHAPTER XXVII.

1 And added Job, taking up parable [5] of him, and said:

2 Liveth God [6] who has taken away right [7] of me, and Almighty who has made bitter breath [8] of me:

3 That while yet breath [9] of me in me, and breath [10] of God in nostrils of me:

---

1. Heb. *ruh*—breath,—wind: Douay....spirit: Ital....*spirito:* E. V. ....spirit: Am. Bib. Un....By his spirit are the heavens adorned: Noyes....By his spirit.

2. Used, says Ges., under *nhsh.* citing this v., of the constellation of the serpent or dragon in the northern part of the sky.

3. Metaphorical, says Ges., for a small part, as it were the extreme lines of the divine works, citing this v. under *qtse.*

4. Metaphor., says Ges., for the whole circuit of the divine power, all the mighty deeds which can be declared of God.

5. Heb. *mshl*—parable, similitude: Douay....parable: Noyes....discourse: E. V....parable: Am. Bib. Un....discourse. It is the same Heb. word used in Isai. 14: 4, and for which the Douay there rightly gives, parable; but the E. V. there, wrongly, and for a purpose, gives, proverb.

6. i. e., says Ges. under *hi*, "as God liveth," an accustomed formula in swearing, says he.

7. Heb. *mshphth:* Douay....my judgment; E. V....my judgment; Am. Bib. Un....my right; Noyes....who hath rejected my cause.

8. Heb. *nphsh*—breath; Douay....soul; Ital....*anima*; E. V....hath vexed my soul: Am. Bib. Un....has afflicted my soul. (To make bitter the breath is a Hebraism for, to make one sad, sorrowful; sadness and sorrow affect the breath, and are shown by it.)

9. Heb. *nshme*—breath; Douay....breath; E. V....breath; Ital.... breath; Am. Bib. Un....breath. In chap. 26: 4, for the same word, *nshme*, the Ital. gives, *spirito*; and the E. V., *spirit.*

10. Heb. *ruh*—breath; Douay....spirit; Ital....breath; E. V....

4 If shall speak¹ lips of me wickedness, and tongue of me, it shall utter deception:²

5 Far be from me when I shall declare righteous you; until I breathe out³ not will I cause to depart integrity of me from me:

6 On rectitude of me I hold fast, and not will I let go; not reproaches heart of me of day of me: (i. e., says Ges., under *hrph*, citing this v., I do not repent of any day.)

7 Let be as wicked adversary of me, and him that rises up against me as evil:⁴

8 For, what, hope of unpious when he has got unjust gain, when shall draw out God breath⁵ of him:

9 Whether outcry of him will attend to, God, when shall come upon him distress:

10 Whether in Almighty can he delight himself; can he call upon God at all times:

11 I will teach you about hand⁶ of God; what with Almighty not will I hide:⁷

---

spirit; Am. Bib. Un....spirit. Ges. under *ruh*, citing this v., gives, "breath of God, as being breathed into man by God, and, returning to him:" Noyes gives this v. thus: As long as I have life within me, and the breath imparted by God in my nostrils.

1. i. .e, not shall speak. Am. Bib. Un....shall not speak.
2. How are tongue and lips to speak without breath.
3. Heb. *aghuo*—from *ghuo*—to breathe out, the same Heb. word is used where the E. V., so often has, give up the ghost: The Douay, E. V., Ital., Am. Bib. Un....till I die: Noyes....to my last breath, equivalent to "until I breathe out." (See fully as to *ghuo* in a note to *ghost* at end of chap. 3.)
4. Heb., as *opl*, which Ges. defines *evil*, citing this v., and Job 18 : 21 ; 29 : 17 : Am. Bib. Un....as the unrighteous.
5. Heb. *nphsh*—breath: Douay....and God deliver not his soul: E. V....when God taketh away his soul: Am. Bib. Un....when God shall take away his soul: Noyes....For what is the hope of the wicked, when God cutteth off his web, and taketh away his life?
6. For, power.
7. i. e., says Ges. under *om*, citing this v., what his mind is.

12 Lo, you all of you have beheld, and why this breath [1] do you breathe out: [2]

13 This, portion of man wicked with God, and lot oppressors from Almighty will receive:

14 If be multiplied children of him, for sword; and springing up of him not shall be satisfied of bread:

15 Survivors of him in death shall be buried, [3] and widows of them not shall bewail:

16 If he heap up as dust silver, and as clay prepare garment:

17 He may prepare, but just shall put on, and silver innocent shall divide:

18 He builds like moth house of him; and as booth made to watch over: [4]

19 Rich [5] shall lie down and not shall be gathered; eyes of him he opens and not there is of him: [6]

20 Shall overtake him like waters, terrors; of night shall steal him whirlwind:

---

1. Heb. *ebl*—a noun, breath.

2. *ebl*, a verb, to breathe out: Ges. citing this v. under the verb *ebl*, says: i. e., Why then do ye speak so vainly?

3. Douay....shall be buried in death: The Latin is....shall be buried in *interitu*—annihilation, so defined by Anthon, citing from Cicero: The Greek is....in death *teleutesousi*—shall be ended: Ital....shall be buried in death itself: E. V....shall be buried in death: Noyes....shall be buried by death: Am. Bib. Un....In the pestilence shall they that remain to him be buried; evading the idea so plainly expressed that death is the end of the wicked.

4. Namely, a vineyard, says Ges., under *ntsr*, citing this v.

5. Ges. under *oshir*—rich, says: "in a bad sense, haughty, impious; inasmuch as riches are the fountain of pride, and pride is used in the Hebrew as equivalent to impiety," citing Isai. 53: 7, and saying, compare Job 27: 19.

6. A bold figure, of a dead man that is not to rise from the dead, of opening his eyes and finding that he is not: Douay....he shall open his eyes and find nothing, (a characteristic evasion:) E. V....he openeth his eyes and he *is* not: Am. Bib. Un....The rich man shall lie down, and shall not be gathered; he opens his eyes, and he is gone: Noyes... The rich man falleth, and is not buried; in the twinkling of an eye he is no more.

21 Takes him east¹ and he goes away, yea, he is swept away in storm from place of him:²

22 And he will cast upon him and not will spare: from hand of him on wind³ he would flee away:

23 They shall clap at him hands of them, and they shall hiss him out of place of him:

---

1. Heb. *qdim*—East, poetical for *ruh qdim*—wind East, says Ges., by far the most violent, says he, in Western Asia.
2. So Ges., under *shor*, citing this v.
3. Heb. *ruh*, often used for wind: the winds are called the breaths of God; generally, *ruh* is breath. Neither the Douay, nor the Ital., nor the E. V. gives anything for *ruh* in the verse; nor does the Am. Bib Un., that gives he would fain flee out of his hand: nor Noyes; he gives "he would fain escape from his hand."

NOTE.—Froude, on page 254, says: "So far all has been clear, each party, with increasing confidence, having insisted on their own position, and denounced their adversaries. A difficulty now arises which, at first sight, appears insurmountable. As the chapters are at present printed, the entire of the 27th is assigned to Job, and the paragraph from the 11th to the 23d verses is in direct contradiction to all which he has maintained before—is, in fact, a concession of having been wrong from the beginning." That Dr. Kennicott attributes the verses in question to Zophar. That the attributing them to Job might have arisen from inadvertence; it might have arisen from the foolishness of some Jewish translator, who resolved, at all costs, to drag the book into harmony with Judaism, and make Job unsay what was thought heresy. That this view has the merit of fully clearing up the obscurity. Another, however, has been suggested by Eichorn, who origininally followed Kennicott, but discovered, as he supposed, a less violent hypothesis, which was equally satisfactory. That Eichorn imagines the verses to be a summary by Job of his adversaries' opinions, as if he said—"Listen now; you know what the facts are as well as I, and yet you maintain this:" and then passed on with his indirect reply to it. That it is possible Eichhorn may be right; that at any rate, either he is right, or else Dr. Kennicott is right. That certainly Ewald (who as Froude has before said, supposes that Job is receding from his position,) is not. That, taken as an account of Job's own conviction, the passage contradicts the burden of the whole poem. Passing it by, therefore, and going to what immediately follows, we arrive, says Froude, at what, in a human sense, is the final climax—Job's victory and triumph. He, too, had been taught to look for God in outward judgments; and when his own experience had shown him his mistake, he knew not

CHAPTER XXVIII.

1 Truly there is to silver, vein, and place for gold they refine it:

2 Iron out of dust is taken, and stone ore is poured out brass:

3 End he sets to darkness, and to all extremities [1] he searches out stone of thick darkness and shadow of death:

4 He breaks through [2] mine with lamp,[3] forgotten of foot [4] they hang down from man and swing: [5]

5 Ground, from it goeth forth bread, and lower part of it is changed as with fire:

6 Place of sapphire, stones of it, and lumps of gold in them:

7 By-way, not knoweth it rapacious bird, and not has scorched it eye of falcon:

8 Not have trod it children of pride ; [6] not has passed over it roaring lion:

---

where to turn. But when he saw the defenders of it (the Jewish theory) wandering further and further from what he knew to be true, the scales fell more and more from his eyes—he had seen the fact that the wicked might prosper, and in learning to depend upon his innocency he had felt that the good man's support was there, if it was any where ; and at last, with all his heart was reconciled to the truth. The mystery of the outer world becomes deeper to him, but he does not any more try to understand it. The wisdom which is alone attainable is resignation to God. "Where," he cries, "shall wisdom be found, and where is the place of understanding." "And unto man he said, Behold! the fear of the Lord, that is wisdom ; and to depart from evil that is understanding." "There is no clearer or purer faith possible for man ; and Job had achieved it."

1. i. e., says Ges., under *tklit*, citing this v., in the most profound recesses of the earth.

2. So Ges., citing this verse under *phrts* and *nhl*.

3. The Heb. word *gr* in my copy here I think must be a mistake for *nr*—lamp: the Heb. *g* and *n* are very much alike.

4. i. e., says Ges., under *shkh*, citing this v., void of the aid of feet.

5. Used of miners letting themselves down into the shafts, says Ges., under *dll*, citing this v. This v. is wholly misconceived by the Douay, the Ital., and the E. V. The Am. Bib. Un. of the v. is, He drives a shaft away from man's abode ; forgotten of the foot, they swing, suspended far from men.

6. i. e., says Ges., under *shhts*, citing this v., the larger ravenous

9 On flint he puts hand of him; he overturns from root mountains:

10 In rocks channels he cleaves, and every precious, seeth eye of him:

11 From flowing by drops he binds up streams,[1] and of hidden goeth forth light:

12 But this wisdom, from where shall it be come to, and where this place of insight:

13 Not knoweth man price of it, and not can it be come to in land of living:

14 Deep says, not in me; and sea says not with me:

15 Not can give shut up[2] in place of it, and not can be weighed silver of price of it:

16 Not can it be lifted up[3] with gold of Ophir, with onyx precious and sapphire:

17 Not can be compared with it gold and crystal, and *not* exchange of it vessels of pure:[4]

18 Corals and crystals not to be made mention of, and possession of wisdom more than red corals:[5]

19 Not to be compared with it topaz of *Kush*;[6] by hid away[7] not can it be lifted up:

20 But this wisdom, from whence comes it; and where this place of unsight:

21 Even hid from eyes of all living, and from winged of these heavens[8] concealed:

---

beasts, as the lion, so called, says he, from the pride of walking; citing also Job 41 : 26.

1. Spoken, says Ges., under *hbsh*, citing this v., of a miner stopping off the water from flowing into his pits.

2. Equivalent to gold shut up, says Ges., under *sgur*, citing this v. Douay....the finest gold: Am. Bib. Un....choice gold.

3. i. e., put in one scale, no amount of gold in the other will lift it up.

4. An epithet of gold, says Ges., unde *phz*.

5. Ges., under *ramut*, citing this v.

6. We write it *Cush*, i. e. Ethiopia.

7. The Heb. word is *ktim*, a poetical word, says Ges.; properly, says he, that which is hidden away in treasuries.

8. Douay....the fowls of the air: E. V....the same: Ital.. .the

22 Place of destruction¹ and death² say: with ears of us have heard we fame of it:

23 God³ discerns way of it, and he knows place of it:

24 For he, to extremities of this earth he looks, under all these heavens he sees:

25 To make to wind⁴ weight, and waters he meted out by measure:

26 At making of him for rain law, and path for lightning of thunders: Am. Bib. Un., "the thunders' flash:" Noyes, "the glittering thunderbolt."

27 Then saw he and recounted it,⁵ he founded it and also explored it:

28 And he said to man: Lo, fear of Lord, it, wisdom, and to depart from evil, understanding:

---

birds of heaven: Noyes....the fowls of the air: Am. Bib. Un....the fowls of heaven.

1. The Heb. here is *abdun*, place of destruction, nearly synonymous with *shaul* (the grave,) says Ges., citing this v., and Job 26 : 6; Prov. 15 : 11: Noyes....The realms of Death say; Ital....The place of destruction; Douay, E. V., and Am. Bib. Un....Destruction. (See note to *abdun* at end of chapter.)

2. Sometimes used as personified, says Ges., citing Ps. 49 : 15, E. V. v. 14. He gives for *mut*—death, the place of the dead, citing this v. Job 28 : 22.

3. Heb. *aleim*—plural of majesty, says Ges.

4. Heb. *ruh*, wind: Douay....a weight for the winds Ital....the weight to the wind: Am. Bib. Un....the weight for the wind.

5. i. e., wisdom.

NOTE.—*Abdun*—place of destruction—is equivalent to the Heb. *shaul*—grave, in Deut. 32 : 22, where the Douay is: A fire is kindled in my wrath and shall burn even to the lowest hell: Ital....to the place more low *sotterra*—under ground: E. V....unto the lowest hell.

We thus see that *abdun*—place of destruction—is a poetical word for the grave, found in Job, the oldest of the Bible writings. It will be interesting to learn what is made of this Heb. word *abdun* by the Rheims and Italian versions, and our English version, of that "mystical book," Revelations. The first ten verses of chap. 9 describe locusts from what the Rheims and the E. V. call the bottomless pit. The Ital. calls it the well of *abisso*, defined in Graglia's Romish Ital. Dict., abyss, obscurity, hell. And we all learned as children that "the bottomless pit" meant orthodoxy's hell. And how many have lived long enough, or have ever become wise enough to know better? A foot note to the Rheims of v. 3, chap. 9, says: " These (locusts) may be devils in Antichrist's time, having the appearance of locusts, but large and monstrous, as here described. Or they may be real locusts, sent to torment those who have not the sign or seal of God on their foreheads. Some commentators by these locusts understood heretics, that sprung from Jews,....who were great enemies to the christian religion; they tormented and infected the souls of men, stinging them, like scorpions, with the poison of their heresies. Others have explained these locusts, and other animals, mentioned in different places throughout this sacred and mystical book, in a most absurd, fanciful and ridiculous manner: they make Abaddon the Pope, and the locusts to be friars mendicant, etc."

The Rheims of v. 11 is: "And they had over them a king, the angel of the bottomless pit, whose name in Hebrew is *Abaddon*, and in the Greek *Apollyon;* in Latin *Exterminans*, i. e. Destroyer:" Ital....And they had for a king over them the *angelo* of the *abisso*, whose name in Hebrew is *Abaddon*, and in Greek *Apollion:* E. V....And they had a king over them, which is the angel of the bottomless pit, whose name in the Hebrew tongue *is Abaddon*, but in the Greek tongue hath *his* name *Apollyon*. The three versions make *Abaddon*—Greek *Apollyon*, the name of the king of the locusts, which, if locusts means devils, would make *Abaddon* —*Apollyon*—the king of the devils, i. e., orthodoxy's Head Devil. And this is in fact what children, and the misinformed, understand by *Abaddon*—*Appollyon*.

Now *Abaddon* is the Heb. word *abdun*, spelled in the three versions *Abaddon;* and it is the name given, not of the king of the locusts, but the name of the place of destruction, nearly synonymous with *shaul*—the grave, says Gesenius. And for *abde* Ges. gives, "equivalent to *abdun*— place of destruction, abyss," citing Prov. 27: 20, where the Heb. is, *shaul u abde*—grave and place of destruction—not can be satisfied: Douay....Hell and destruction are never filled: Ital....The sepulchre and place of destruction not are ever full: E. V....Hell and destruction are never full.

The grave may well be called a bottomless pit, as it is in the Rheims Romish English version, followed by the E. V. A pit without a bottom can never be filled.

The Greek word *Apollyon* (given for *abdun*—spelled *Abaddon*) is the neuter of the present participle of the Greek verb *apolluo*—defined in Liddell & Scott's Greek Lexicon, to destroy utterly; and putting *y* for the Greek *u*, as is generally done, we have the very word *apollyon*—destroying utterly, given in the v. by the Rheims and the E. V. as equivalent to their word *Abaddon*. The Rheims in v. 11, gives for *Abaddon* and *Apollyon*, the Latin participle *exterminans*—(exterminating,) and adds in in italics, "i. e. Destroyer"—making a noun from the participle, as is often done; and so making a personification of *Abaddon—Apollyon*, and in the Heb. of Job. 28 : 22, *abdun*—place of destruction, and *mut*—death, are both personified. But the Ital. gives no such information in reference to v. 11, as the Rheims does; nor does the E. V. In Prov. 15 : 11 also, the Ital. for Heb. *abdun*, gives the place of destruction : The Douay there is, Hell and destruction : E. V.... Hell and destruction.

It might afford amusement to ask a good orthodox lady or gentleman, whether Romanist or Protestant, what these formidable words *Abaddon* and *Apollyon*, with their capital *A*, mean. I am disposed to think that very few of the readers of that "mystical book" have understood them rightly. I have asked several persons what they have understood those words, in Rev. 9 : 11, to mean; and they answered, they had supposed them to mean the Devil.

Eadie, Professor of Biblical Literature and Exegesis to the United Presbyterian Church, in his Biblical Cyclopædia, defines *Abaddon*, "the Hebrew name for the angel of the bottomless pit," and says, it answers to the Greek name *Apollyon*; and he says they both signify the destroyer. Surely the Professor knew that *angel* is the Greek word for *messenger*, not translated, but the Greek termination *os* cut off: the word *angel* is not given for the Greek *aggelos* (pronounced *angelos*) in any Greek Lexicon I have ever seen. And the Professor is wrong in saying, and will mislead many by saying, that *Abaddon* is the name of the angel of the bottomless pit, (as the Rheims, E. V., and the Professor, give for the Heb. *abdun*—place of destruction;) It is the name of the place of destruction, as the Italian rightly gives it in Prov. 15 : 11, and Prov. 27 : 20, and Job 28 : 22.

Perhaps we ought to feel some consolation from the assurance in chap. 9 : 4 of the "mystical book," that the locusts, whether orthodox devils or mendicant friars, only had power to torment the men who had not the seal of God in their foreheads.

CHAPTER XXIX.

1 And added Job, taking up parable of him, and said:

2 Who will give to me as months before, as days God kept me:

3 When shone lamp of him over head of me, and in light of him I walked through darkness:

4 Like as was I in days of autumn of me,[1] with counsel of God over tent of me:

---

1. Metaphor., for mature age, manly vigor, says Ges., citing this v. under *hrph*.

5 While yet Almighty with me; round about me children of me:

6 At to wash¹ goings of me in milk, and rock poured out with me streams of oil:

7 At to go out I gate near city, in broad space setting up seat of me:²

8 Looked at me youths and hid themselves,³ and old men rising stood:

9 Princes held back as to words, and hand put to mouth of them:

10 Voice of Nobles hid itself,⁴ and tongue of them to palate of them cleaved:

11 For ear heard and pronounced happy⁵ me, and eye saw and bore witness for me:⁶

12 For I delivered poor crying for help, and orphan and no helper to him:⁷

13 Blessing of wretched upon me came, and heart of widow I made shout for joy:

14 Righteousness I put on, and it put on me,⁸ as upper garment and tiara rectitude⁹ of me:

15 Eyes was I to blind, and feet to lame I :

---

1. We use the participle, washing, instead of the infinitive, to wash.
2. So Ges., under *kun* citing this v.
3. i. e., gave place to me out of respect and modesty, says Ges., under *hba*, citing this v.
4. i. e. they were silent, says Ges., citing this v. under *hba*.
5. So Ges., under *ashr*, citing this v.
6. i. e. praised me, says Ges., under *oud*, citing this v.
7. i. e. the orphan who had no helper, says Ges., citing this v. under *u*: Douay, " and the fatherless, that had no helper:" And the Ital. is right: Am. Bib. Un....and the orphan and him that had no helper: The E.V. also, is wrong: Noyes is right.
8. i. e. says Ges., under *lbsh*, citing this v., I am covered without with righteousness, and within it wholly fills me. He says, There is a play on the double use of *lbsh* in the verse: Am. Bib. Un....and it clothed itself with me: Noyes....and it clothed me.
9. Heb. *mshphth*—right, rectitude: For it the Douay gives....judgment: E. V....judgment: Ital....integrity: Am. Bib. Un....rectitude: Noyes....justice. (It should be justness.)

16 Father I to needy, and many¹ not knew I, I searched out them:

17 And I broke biters² of evil, and from teeth of him I plucked prey:

18 And I said, in nest³ of me I shall breathe out,⁴ and as sand I shall multiply days:

19 Root of me is open to water, and dew lodges⁵ on bough of me:

20 Liver⁶ of me new with me, and bow of me in hand of me strengthened:⁷

21 To me listened they and waited, and were silent for counsel of me:

22 After word of me not repeated they, and on them dropped speech of me:

23 And they waited as for rain for me, and mouth of them they opened wide for latter rain:⁸

24 Smiled I upon them, not were sure they, and light of face⁹ not would they cast:

---

1. Douay....and the cause which I knew not I searched out: Ital.... and the cause: E. V....and the cause: The Heb. word used in the v. is *rb*—many: The Douay and Ital. must have taken it for *rib*—forensic cause: And the Am. Bib. Un. is....and the cause of him I knew not, I searched it out.

2. Poetically used for teeth, says Ges., under *mltout*, citing this v.

3. Metaphor., abode says Ges., under *qn*, citing this v.

4. The Heb. word here is *aghou*—I should breathe out. See fully as to the Heb. verb *ghuo* in a note to *ghost* at the end of chap. 3. In this v. the Douay gives, I shall die: Ital. and E. V....I shall die: Am. Bib. Un....I shall expire: i. e. out-breathe: It should be exspire: Noyes.... I shall die.

5. Poetical, for, passes the night, says Ges., under *lun*, citing this v.

6. Heb. *kbud*, which Ges. says may be the same as *kbd*—liver; and I see no reason why the sense here may not be liver of me renewed with me: The Douay is....my glory shall always be renewed: See E. V.: Noyes....my glory is fresh with me: Am. Bib. Union....my glory is fresh upon me.

7. This would be the effect of renewing the liver.

8. Ges., under *mlqush*, citing this v., says: Poetically an eloquent and profitable discourse is compared to the latter rain.

9. i. e., says Ges., brightness of countenance, under *aur*, citing this v.:

25 Approved I way of them, then sat I head, and dwelt as king among troop,¹ as one who the mourning comforts:

CHAPTER XXX.

1 But now jest at me younger than I in days, who I would have despised fathers of them to put with dogs of flocks of me:

2 Truly, strength of hands of them, what to me, in whom is perished completion:²

3 With want and with hunger lean, they flee into desert, and darkness of desolate waste:

4 Pluckings off of sea-purslain by the hedge, and root of broom, food of them:

5 From midst they are driven;³ they cry out against them as thief:

6 In horror of valleys⁴ to dwell, caverns of dry earth and rocks:

7 Between bushes they bray, under nettles they are gathered together:

Douay.... and the light of my countenance fell not on the earth : Ital.... and not made they to fall the brightness of my face : E. V....and the light of my countenance they cast not down : Am. Bib. Un....nor let the light of my countenance fall. The using of the word *my* is plainly wrong. The Heb. word used here is *phni*—face. Ges., under *phne*—gives also *phni*—face, citing Ezek. 21 : 2, where the Heb. is *phni*—face—of thee : Douay, Ital. and E. V., "thy face ;" and citing Ezek. 21 : 21, where the Heb. is *phni*—face—of thee : Ital., v. 21, "thy face :" The Douay is, v. 16, " thy face :" and the E. V. is, v. 16, " thy face." And in Job 33 : 26 the Heb. is, *phni*—face—of him. The *i* belongs to the word *phni*—face, and is not the *i*, of me—my.

    1. Band of soldiers, says Ges., under *gdud*.

    2. i. e., says Ges., under *klh*, citing this v., who cannot complete any thing, used, says he, of very despicable men. Am. Bib. Un....they in whom old age is perishing. Noyes. ..in whom activity is perished!

    3. i. e., says Ges., from among men under *gu*, citing this v.

    4. i. e., says Ges., in *the* horrid valleys, under *oruts*, citing this v.

8 Sons of impious[1] and sons without name, they are cast out of this land:[2]

9 And now, song of them I am become, yea, I am become to them for speech:

10 They abhor me, they go away far from me, and from face of me they spare not spittle:[3]

11 So that bridle of them they loose and oppress me, and curb before me they let hang down:[4]

12 On right side offspring of beasts[5] rise up; feet of me they push aside; and they cast up against me ways of destruction of them: Am. Bib. Un....their ways of destruction:

13 They tear up footpath of me; to fall of me they help;[6] not helper to him:[7]

14 As if of breach[8] wide they came in; under crash they were rolled:[9]

---

1. A Hebraism for *the* impious.

2. Ges., under *kae*, citing this v., renders, "they are cast out of the land;" Ital....more vile than earth itself; E. V....they were viler than the earth; Am. Bib. Un....they are beaten out of the land.

3. Noyes and Am. Bib. Un....they forbear not to spit before my face.

4. The Douay of v. 11 is, For he hath opened his quiver, and hath afflicted me, and hath put a bridle into my mouth: Ital....For *God* has untied my ligature, and me has afflicted; whereupon they have shaken the bridle *for not* to revere *more* my face: Am. Bib. Un....Because He has let loose his rein and humbled me, they also cast off the bridle before me. *He*, with capital H, used here in the Am. Bib. Un., is equivalent to *God*, interpolated in the Italian; just as *His*, in the Am. Bib. Un. of Job 15 : 30 means *God's* breath. This v. 30 : 11, has no reference to God; and it was entirely misconceived by the Douay, the Ital., the E. V., and the Am. Bib. Un. See E. V. Noyes....They let loose the reins, and afflicted me, they cast off the bridle before me.

5. Used in contempt of vile and wicked men, says Ges., under *phrhh*, citing this v.

6. They help my fall, says Ges., under *iol*, citing this v.

7. i. e. to Job; him being here used for *me*. See Ges under *lmu*, citing Isai. 53 : 8.

8. Ges., under *phrts*—breach, citing this v., says, "rightly rendered by the Latin Vulgate," giving the Latin; a metaphor, says he, taken from besiegers who rush into a city through breaches in the wall in great numbers and in great violence.

9. Douay....and have rolled themselves down to my miseries: Ital.

15 Are turned against me terrors; they pursue like wind;[1] free will[2] of me, and as cloud has passed quickly by, welfare of me:

16 And now upon me pours itself breath[3] of me; have taken hold of me days of affliction:

17 Night, bones of me pierces upon me,[4] and they that gnaw me[5] not are quiet:

18 By great power is changed garment of me;[6] as mouth of tunic[7] it girds me:

19 He has cast me into mire, and I am become like dust and ashes:

---

they are rolled under the ruins: Am. Bib. Un....they roll on beneath the ruins.

1. Heb. *ruh*—wind.

2. Heb. *ndbe*—free will, readiness of mind: Douay....as a wind thou hast taken away my desire: Ital....they pursue my *anima* like the wind: E. V....they pursue my soul as the wind: Am. Bib. Un....they chase away, like the wind, my princely estate: Noyes....my prosperity.

3. Heb. *nphsh*——breath: Douay....and now my soul fadeth within myself: Ital....And now my *anima* pours itself out upon me: E. V.... And my soul is poured out upon me: Am. Bib. Un....And now my soul is poured out within me: Noyes....And now my soul is poured out in grief. Ges., under *ol*, citing this v., says: i. e., being poured out into tears, it wholly covers me as it were with them; citing also Ps. 42 : 5, E. V. v. 4. And under *shphk*—to pour, pour out, he gives: "metaphorically, *shphk nphsh*—(to pour out *the* breath,) i. e., says he, to be poured out in tears and complaints, citing 1 Sam. 1 : 16, where the Heb. is, but have poured out *nphsh*—breath—of me to face of Jehovah. And citing Jer. 4 : 10, in which the Heb. is *nphsh*—breath. I add Lament. 2 : 12, where the Heb. is....in fainting of them....in pouring out *nphsh*—breath—of them into bosom of mothers of them. The E. V. there is....when they swooned....when their soul was poured out into their mother's bosom. [Affliction causes sorrowful *nphsh*—breath, and sorrowful breath causes tears.]

4. i. e., says Ges. under *nqr*, citing this v., by night my bones are, as it were, pierced with pain: Am. Bib. Un....By night my bones are pierced and severed from me.

5. i. e., pains, says Ges., under *orq*, citing this v.

6. Ges., under *hphsh*, citing this v. renders, "by *its* great power my garment (i. e., says he, my skin) is changed. Am. Bib. Un....By sore violence, my covering is disfigured.

7. i. e., an inner garment next the skin, says Ges., under *ktnt*.

20 I cry for help to thee and not answerest thou me; I stand up, and not¹ turnest thou mind to me:

21 Thou hast turned thyself into cruel to me; in strength of hand of thee thou hast laid snares for me:

22 Thou hast lifted me up to wind;² thou hast caused me to ride;³ and thou hast made me to melt terrified:⁴

23 For know I death will return me,⁵ and house of assemblage to every living:⁶

24 Surely, not prayers, stretches out he hand, though in calamity of him he cry for help:

---

1. The *not* in the first hemistich belongs also to the last, in the Heb. usage. The Douay, and the Ital., use *not* twice in the v.; and the E. V. inserts a second *not:* Am. Bib. Union....I stand, and thou observest me: Noyes....but thou regardest me not.

2. Heb. *ruh*—wind.

3. Metaphor., says Ges., under *rkb*, citing this v., "caused me to ride upon the wings of the wind:" Ital...Thou me hast lifted on high; thou me hast caused to ride on horse back upon the *vento*—wind: See E. V.: Am. Bib. Un....Thou dost lift me to the wind, and let me be borne away.

The Heb. *ruh*, defined breath, wind, is the word where the Douay, and the E. V., so often have spirit, from the Latin noun *spiritus*—breath. The writer of Job had no knowledge of the Latin language, and so no knowledge of what self-styled orthodoxy and modern spiritism would have us believe the Latin *spiritus*, Douay and E. V., spirit, means. Now by some one disposed to be facetious a laugh might be provoked by giving for *ruh* here the word *spirit* in the same sense in which it is used in orthodoxy and spiritism, and so setting Job astride an orthodox *spirit* to ride it. But what if Job should have thought its gait too slow? could he have made it feel the spur?

4. Figurative, says Ges., "to be dissolved with fear and alarm."

5. i. e., to dust: The writer of Job had not learned to say *my body*. Douay....I know that thou wilt deliver me to death: Ital....that thou me wilt reduce to death: Am. Bib. Un....For I know thou wilt bring me to death: Noyes....the same. [The Heb. is evaded.]

6. Ges., under *muod*, citing this v., renders, "the place of the assemblage of all living. Under *mut*—death, he says, it is used of death, whether of men or beasts, citing Exod. 11 : 5; Eccles. 9 : 4; and he says, death is sometimes used as personified, citing Ps. 49 : 14, death shall feed on them: and that death is poetically used for the dead, citing Isai. 38 : 18, under *mut*—death; and also that *mut*—death—is used for the place of the dead, i. e., says he, *Hades*, citing Job 28 : 22; see it in its place.

25 Whether not have wept I for hard of day,[1] been sad breath [2] of me for needy:

26 When good I looked for, came evil, and I hoped for light, and came thick darkness:[3]

27 Intestines of me boiling,[4] and not are quiet: have met me days of misery:

28 Of dirty color [5] I go along, not by heat;[6] rise I in congregation, I cry for help:

29 Brother am become I to jackals,[7] and companion to children of female ostrich:[8]

30 Skin of me black upon me, and bones of me are kindled with heat:

31 And is become for mourning harp of me, and pipe of me for voice of them that weep:

CHAPTER XXXI.

1 Covenant have cut I [9] with eyes of me, and how could I show myself attentive upon virgin:

---

1. Ges., under *qshe*, cites this v., and renders, "whose day is hard, i. e., says he, whose lot is hard.

2. Heb. *nphsh*—breath; poetically for whether not have I been sad; sadness affects, and is shown by the breath. The Douay, E. V., and Am. Bib. Un., give my soul.

3. Light, says Ges., citing this v., is sometimes used for prosperity itself: and *aphl*—thick darkness—is a poetic word, says he, citing this v. and Job 3 : 6; 10 : 22; 28 : 3 : metaphor., says he, of misery, misfortune.

4. Metaphor., of an emotion of the mind, says Ges., citing this v. under *rth*.

5. As of a sunburnt skin, says Ges., under *qdr*, citing this v.

6. Poetically, says Ges., for the sun itself, citing this verse under *hme*—heat.

7. i. e., says Ges, under *ah*, citing this v., I am forced to howl like a jackal.

8. i. e., a companion of ostriches, see Ges., under *ione*.

9. So Ges., under *krt*—to cut; so used, says he, from slaying and dividing the victim, as was customary in making a covenant, citing this v. and other passages.

2 And what, portion of God from above, and iot of Almighty from heights:

3 Whether not destruction to wicked; and misfortune to workers of iniquity: Noyes, and ruin: Am. Bib. Un., calamity.

4 Whether not himself he sees ways of me, and every step of me he numbers:

5 If have walked I with falsehood, and has made haste towards fraud [1] foot of me:

6 Let him weigh me in scales just, and he will get to know innocence of me: [2]

7 If has turned aside goings of me from that way, and after eyes of me has gone heart of me, and on hand of me has cleaved spot,

8 Let me sow and another let eat, and springing up of me [3] let be rooted out:

9 If has been enticed heart of me on woman, and at door of companion of me I have lain in wait,

10 Let grind for another wife of me, and upon her let bow down another: [4]

11 For that, wickedness, and it, crime of judges: [5]

12 For, fire it *which* to place of destruction [6] would consume, and all gain of me would root out:

---

1. Metonymy for, riches gained by fraud, says Ges., under *mrme*.

2. Am. Bib. Un....He will weigh me in scales of justice, (it should be justness:) The E. V. is better: Let him weigh me in an even balance.

3. Metaphor., descendants, children, says Ges., under *tsatsaim*, citing this v. and others: Douay, and E. V....my offspring: Am. Bib. Un.... my products.

4. Douay....and let other men lie with her: Am. Bib. Un....and let others lie with her: Ital....and let bow down others upon her: E. V... the same.

5. i. e., says Ges., under *oun* citing this v., to be punished by the judges.

6. The Heb. is *abdun*, see before, Job 26 : 6 ; 28 : 22.

13 If I reject right¹ of servant of me and handmaid of me in contention of them with me:

14 Then what should I do when should arise God; and when he should visit, what could I answer him:

15 Whether not in belly *who* made me made him, and fashioned us in womb One:

16 If I have kept back from desire, weak, and eyes of widow have caused to pine away:

17 And have eaten morsel of me alone of me, and not hath eaten orphan of it;

18 For from boyhood of me he grew up to me as father,² and from womb of mother of me I have led her:

19 If I have seen ready to perish because not clothing, and not was covering to needy;

20 If not have blessed me loins of him, and from fleece of lamb of me he has *not* been warmed;³

21 If I have shaken at orphan hand of me⁴ when I looked at gate of court⁵ of me:

22 Shoulder of me from shoulder blade of it let fall, and arm of me from higher bone of arm let be broken:

23 For terror to me, destruction of God,⁶ and because of majesty of him not could I:⁷

24 If made I gold confidence of me, and to hid away⁸ have said I, security of me:

---

1. Heb. *mshphth*—right: Douay....judgment: E. V....the cause: Am. Bib. Un....right.

2. i. e., says Ges., under *gdl*, citing this v., under my care.

3. The *not* in the first clause belongs also to the second.

4. i. e., threatened, says Ges., under *nuph*, citing this v. and others.

5. The Heb. word here is *ozrt* for *ozre*, which, says Ges., is for the older Heb. *htsr*, which he defines, an enclosure, a court, an enclosure before a building: The Douay is....even when I saw myself superior in the gate: Ital....though I saw who me would have aided in or at the gate: E. V., Am. Bib. Un....because I saw my helper in the gate:

6. i. e., sent by God, says Ges., under *aid*, citing passages.

7. i. e., says Ges., do any thing of the kind, citing this v. under *la*.

8. Heb. *ktm*, a poetical word, says Ges., properly, says he that which is precious.

25 If I rejoiced that great, wealth of me, and that much had come to hand of me:

26 If I looked at [1] light [2] which brilliant, and moon splendid [3] going along:

27 And was beguiled in secret heart of me, and has kissed hand of me to mouth: [4]

28 Also it, crime of judges, for I should have feigned to God above:

29 If I rejoiced at calamity of hater of me, and made myself naked [5] when met him evil:

30 But not have given I to sin palate of me, to ask with curse breath [6] of him:

31 Whether not have said men of tent of me, who will give forth, from flesh of him not was he satisfied: [7]

32 On outside not passed night stranger; doors of me to way [8] I opened:

33 Whether have covered I like men [9] fault of me, to hide in bosom of me guilt of me:

---

1. i. e., specially regarded.

2. Of the sun, or the sun itself, says Ges., citing this v., and Job 37 : 21, that brilliant.

3. Heb. *iqr*, magnificent, splendid, says Ges., citing this v.

4. Ges., under *nshq*, to kiss, citing this v. says: "To kiss idols is a term applied to those who worship them, which was done by kissing the hand to them:" Am Bib. Un....and my hand my mouth hath kissed.

5. For, was tumultuously joyful: Douay....and have rejoiced: Ital... tumultuous *with joy*: Am. Bib. Un....and triumphed.

6. Heb. *nphsh*—breath; Douay....by wishing a curse to his soul; E. V....the same; Ital....to ask his death with curse; Am. Bib. Un.... to asking with cursing his life; Noyes....his life.

7. Ges. under *bshr*—flesh, citing this v., renders, "who is there that was not satisfied with his flesh," i. e., says he, in his feasts.

8. Heb. *ark*—way, poetically used for traveler, says Ges., citing this v. Noyes....to the traveler; Am. Bib. Un....to the traveler.

9. Heb. *adm*; Ges. says, it is very often used to denote men, citing Gen 6 : 1; Job 21 : 32, and other passages; The Douay in Job 31 : 33 is, If as a man I have hid my sin; Ital....as do men; E. V....as Adam; Am. Bib. Un....like Adam; Noyes....after the manner of men.

34 That I should fear multitude great, and contempt of families should prostrate me, and I should be silent, not should go out of door:

35 Who will give to me to listen to me: Behold sign [1] of me; let Almighty answer me, and accusation write man of contention with me:

36 Whether not on shoulder of me I would take it up, would bind it crown to me:

37 Number of steps of me I would tell him, like as prince [2] would I come near him:

38 If against me land of me cries out, and together furrows bewail:

39 If strength [3] of it I have eaten without silver, and breath [4] of owners of it I have caused to breathe out:

40 Instead of wheat let go forth thornbush, and instead of barley, useless plant : Are ended words of Job.

---

1. Ges., under *tu*—a sign, says: "sign cruciform, mark subscribed instead of a name to a bill of complaint, hence subscription," citing this v. He says: "It is stated that at the Synod of Chalcedon and other synods, principally in the East, some even of the bishops being unable to write, put the sign of the cross instead of their names."

2. Ital....as a commander: E. V....as a prince: Noyes....like a prince: Douay....as to a prince: Am. Bib. Un....the same.

3. Ges. under *kh*—strength, citing this v., says: "The strength of the earth is used for its product," citing also Gen. 4 : 12.

4. Heb. *nphsh*—breath, *ephhti*—have caused to breathe out I. The verb here used is the causative form of the verb *nphh*, defined by Ges., to breathe out: He says it is onomatopoietic, [i. e., it expresses its meaning by the sounds of it—*en-phh*.] The Douay is....and have afflicted the soul of the tillers thereof: Ital....have made to sigh the *anima*—breath —of its lords: E. V....have caused the owners thereof to lose their life: Noyes....and extorted the life of its owners: Am. Bib. Un....and made its tenants sigh out their breath, [showing that the Ital. *anima*, which is the Latin *anima*, means breath. The only definition Graglia's Ital. Dict. gives of *anima* is, soul.]

NOTE.—There is a note on page 257 of Froude's book, thus: "The speech of Elihu, which lies between Job's last words, (the end of chap.

31,) and God's appearance; (God's answer to Job at the beginning of chap. 38,) a speech of six chapters, is now decisively pronounced by Hebrew scholars not to be genuine. The most superficial reader will have been perplexed by the introduction of a speaker to whom no allusion is made, either in the prologue or epilogue; by a long dissertation which adds nothing to the progress of the argument, proceeding evidently on the false hypothesis of the three, and betraying not the faintest conception of the real cause of Job's sufferings. And the suspicions which such an anomaly would naturally suggest are now made certainties by a fuller knowledge of the language, and the detection of a different hand. The interpolater has unconsciously confessed the feelings which allowed him to take so great a liberty. He, too, possessed with the old Jewish theory, was unable to accept in its fullness so great a contradiction to it; and, missing the spirit of the poem, he believed that God's honor could still be vindicated in the old way. " His wrath was kindled " against his friends because they could not answer Job; and against Job because he would not be answered; and conceiving himself 'full of matter,' and ' ready to burst like new bottles,' he could not contain himself, and delivered into the text a sermon on the Theodice, such, we suppose, as formed the current doctrine of the time in which he lived."

On page 260, Froude says: " Such in outline is this wonderful poem. With the material of which it is woven we have not been concerned, although it is so rich and pregnant that we might with little difficulty construct out of it a complete picture of the world as it then was ; its knowledge, arts, habits, superstitions, hopes and fears. The subject is the problem of all mankind. And its composition embraces no less wide a range. But what we are here most interested upon is the epoch which it marks in the progress of mankind, as the first recorded struggle of a new experience with an established orthodox belief. True, for hundreds of years, perhaps for a thousand, the superstition against which it was directed continued. When Christ came it was still in its vitality, nay, it is alive, or in a sort of mock life, among us at this very day. But even those who retained their imperfect belief had received into their canon a book which treated it with contumely and scorn, so irresistible was the majesty of truth."

We accept the account given in this note of Elihu's "sermon." But as it is in the Hebrew language, we will select some verses in each chapter, for the purpose of illustrating the meaning of some leading Hebrew words used in Scripture. Froude does not go to the original. His quotations are from the E. V.

CHAPTER XXXII.

2 And breathed hard[1] nostril of Elihu, son,&c., at Job; was kindled nostril of him at his declaring just breath of him[2] more than God:

6 ...therefore was afraid I, and feared to breathe out[3] opinion of me with you:

8 Surely breath[4] it in men, even breath[5] of Almighty causes them to have understanding:

18 For am full I of words; compresses me breath[6] of belly of me:
[See note to this v. at the end of the chapter.]

---

1. The Heb. verb here is *nhr*, defined by Ges., to breathe hard through the nose; an onomatopoietic, says he, i. e. expressing its meaning by the sounds of it: Am. Bib. Un....then was kindled the anger of Elihu.

2. Heb. *nphsh u*—breath of him, i. e. himself: Ges. under *tsdq*—"to declare any one just or innocent," says, "followed by *nphsh u*—(breath of him)—one self," citing this v., and Job 33 : 32: and under *nphsh* he gives "*nphsh i*—(breath of me) I myself;" and *nphsh k*—(breath of thee)—thou thyself." For *nphsh u*—breath of him, in Job 32 : 2, the Douay gives *he*: Ital....himself; E. V....himself; Am. Bib. Un....himself; Noyes ....himself.

3. The Heb. verb used here is *hue*, defined to breathe out; a word used in poetry says Ges., citing Job 32 : 10, 17, where the same verb is used: The Douay is....to shew you my opinion: Am. Bib. Un....to show you my opinion.

4. Heb. *ruh*.

5. Heb. *nshmt*, (the same word used in Gen. 2 : 7; *nshme* is the true word, sometimes written *nshmt*:) for *ruh* in the v. the Douay gives, a spirit; and for *nshmt*, inspiration: Ital....the *spirito;* the inspiration, &c.; Am. Bib. Un....But a spirit there is in man; and (in a foot note, even) the breath of the Almighty gives them understanding: Noyes.... But it is the divine spirit in man, even the inspiration of the Almighty, that giveth him understanding.

6. Heb. *ruh*—breath or wind, of *bthn*—belly—of me: Douay....the spirit of my bowels straiteneth me: Ital....the *spirito* of my belly me draws together: Am. Bib. Un....the spirit within me constrains me: Noyes....The spirit within constraineth me. [See note to this verse at the end of the chapter.]

19 Lo belly of me like wine not opened, as bottles new burst:[1]
20 I will speak and it will be airy[2] to me:
22 ....as suddenly might take away me Maker of me:

---

1. Ges., under *aub*, citing this v. renders, "like new bottles," i. e., says he, full of new wine, *which* burst: Douay....Behold my belly is as new wine which wanteth vent, which bursteth the new vessels: Ital.... my belly: E. V....my belly: Am. Bib. Un....my breast is as wine that has no vent: Noyes....Behold my bosom is as wine that hath no vent... it is bursting.

2. Ges. under the verb *ruh*, defined, to be airy, gives, *iruh li*, (the words used in this v.)—it will be airy to me; hence says he, "spacious to me," i. e., says he, I shall breathe,—be refreshed, citing this v. and 1 Sam. 16 : 23: The Douay is....I will speak and take breath a little: E. V....I will speak that I may be refreshed: Am. Bib. Un....I will speak and be relieved: Noyes....that I may be relieved.

NOTE to the words "the spirit within me," used by the E. V., and the Am. Bib Un., in Job 32 : 18.

In 1 Kings 17 : 21, the Heb. is....let return, I pray thee, *nphsh*—breath of this child into *qrb*—entrails of him: Latin....the *anima*—breath—of this child into *viscera*—entrails—of him: Douay....let the soul of this child return into his body: Ital....the *anima* of this child into him: E. V....let this child's soul come into him again.

1 Kings 17 : 22, Heb.....and returned *nphsh*—breath—of this child into *qrb*—entrails of him, and *ihi*—he lived again: Douay....and the soul of the child returned unto him, and he revived, (i. e. lived again:) Ital....and the *anima* of the child returned into him, and he came to life again: E. V....and the soul of the child came into him again, and he revived.

Ps. 40 : 9, Heb., law of thee in midst of *moi*—intestines of me: Douay, Ps. 39 : 9....thy law in the midst of my heart: Ital. 40 : 9....in the midst of my *interiora*—entrails—of me: E. V....within my heart.

Ps. 51 : 12, E. V. v. 10, Heb....and *ruh*—breath—straight (metaphor., for upright, just, says Ges., under *nkh*, citing Prov. 8 : 9) renew in *qrb*—entrails—of me: Douay, 50 : 12....and renew a right spirit within my bowels: Ital., 51 : 12....and renew within me a *spirito* straight: E. V., 51 : 10....and renew a right spirit within me.

Psal. 103 : 1, Heb....Bless *nphsh*—breath—of me Jehovah, yea all *qrb* —entrails of me *bless* name holy of him: Douay, 102 : 1....Bless the Lord, O my soul: and let all that is within me *bless:* Ital., 103 : 1....

and all my *interiora*—entrails—*bless:* E. V....and all that is within me bless.

Isai. 63 : 11, Heb....who put in *qrb*—entrails—of him *ruh*—breath—holy of him : Douay....that put in the midst of them the spirit of his holy One? Ital....that put his *spirito* holy in midst of them : E. V....that put his holy spirit within them.

Isai., 26 : 9, Heb. *nphsh*—breath—of me desireth thee in night, (i. e., says Ges., citing this v., " I desire thee in the night,") also *ruh*—breath—of me in *qrb*—entrails—of me shall break forth at dawn to thee : Douay ....My soul hath desired thee in the night: yea, and with my spirit within me in the morning early I will watch to thee: Ital....with my *spirito that is* within me : E. V....with my spirit within me.

Ezek. 11 : 10, Heb....and *ruh*—breath—new I will give in *qrb*—entrails—of you: Douay....a new spirit in their bowels: Ital....a new spirit within them : E. V....and I will put a new spirit within you.

Ezek. 36 : 26, Heb....and *ruh*—breath—new will I give in *qrb*—entrails—of you: Douay....and put a new spirit within you: Ital....a *spirito* new within you : E. V....a new spirit within you.

Ezek. 36 : 27, Heb....*ruh*—breath—of me I will give in *qrb*—entrails—of you: Douay....my spirit in the midst of you: Ital. ..I will put my *spirito* within you: E. V....my spirit within you.

Habak. 2 : 19, Heb....and any *ruh*—breath—not there is in *qrb*—entrails—of it: Douay....and there is no spirit in the bowels thereof: Ital....and not there is within it *spirito* any: E. V....and no breath at all in the midst of it.

In Baruch 2 : 17 we have in the Greek, (my copy of the Hebrew has not the so-called Apocrypha,) " for not those lying dead in the *hades*, (grave,) of whom is taken away the *pneuma*—(the Greek word uniformly used, for the Heb. *ruh*)—breath—of them from the entrails of them will give glory....to the Lord : The Latin there is, for not dead, who are in *inferno*, (from *infernus*, defined " lower, situate beneath or under,") of whom *spiritus*—breath—was taken from the entrails of them, shall, &c. The Douay there is....for the dead that are in hell, whose spirit is taken from their bowels, shall not give glory, &c. : The E. V. there is....for the dead that are in their graves, whose souls (margin, "Greek, spirit, or life,") are taken from their bodies, will give unto the Lord neither praise, &c.

The E. V. persistently avoids giving *nphsh*—breath—soul—in entrails, or *ruh*—breath—spirit—in entrails. So persevering a use of its word "within" could not be other than designed—more persevering even than either the Douay or the Italian. The purpose of the evasion is too manifest to need remark. The reader may do the thinking.

CHAPTER XXXIII.

4 Breath[1] of God made me, and breath[2] of Almighty caused me to live:

18 May keep safely breath[3] of him from pit, and life[4] of him from to perish by weapon:[5]

20 And loathes life of him bread, and breath[6] of him food of delight:

22 And draws near to pit breath[7] of him, and life of him to killers:[8]

---

1. Heb. *ruh*—breath.
2. *nshmt*——breath. This verse expresses what is expressed in Gen. 2 : 7. By the *ruh*—breath—word—of God, the inanimate organism, man, was made, and by the *nshmt*—breath—of Almighty, breathed into the breathing organs, the inanimate man was caused to live. The Douay of the v. is....The spirit of God made me, and the breath of the Almighty gave me liife : The Ital. here uses, first *spirito*, and then *alito*—breath....hath given me life; Noyes....the spirit of God made me and the breath....gave me life: Am. Bib. Un....The spirit....made me, and the breath...gives me life: (an evident evasion :) The verse plainly teaches the same that Gen. 2 : 7 teaches—that the inanimate organism was first created, and that then it was made alive by the breath of lives imparted to it.
3. Poetical for him : Douay....his soul from corruption : Ital....his *anima* from the grave : Am. Bib. Un....his soul from the pit : Noyes....him from the pit.
4. Heb. *hie*—life, equivalent, says Ges., to *nphsh* No. 4, "vital power," citing Job 33 ; 20 ; 38 : 39.
5. Ges., under *obr*, gives, "from to perish by the weapon (of death.)" citing this v., and Job 36 : 12.
6. Heb. *nphsh*—breath : The Douay of the v. gives....his life....his soul : The Ital....his life....his *anima* : E. V....his life....his soul : Am. Bib. Un....And his spirit (Heb. *hie*—life) ...his soul : Noyes.... So that his mouth abhorreth bread, and his taste the choicest meat.
7. Heb. *nphsh u*—breath of him—poetical for he : Douay....his soul to corruption : Ital....his *anima* to the grave : Am. Bib. Un....his soul comes nigh to the pit : Noyes....his soul draweth near to the pit.
8. Often used, says Ges., under *mut*—death, of death sent by God himself, by diseases, famine, etc., citing this v.

23 If there be to him messenger,[1] interpreter, one out of a thousand, to show to man straightness of him:
   [See note to this v. at the end of the chapter.]

24 Then he will be gracious to him, and will say, set him free from descending pit,[2] I have found covering, (or expiation:)

26 He may intreat God, and he will receive him graciously, and he shall see face of him[3] with rejoicing:

28 Redeeming breath[4] of me from to perish in pit, that life of me in light I may see:

29 Lo, all these things doth God treads three[5] with man:

30 For to bring back breath[6] of him from pit, to light in light of lives:

---

1. Heb. *mlak*—messenger; Douay....Angel; Ital....messenger; E. V....messenger; Noyes....messenger; Am. Bib. Un,...messenger.
   [See note to this v. at the end of the chapter.]

2. Heb. *shht:* Douay....that he may not go down to corruption; Ital. ....the grave; E. V....pit; Noyes....him from the pit; Am. Bib. Un. ....the pit. [By comparing verses 22 and 24 we see that his soul to the pit and him to the pit mean the same.]

3. i. e., enjoy his favour; the Heb. here is, *phni*—face—of him.

4. Heb. *nphsh i*—breath of me—poetical for me: Douay....his soul from going into destruction, that it may live and see light; Ital....his *anima* that not it pass into the grave; E. V....his soul from going into the pit; Noyes....he hath delivered me from going down to the pit; Am. Bib. Un....He has redeemed my soul from going into the pit: Ges., under *obr* citing this v., renders, "perishing in the sepulchre."

5. i. e., thrice, says Ges., citing Exod. 23:17, etc. Noyes....time after time; Am. Bib. Un....thrice.

6. Heb. *nphsh u*—breath of him—poetical for him or them: Douay... their souls from corruption: Ital....his soul from the grave; E. V.... his soul from the pit, Noyes....that he may bring him back from the grave; Noyes....that he may bring him back from the grave; Am. Bib. Un....to bring back his soul from the pit. See the E. V., of Ps. 30:3.

NOTE TO JOB 33:23.

The Heb. is....If there be to him *mlah*—messenger: Ital.:...*messo*—

messenger; E. V....messenger; Noyes....messenger; Am. Bib. Un. ....messenger; Douay....Angel. The Greek word is *aggelos*, sounded *angelos*, defined in Donnegan's Greek Lex. "a messenger," and in Liddell & Scott's Greek Lex. "a messenger, envoy, often in Homer, Herodotus, and others; in general, one who announces or tells." *Angel* is not given in any Lex. for the Greek *angelos*. This Romish word *angel* has done so much mischief in the world that it is high time its true meaning should be made known.

In Psal. 104 : 4, we have in Latin, (the Papacy says it is the sacred language, and that the Latin version is the only true version of the scriptures,) " Who makest thy *Angelos spiritus*, and thy ministers fire burning, or, lighting up." [The Latin *spiritus* is plural as well as singular.] The Douay is Psal. 103 : 4, and is, " Who makest thy angels spirits; and thy ministers a burning fire; The Ital. 104 : 4, is...." He makes the *venti*—winds—his *Angeli*—messengers; " E. V...." Who maketh his angels spirits; his ministers a flaming fire : The Heb. is, " He maketh *mlaki*—(plural of *mlak*)—messengers—of him *ruhut*—(plural of *ruh*—winds; servants of him lightnings flashing." (And *ruh* is used in the very next preceding verse, and the Douay, Ital., and E. V. there give *wind* for it :) The Greek is, Who making *angelous*—(plural of *angelos*)—messengers—of him *pneumata*—(plural of *pneuma*)—winds, and workmen of him fire blazing.

In Heb. 1 : 7, the Rheims Romish version of the New Testament, (published with the Douay Romish version of the Old Testament,) has, " He maketh his angels, spirits," (with a comma after angels,) and a flame of fire his ministers :" E. V..... " Who maketh his angels spirits, (without comma after angels,) and his ministers a flame of fire : The Ital. there is ...."who makes the *venti*—winds—his *angeli*—messengers, and flame of fire his ministers."

In Zech. 6 : 5, the Heb. is, And answered that *mlak*—messenger, these *the* four *ruhut*—(plural of *ruh*)—breaths—winds—of these heavens : Greek ....the four *anemoi*—winds—of the heaven : Latin....these are the four *venti*—winds—of heaven—the sky : Douay....And the Angel answered, and said to me, these are the four winds of the heaven : Ital....And the *Angelo*—messenger—answered, and to me said : These *are* the four *spiriti* of the heaven—air—sky : E. V....And the angel answered....these *are* the four spirits (margin, or, winds.)

In Ezek. 37 : 5, the Heb. has *ruh*—breath ; Douay....spirit; Ital.... *spirito;* E. V....breath.

In Ezek. 37 : 6, the Heb. is *ruh*—breath ; Douay....spirit; Ital.... *spirito;* E. V....breath.

In Ezek. 37 : 8, the Heb. is *ruh*—breath ; Douay....spirit; Ital.... *spirito;* E. V....breath.

In Ezek. 37 : 9, the Heb. has *ruh*, twice, then *ruhut*, and then *ruh* again : The Douay has *spirit* twice, and then, " come, spirit, from the four winds, and blow upon these slain, and let them live again:" The Ital. has *spirito* twice, and then, come *O spirito* from the four *venti*—winds, and blow into these slain, that they may live again: The E. V. has *wind* twice, and then "Come from the four *winds, O breath*, and breathe upon these slain, that they may live," (omitting to add *again*, though it is plain that the slain had once lived before. The omission was not without purpose.)

Ezek. 37 : 10, Heb....and came into them that *ruh*—breath, and they lived again ; Douay....and the spirit came into them ; Ital....and the *spirito* entered into them and they returned to life; E. V....and the breath came into them, and they lived: (again omitting "again.")

Ezek. 37 : 14, Heb...And I will give *ruh*—breath—of me into you, and ye shall live again ; Douay.. .my spirit; Ital....my *spirito*, and ye shall return into life; E. V....my Spirit in you, and ye shall live: (again omitting the word "again :" See Job 14 : 14 and note.)

After I had translated beyond Psalm 104 : 4, in preparing the work entitled "The Theology of the Bible," a gentleman who knew I was engaged in that work happened to see the work of Alex. Geddes, LL.D., in a book store in New York, and thinking I would like to have it, he brought it to me,—three large folio volumes, and his Prospectus, etc., a smaller fol. vol. ; a very expensive work, and not likely to have obtained more than a very limited circulation. I at first told the gentleman I did not desire to have the books. But it occurred to me to look at a few passages. I found that in Gen. 1 : 2, he rendered " a vehement wind:" The Heb. there is, *ruh aleim*—a breath, or, wind, of God: Douay....the spirit of God moved over the waters; Ital....and the *Spirito*—breath, or, wind, of God was moved upon the face of the waters. And that in Psal. 104 : 4, he rendered, " Who maketh the winds his messengers." These renderings, by which I found myself supported by so accomplished a Hebrew scholar, induced me to say to the gentleman he might leave the books.

I give what Geddes says of Psal. 104 : 4. "Another instance I shall give, says he, from the Psalms : Ps. 104 : 4, is thus rendered by our last translators : 'Who maketh his angels spirits, and his ministers a flaming fire.'" He then says: "That a servile translator from the Vulgate (the Latin) should be guilty of so egregious a mistake is not, perhaps, to be wondered at. He had before him an ambiguous text, and might think it incumbent on him to be as obscure and unintelligible as *his* original ; but that one who translates immediately from the Hebrew, and is but moderately acquainted with its genius, should so miserably degrade this sublime passage is surprising indeed." He renders: "Who maketh the winds his messengers, and his ministers the flashing lightning." "A bold and sublime idea," says he, "and worthy an Oriental bard."(David.) A note says: Bishop Hare has well rendered this verse in Latin, "faciens angelos suos ventos, ministros suos ignem flammantem,"—making his messengers *the* winds, his ministers (servants) fire flaming. "But Green says Geddes, who took Bishop Hare for his model, has ill translated into English the first line thus, who maketh his angels winds." "That Green's mistake is in not putting a comma after his word angels, as Bishop Hare does."

The Rev. Alex. Geddes, LL.D., was an eminent Scottish Rom. Cath. divine, distinguished as a learned writer. The distinction LL.D., was conferred on him by a Presbyterian University, the only instance of the kind. He was born in 1737. Finding that the Latin Vulgate was in many instances inaccurate, he resolved to translate the Bible from the originals. In 1799 he gave to the world his first volume; and in 1800 the second, which brought the work to the end of Ruth. He died in 1802, while engaged in translating the Psalms. His version of the Psalms, which he completed as far as the 118th, was published in 1807. His version showed, (as all will see who will fully prepare themselves to read the Scriptures in the originals,) that the current so-called theology was radically wrong: and he became an object of equal alarm and hostility to his own church and all the Protestant denominations. A majority of the Rom. Cath. bishops in England forbade the use of his work in their sees; while the apostolic vicar of the London district interdicted him from officiating as priest. Accusations of infidelity, and a desire to destroy the authority of Scripture, were heaped upon him from all quarters. To dissipate these charges he published an "Address," in which he proclaimed himself "a sincere though unworthy disciple of Christ," and denounced those as the real enemies of religion "who seek to support her on rotten props, which moulder away at the first touch of reason, and leave the fabric in the dust." The foregoing brief account of Geddes and his work we have collected from different notices of him.

CHAPTER XXXIV.

14 If he should turn to it[1] mind of him, breath[2] of him, yea breath[3] *of lives* of him to himself draw back,

15 Would breathe out[4] every flesh at once, and man[5] to dust would return:

---

1. Heb. *u*—it, the *tbl*—habitable globe, in v. 13.
2. Heb. *ruh*—breath.
3. Heb. *nshmt*—breath (of lives.)
4. Heb. *ighuo*, from the verb *ghuo*—to breathe out.
5. Heb. *adm*—used here for each—every one. In Ps. 104: 25—29, small and great beasts are said to breathe out, and return to dust of them:

and see page 22 of this book, in note. And Ges. under *adm* (3) says, "compare *aish* [man] No. 4;" and for *aish* No. 4, he gives, each, every one, citing 1 Kings 20 : 20, where, for *aish*, the Douay and the E.V. give "every one;" and citing Gen. 15 : 10, where for *aish*, Ges. gives "each," thus: "and he set each" [Heb. *aish*] "of the several (*animals*, inserted) part over against part;" and he adds, "*aish btru* is equivalent to *kl btru*" —each part of them; "but the sacred writer has put *aish*—man—'for *kl*' —each:" The Douay in Gen. 15 : 10 is...."and laid the two pieces of each one"—Heb. *aish*—"against the other:" See E. V. And for the Heb. *aish*—man—in Job 1 : 4, the Douay and the E. V., give, "every one:" Noyes and Am. Bib. Un...."each." And in Job 2 : 11, the Heb. *aish* is used for each one: the Douay and the E. V. there give for it "every one:" Noyes gives "each one," and the Am. Bib. Un. gives, "each." The Ital. of v. 14 is ....If he should put mind to man, (interpolating the word man as being in the original,) should draw back to himself his *alito*—breath, and, or, yea, his *soffio*—breath: v. 15, Every flesh together would end, or, cease, and man would return into dust. The E. V. follows the bold interpolation by the Ital. of the word "man" in v. 14; and for the Heb. *ruh* and *nshmt* gives his "spirit and his breath." And Noyes uses the Ital. word "man" in v. 14, and gives, "take back his spirit, and his breath, all flesh would then expire together:" The Douay in the two verses is, If he turn his heart to him [it should be *it*, "the world which he made," as the Douay gives in v. 13,] "he should draw his spirit and his breath unto himself, all flesh shall perish together, and man shall return unto dust." The Am. Bib. Un. is...."should he set his thoughts upon him" [it should be *it*,] "withdraw to himself his spirit and his breath, all flesh would expire together, and man return to dust." The Heb. *nshmt* in v. 14 is the word used in Gen. 2 : 7, where the Heb. is *nshmt hiim*—breath of lives; and it is plain from the words "to himself draw back" in v. 14, that *nshmt* here means breath of *lives:* "Every flesh," in v. 15, "All flesh," as the Douay, E. V., Noyes, and Am. Bib. Un. give, means, every breathing flesh, no other could breathe out,—Latin, exspire. And surely, if God should draw back to himself the breath of lives, every breathing creature would breathe out. And the two verses show plainly, that the Heb. *adm* in v. 14 means *each*, or, every one, i. e. every flesh, every breathing flesh, would breathe out, and return to dust of them, as is said in Ps. 104: 25—29, before given. And the two verses in the Heb. plainly teach, that every breathing creature dies by breathing out, i. e. by giving up the ghost (breath,) as the E.,V. gives for the same Heb. verb *ghuo* in Job 3 : 10; 10 : 18; 13 : 19; 14: 10. But the Romish Ital. version by substituting the word *man* for the Heb. *u—it*, in v. 14, attempts to make the two verses apply only to man, and to make "every flesh," in v. 14 apply only to man. And why did they who gave us the E. V. follow the Ital. substitution of the word "man" in v. 14, which could not be other than a

19 Who not accepts faces [1] of princes:
36 Breathe after I,[2] may be tried Job to completeness because of answers like as men of wickedness.

CHAPTER XXXV.

11 Who teaches us more than beasts of earth; and more than birds of these heavens [3] made us wise:
14 ....cause [4] is before him; and wait thou for him:
16 Therefore Job with breath [5] opens mouth of him; without knowledge words he multiplies.

---

willful perversion. No other reason can be given than that they chose to evade the teaching of the Hebrew, that every breathing creature has a ghost—breath—to give up; which teaching they evade also in Gen. 6 : 17 ; 7 : 22 ; Ps. 104 : 25—29 ; see pages 21, 22 of this book in note.

Our word *it* is often given for the Heb. *u*, meaning in v. 14, the habitable earth, or, globe. I give a few instances : Job 31 : 36, Heb. *u*, twice: E. V., and Noyes, and Am. Bib. Un., *it*, twice : Job 37 : 13, Heb. *u*, Am. Bib. Un., *it :* Job 36 : 30, Heb. *u :* Ital., and E. V., *it :* Job 36 : 25, Heb. *u*, E. V, *it :* Job 38 : 10, Heb. *u*, Am. Bib. Un. *it :* Job 38 : 20, Heb. *u*, twice ; E. V., and Am Bib. Un., *it*. The instances might be multiplied. For the meaning of the E. V. word "ghost," and of the Heb. verb *ghuo*, more at large, see note at the end of chap. 3 : near the end of which note the reader will find what Noah Webster's Dictionary makes of the word "ghost."

1. For persons.
2. i. e., I desire ; the Heb. verb used here is *aeb*, defined, to breathe after, to desire.
3. Douay....than the fowls of the air: Ital....the birds of heaven : E. V....the fowls of heaven: Am. Bib. Un....the birds of heaven : Noyes....the birds of heaven.
4. Heb. *din*, defined, cause, controversy, right: Douay....be judged before him, and expect him : E. V....*yet* judgment *is* before him, therefore trust thou in him : Am. Bib. Un....the cause is before him ; and wait thou for him : Noyes....justice is with him.
5. Heb. *ebl*—breath ; hence, says Ges., in vain, citing this v. and others: Douay....Job openeth his mouth in vain : E. V....the same : Am. Bib. Un....fills his mouth with vanity : Noyes....Job hath opened his mouth rashly.

CHAPTER XXXVI.

6 Not will he give life[1] to wicked; but that which is just,[2] meek he will give:

[For Job's hope see further in note at the end of chap. 40.]

11 If obey they and serve[3] they shall fulfill days of them in good, and years of them in pleasures:

12 But if not obey they, by weapon[4] they shall perish;[5] they shall breathe out[6] without knowledge:

14 Shall die in youth breath[7] of them; and life of them like as *those* prostituting themselves in honor of Astarte, (—Venus.)[8]

---

1. Ges., under *hie*, the verb used here, gives, cause to live, make alive, give life to, citing Job 34 : 4; and call back to life, citing 1 Sam. 2 : 6, etc.: Am. Bib. Un....He will not prosper the wicked.

2. Heb. *mshphth*, that which is just: Douay....judgment: Ital.... reason: E. V....right: Am. Bib. Un....right: Noyes....But rendereth justice to the oppressed.

3. Jehovah, says Ges.

4. "The weapon of death," says Ges., under *shlh*, citing this v., and Job 33 : 18.

5. The Heb. verb here is *obr*, which Ges. defines, to perish, citing Ps. 37 : 36, where the Heb. is, And *iobr*—he perished, and not was there of him: Douay....and lo, he was not: Ital....but he is passed away; and lo, he not *is more:* E. V....Yet he passed away, and lo, he was not.

6. Heb. *ighuo*—they shall breathe out: The Douay in Job 36 : 12 is... they shall pass by the sword and be consumed in folly: Ital....they shall pass by the sword, and die for want of understanding: E. V.... and they shall die without knowledge: Am. Bib. Un....by the dart they perish, and expire (from the Latin verb *exspiro*, defined in Anthon's Latin Dict. " to breathe out," " breathe one's last ") without knowledge: Noyes....they die in their own folly.

7. Heb. *nphsh*—breath—of them—poetical for they: Latin, *anima*—breath—of them.

8. So Ges., under *qdsh*, citing this v. and others: The Douay of the v. is....Their soul shall die in a storm, and their life among the effeminate: Ital....Their person (Heb. *nphsh*) shall die in youth, and their life among the *cinedi:* This word is not given in Graglia's Ital. Dict.: it is the Latin *cinœdus*, one guilty of unnatural lewdness: The E. V. of the verse is

17 But cause[1] of wicked fillest thou, (i. e. if thou fillest,) cause[2] and right[3] hold together:[4]

18 So that beware lest he drive thee out by chastening,[5] and great redemption price not can save (or deliver) thee:

20 Breathe not after[6] that night[7] of being made to pass away peoples underneath them:[8]

....They die in youth, and their life *is* among the unclean: Am. Bib. Un....Their breath shall expire in youth, and their life with the unclean: " Their breath shall expire, " is saying, Their breath shall breathe out: This is not the Heb.: the Heb. is *tmt*—(from *mut*—to die)—shall die breath of them, poetical for, they shall die. The Am. Bib. Un., to avoid the idea of a soul dying, gives, Their *breath* (the right word for the Heb. *nphsh*,) and gives *expire*, i. e. breathe out, a wrong word for the Heb. *imt*—shall die, in the verse. It is one of the many evasions which a translation " on the basis of the common and earlier English versions " required; Noyes....They die in their youth.

1. Heb. *din*—cause, so Ges., under *din*, citing this v.
2. Heb. *din*—cause.
3. Heb. *mshphth*—right.
4. Heb. *tmk*—hold together: Ges., under the verb *tmk* cites this v., and renders, " cause and judgment follow one another : Am. Bib. Un... But if thou art filled with the judgment of the wicked, judgment and justice will lay hold of thee: The Heb. *k* is generally thee ; but here it is part of the Heb. verb *tmk*—to hold together. Noyes renders the v. ....But if thou lade thyself with the guilt of the wicked,—guilt and punishment follow each other.
5. So Ges., under *sut*, citing this v.
6. i. e., desire not.
7. i. e., death, says Ges., under *shaph*, citing this v.
8. The Douay of this v. is: Prolong not the night, that people may come up for them: Ital....Pant not after the night in which the peoples, (or, nations) perish to bottom: E. V....Desire not the night, when people are cut off in their place: Am. Bib. Un....Long not for that night, where the nations are gathered to the world below them: Noyes.... Long not for that night to which nations are taken away from their place.

Finding in this verse the E. V. words "cut off," I give an incident: Meeting a Presbyterian clergyman, a graduate of a theological seminary, and in whose hearing I had previously had a short conversation with a lady, he at once asked me, how I got over Matt. 25 : 46. The E. V. of it is: And these shall go away into everlasting punishment: but the righteous into life eternal. I as promptly said: I'll bet a fippenny bit you don't know what the word is in the original—the Greek— where the E. V. gives the word punishment. He did not know. I repeated what I had said. He then asked what the word was. I told him it was *kolasin*—cutting off, from the Greek verb *kolazo*, defined in Donnegan's Greek Lexicon, to cut off. He then asked: Do you undertake to say that *kolasin* is the word used there? I answered, I know it was; and that the Old Testament would teach him what "to cut off," in such connection, meant.

The Heb. verb is *krt*, defined by Ges., "to cut off," as the branch of a tree, says he ; " to be exterminated, destroyed," used of persons, says he, citing Gen. 9 : 12, where the verb *krt* is used, and for which the Douay there gives, " be destroyed :" The Ital....be destroyed : E. V....be cut off. And Ps. 37 : 9, where the same word is used, and for which the Douay, Ps. 36 : 9, gives, For evil doers shall be cut off: but they that hope upon the Lord shall inherit the land : Ital....Ps. 37 : 9....For the wicked shall be exterminated ; but they that hope upon the Lord shall possess the earth: E. V. 37 : 9,....For evil doers shall be cut off: but those that wait upon the Lord, they shall inherit the earth. And citing Prov. 2 : 22, where the same Heb. verb is used, and where the Douay gives, But the wicked shall be destroyed from the earth : The Ital.... But the wicked shall be exterminated from the earth : E. V....But the wicked shall be cut off from the earth. The verse gives to the just, i. e. to them who shall be accounted just, a life eternal ; and to the wicked the opposite. But orthodoxy would make the verse give a life eternal to the wicked also. It would make the verse give a life eternal of happiness to the one class, and a life eternal of misery to the other !

The Douay of Matt. 25 : 46 is, And these shall go into everlasting punishment: but the just into life everlasting: The Ital....And these shall go to the pains eternal, and the just to the life eternal.

The Douay gives, "into life everlasting," and the E. V...."into life eternal ; " both omitting our article *a* before life. The true rendering of the Greek into English is, a life everlasting, or eternal. Thus distinguishing the life eternal—the immortality—to which they who shall be accounted just will be raised, from this life of an inch of time. The Greek has no indefinite article ; and the rule is given in the Greek grammars, that where no article is used before a noun in the Greek our article *a* is to be supplied in rendering Greek into English. Why should the Douay and Ital. Rom. Cath. versions of the verse have been followed by our English version.

The Greek very uniformly puts the noun before the adjective : (and so does the Hebrew.) The E. V. generally puts the adjective first. So that whenever the reader finds in the E.V., "eternal life," "everlasting life," he must, in order to get the true rendering from the Greek into English, put the noun first with our article *a* before it, and read a life eternal, a life everlasting. Eternal life may be thought somewhat accordant to the immortal soul theory; but a life eternal is unsuitable to it.

The Greek of Matt. 25 : 46 is: And *apeleusontai* (from *aperchomai*)—shall go away; metaphor., die, drop off, says Donnegan; depart from life, die, says Liddell and Scott's Greek Lexicon; *houtoi*—these—*eis*—to —*kolasin*—cutting off—eternal; but the just *eis*—for—a life eternal. *Kolasin* is the accusative of *kolasis*, from the Greek verb *kolazo*—to cut off.

The same Greek word *kolasis* occurs in the Greek of the Septuagint in Ezek. 18 : 30, and 44 : 12. In 18 : 30 the Greek is....turn away from all the impieties of you, and not shall they be to you *eis*—for—*kolasin*—cutting off—by reason of iniquity. (The Heb. preposition in the v. is *l*—for —*mkshul*, the Heb. word for which the Septuagint gives *kolasin*: for *mkshul* Ges. gives, cause of falling, citing this v. and Ezk. 44 : 12.) In Ezek. 18: 20, the Douay gives....and iniquity shall not be your ruin: E. V....so iniquity shall not be your ruin. In Exek. 44 : 12 the Heb. is... and were *l*—to—house of Israel *l*—for—cause of falling by reason of iniquity: Greek....and were to house of Israel *eis*—for—*kolasin*—cutting off—by reason of iniquity: Douay....and were a stumbling block of iniquity to the house of Israel: E. V....and caused the house of Israel to fall into iniquity. The Heb. preposition *l* is defined by Ges., to, towards, unto, for, etc.; and the Greek preposition *eis* is defined by Donnegan, to, towards, for, in order to, etc.; and by Liddell and Scott, to, towards, for, for the purpose of, etc. The sense requires a different English preposition for the second *l* and for the second *eis* in these two verses, from that for the first *l* and *eis*.

Kolasin—cutting off—in Matt. 25 : 46, is *death*; and everlasting cutting off is everlasting death: but to the just, says Matthew, a life eternal. Paul teaches the same in Romans 6 : 23. He says: Death is the *opsonia* of sin; (*opsonia* is defined, pay, stipend; the E. V. is, wages. It is used figuratively for penalty—punishment;) but the gift of God, a life eternal through Jesus Christ. The gift of God is not a life eternal to the wicked, but a life eternal through Christ, i. e. to them who die in Christ. To them who die in sin death is everlasting, and death being the pay—penalty—punishment—of sin, everlasting death is everlasting punishment. The one—death, is the penalty—punishment—of sin, i. e. of the wicked: the other—a life eternal, is the gift of God, and not a gift to all, but the gift through Christ, i. e., through faith in Christ, equivalent to life and immortality through the gospel, which Christ is said (2 Tim. 1 : 10) to have brought to light. *Wages* is defined by Webster, recompense; and *pay* is defined by him, compensation; and stipend is defined by him, wages. But some say, Death is no penalty for sin; and hold, that the penalty—wages—meant is eternal life in misery; so that the penalty for

sin in this short life can never be paid, as there is no end to eternity.
For Matt. 25:46, see further " The Theology of the Bible," p. 586.

CHAPTER XXXVII.

10 From breath¹ of God is given ice, and breadth of waters into narrow:²

21 And now not can they³ look at light,⁴ bright in clouds,⁵ and wind⁶ has passed over and cleansed them:⁷

22 Out of north gold⁸ cometh;

CHAPTER XXXVIII.

1 Then began to speak⁹ Jehovah with Job out of that storm, and he said:

---

1. Heb. *nshmt*, defined by Ges., breath, spirit, (spirit means breath.) Ital., E. V., Am. Bib. Un., and Noyes. ..breath.

2. i. e., contracted, says Ges., under *mutsq*, citing this v.

3 Impersonal.

4. Heb. *aur*—light, used of the sun itself, says Ges., citing this v.

5. By metonymy used of the firmament of Heaven, says Ges. under *shhq*, equivalent, says he, to *shmim*—heavens, and to *rquio*, "the firmament, of heaven spread out like a hemisphere above the earth, like a splendid and pellucid sapphire to which the stars were supposed to be fixed, and over which the Hebrews believed there was a heavenly ocean," citing Gen. 1:7; 7:11; Ps. 104:3, E. V., v. 2; Ps. 148:4, E. V., v. 3, 4.

6. Heb. *ruh*.

7. Ges., under *ther*—to cleanse, gives, "the sky from clouds," citing this v. The Ital. in Job 37:21 is: Lo yet *man* not can look at the sun, *when* he shines in the heaven, after that the wind is passed and it has cleaned: Am. Bib. Un....For now, they look not on the light, when it is shining in the skies and the wind has passed over and cleared them.

8. Metaphor., says Ges., of the golden splendor of the heavens, perhaps the sun itself, citing this verse under *zeb*—gold: Douay....Cold cometh out of the north: Ital....the gilded brightness: E. V....Fair weather cometh out of the north: Noyes....And a golden brightness cometh out of the sky: Am. Bib. Un....Out of the north comes gold.

9. So Ges. under *one:* Noyes....Then spake Jehovah to Job: Am. Bib. Un....Then Jehovah answered Job.

2 Who this, darkening counsel in words without knowledge:

3 Gird up now like *a* man loins of thee, and I will inquire of thee and thou mayest cause me to know:

4 Where wast thou at founding of me earth: tell if thou knowest insight:

5 Who set measures of it, for thou knowest; [1] and who stretched out upon it measuring cord:

6 Upon what, foundations of it, were sunk they; or who laid stone of corner of it:

7 When shouted together stars of morning, and rejoiced all sons of *aleim*:

8 And hedged with doors, sea, when burst out it, from womb came forth:

9 When put I cloud, garment of it, and thick cloud swaddling band of it:

10 And I set upon it bound of me, and put bars and doors:

11 And said: To here mayst thou come and not shalt thou continue,[2] and here shall be set[3] to pride of rollers[4] of thee:

---

1. Ironical, says Ges., under *ki*, citing this v. and Prov. 30 : 4.
2. So Ges., under *isph*, citing this v. and others.
3. There is an ellipsis after "set:" fill it with *bound*, the word used in v. 10.
4. Heb. *gaun* (a noun)—pride, of *gli* for *glili*, plural of *gilil*, an adjective defined rolling, from the verb *gll*, to roll; and in the Heb. says Professor Charles Wilson, p. 85 of his Heb. Grammar, " adjectives and participles are often used as substantives;" so that, giving the English termination of a substantive, we get rollers of thee: For examples, the Professor gives, *shumr*—keeping, i. e. says he, keeper : and *suphr*—writing i. e., says he, writer. Ges., under *sh yod t*, citing this v. says, "elliptical," and renders, " here shall be put, (namely, a bound, says he,) to the pride of thy waves: Douay....and here thou shalt break thy swelling waves: Ital....and here shall be stayed the pride of thy surges. It seems plain that " waves" is not the proper word here. There are waves in mid ocean. They move on without stay. But the poet puts us

12 Whether from days of thee hast thou commanded morning, and made to know dawn place of it:

13 For to take hold on extremities of this land, and might be shaken out wicked from it:

14 It is changed as clay [1] of seal-ring, [2] and they stand forth [3] as in splendid attire:

15 And is taken away from wicked light of them, and arm stretched out is broken:

16 Whether hast entered thou to fountains of sea, and on most secret recesses of deep hast walked:

17 Whether are made naked to thee gates of death, and gates of shadow of death hast thou seen:

18 Whether hast turned mind to broad spaces of earth; tell if thou knowest all of it:

19 Where, that way dwelleth light; and darkness, where place of it:

20 That thou mayest bring it to boundary of it, and that thou mayest understand ways of house of it:

21 Thou knowest, for then wast thou born; and number of days of thee great:

22 Whether hast entered thou to treasuries of snow, and treasuries of hail hast thou seen:

23 Which I have reserved for time of adversary, for day of battle and war:

---

on the shore, the very beach which sets bound to the rollers,—breakers, and where we see the billows raging in all their pride as if mad at the obstruction. Am. Bib. Un....and here shall thy proud waves be stayed.

1. Clay, says Ges., under *hmr*, citing this v.

2. Ges., under *hutm*—a seal-ring, citing this v., and Job 41 : 7; Jer. 22 : 24; Exod. 28 : 11, 21, says: The Hebrews were accustomed, like the Persians in the present day, sometimes to carry a signet ring hung by a string upon the breast, citing Gen. 38 : 18; to which custom, says he, allusion is made in Cant. 8 : 6.

3. Ges., under *lbush*, citing this v., renders, " and (all things) stand forth as in splendid attire." The Am. Bib. Un. of the v. is....It is changed like the signet-clay; and they stand forth as in gay apparel.

24 Where that path divideth itself light; spreads itself east wind upon earth:

25 Who divided for out pouring, channels, and path for lightning of thunders:

26 For to cause to rain on land without men, desert not man in it:

27 For to cause to be satiated desolate regions and waste places, and for to cause to sprout forth tender grass:

28 Whether exists to rain father, or who has begotten storehouses of dew: Am. Bib. Un....the drops of dew.

29 From womb of whom came out that ice, and hoar frost of heavens, who begat it:

30 As stone, waters hide themselves, and face of waters adheres together:

31 Hast thou bound together[1] bands of Pleiades, or cords of *ksil* canst thou loose:[2]

32 Whether canst thou cause to rise signs of Zodiac at time of them and Ursa Major with sons of her canst thou lead them:[3]

33 Whether knowest thou laws of heavens;[4] whether settest thou dominion of them upon (or over) earth:

---

1. Ges. under *kime*, citing this v., renders, "hast thou fastened together the bands of the Pleiades:" Am. Bib. Un....the soft influences of the Pleiades.

2. Ges., under *ksil*, citing this v., renders, "canst thou loose the bands of Orion." He also gives the plural, *ksilim*, citing Isai. 13 : 10: as if, says he, it were the Orions, or the giants of the heaven, i. e., says he, the greater constellations of the sky, such as Orion.

3. Ges. under *osh*, says : It appears to be the same as *oish*, feminine, citing this v., where her sons, says he, are the three stars in the tail of the bear. *Osh*, says he, does not properly signify a bear, but by aphæresis it stands for *nosh*, a bier, which is the name of this constellation in Arabic. They also, says he, call the three stars in the tail daughters of the bier. He says, that Schultens considers *Osh* to be the same as the Arabic nightly watcher, and supposes this constellation to be so called from its never setting.

4. Ges., under *hqe*—"law of heaven," citing this v., and Jer. 31 : 35;

34 Whether canst thou lift up to cloud voice of thee
and abundance of waters shall cover thee:

35 Whether canst thou send lightnings and they go
and say to thee, Behold us:[1]

36 Who put in reins wisdom, or who gave to mind[2]
insight:

37 Who can number clouds by wisdom, and bottles of
heavens[3] who can pour out:

38 When flows dust into molten mass, and clods cleave
together:

39 Whether canst thou hunt for lioness prey, and life[4]
of young lions canst thou fill:

40 When they are famished in caves, remaining in lair
of them lying in wait:

41 Who provides for raven food of him when born of
him to God cry for help, wander without food:

CHAPTER XXXIX.

1 Whether knowest thou time of bearing of chamois
of rock, bringing forth of hinds dost thou observe:

---

33 : 25; "dost thou set its dominion upon earth," citing this v., under
mshthr. [The heavens were known to have some rule, or dominion,
upon, or over, the earth.]

1. Ges., under *ene*, citing this v. and many others, gives, "Behold us;"
showing their ready obedience, says he: Douay....here we are: Am.
Bib. Un....Here are we.

2. Heb. *shkui*, Ges. gives for it "mind," citing this v.: The Douay is....
or who gave the cock understanding: Ital....or who hath given understanding to the mind: Am. Bib. Un....or who gave to the spirit understanding: Noyes....intelligence to the mind. What does the reader
think of the use the word "spirit," here by the Am. Bib. Un.?

3. Ges., "the bottles of heaven," citing this v. under *nbl*, poetical says
he, for the clouds, a metaphor in common use in Arabic, says he.

4. Ges., under *hie*, life, cites this v., and says: equivalent to *nphsh*—
breath: Ital....desire: Douay and E. V....appetite: Am. Bib. Un....
the craving.

2 Canst thou number months they make full, and knowest thou time of bearing of them:

3 They bow themselves, borne of them they cause to to cleave,¹ pangs of them they cast forth: ²

4 Become strong, children of them, large in field; they go forth and not return they to them:

5 Who sent out wild ass free, yea, bonds of wild ass who loosed:³

6 When I made desert house of him, and dwelling place of him salt land: ⁴

7 He laughs at noise of city; clamour of driver not hears he:

8 Searched out ⁵ mountains pastures of him, and every green thing he searches after:

9 Whether will breathe after ⁶ buffalo ⁷ to serve thee; whether he will pass the night at manger ⁸ of thee:

---

1. Ges., under *phlh*—to cleave, gives, "to cause *young ones* to cleave the womb and break forth," citing this v.

2. i. e., says Ges., under *hbl*—citing this v., "they bring forth their young ones with pain." He adds: "Since the pain of parturition ceases with the birth, a parturient mother may well be said to cast forth her pangs with her offspring.

3. So Ges., under *orud*, citing this v.: Am. Bib. Un....and who loosed the wanderer's bands?

4. Ges., under *mlhe*, citing this v., "a salt land," and on that account barren, says he: Douay....the barren land: Am. Bib. Un....the barren waste.

5. Ges., under *itur*—searching out, citing this v., says: Metonymy, that which is found by searching out: Am. Bib. Un....the range of the mountains *is* his pasture.

6. The Heb. word here is *iabe*, from the verb *abe*, defined, "to breathe after," hence, says Ges., to desire.

7. The Heb. word is *rim*: Ges. says: The animal meant is doubtful: that he has no hesitation in agreeing with Albert Schultens and do Wette in understanding it to be the buffalo.

8. So Ges., under *ol*, citing this v.: Am. Bib. Un....Will the wild-ox be willing to serve thee, or abide at thy crib.

10 Whether canst thou bind buffalo in furrow rope of him; whether will he harrow valleys [1] after thee:

11 Whether wilt thou trust in him because great, strength of him; and wilt thou leave to him toil [2] of thee:

12 Whether wilt thou trust in him that he will bring back harvest [3] of thee, and floor [4] of thee will gather:

13 Wing of ostriches [5] exults, [6] whether wing feather pious, and pinion: [7]

14 For she leaves to ground eggs of her, and in dust they are made warm: [8]

15 And she forgets that foot may press upon [9] them, and beast of field trample them:

---

1. i. e., says Ges., under *omq*, low tracts of land, fit for corn land, citing this v., and Ps. 65 : 14, E. V. v. 13.

2. So Ges., under *igio*, citing this v.

3. So Ges., under *zro*, citing this v.

4. Ges., under *grn*—floor, says, "especially used of a floor on which corn is trodden out," and he says that in this verse, citing it, floor is used by metonymy, of the corn itself, Am. Bib. Un.... Wilt thou believe him, that he will bring home thy seed, and gather into thy threshing floor?

5. Ges., citing this v. under *rnnim* (plural,) gives, ostriches, poetically, says he, for the common *bnut ione*—daughters of the female ostrich : Am. Bib. Un.... The wing of the ostrich.

6. i. e., says Ges., under *ols*, citing this v., moves itself briskly.

7. Ges., under *hside*—the stork, says: "properly, the pious *bird*, so called from its love towards its young, of which the ancients made much mention, citing Pliny; as, on the contrary, says he, the Arabs call the female ostrich impious bird on account of her neglect of her young, citing this v. and the following. He says: "*hside* in this v. is not to be taken as the name of the stork, but as the feminine adjective *pious*, yet with an allusion to the stork." He renders, "The wing of the ostrich exults, but *is her* wing and feather *also* pious?" i. e., says he, but she is not *like the stork*, pious or affectionate towards her young, but she treats them cruelly, verses 14—16.

8. So Ges., under *hmm*, citing this v. : Am. Bib. Un....Nay, she abandons her eggs to the earth, and warms them in the dust.

9. i. e., crush, says Ges., under *zur*, citing this v.

16 She treats harshly¹ young of her as if not to her;²
in vain labor of her without fear—(or, caution:)

17 For God has made it³ to forget wisdom, and not
has he apportioned to her of understanding:

18 When she lashes up herself lofty she will laugh at
horse and at rider of him:

19 Whether hast thou given to horse strength; whether hast thou clothed neck of him with trembling:⁴

20 Whether makest thou him to leap like locust;⁵ majesty of snorting⁶ of him, terror:

21 They dig⁷ in valley, and rejoice in strength; he goeth forth to meet arms:⁸

22 He laughs at fear, and not is confounded, and not turneth he from face of sword:

23 Upon him may rattle quiver, flaming spear and javelin:

24 In tumult⁹ and raging¹⁰ he swallows¹¹ ground, and not will stand still when sound of trumpet:¹²

---

1. So Ges. under *qshh*, citing this v.
2. i. e., as if not hers; "as if they were not hers," says Ges., under *l*, citing this v.
3. So Ges., under *nshe*, citing this v.
4. i. e., says Ges., under *rome*, citing this v., with trembling, quivering mane. He says, trembling is poetical for the neck of a horse; Douay... or clothe his neck with neighing: Am. Bib. Un....dost thou clothe his neck with terror?
5. So Ges. under *rosh*, citing this v.: Am. Bib. Un....locust.
6. The Heb. word is *nhr*, for which Ges. gives both snorting and neighing, citing this v. and Jerem 8:16: The Douay is....the glory of his nostrils is terror: Am. Bib. Un....his proud snorting is terrible: The Ital. is....his magnificent neigh is frightful.
7. So Ges., under *hphr*, citing this v. Am. Bib. Un....They paw in the valley.
8. Ital....to meet arms.
9. Of battle, says Ges., under *rosh*, citing this v.
10. So Ges., under *rgz*—raging,—e.g. of a horse, says he, citing Is. 39:24.
11. Poetically applied to a horse, as it were swallowing the ground in his rapid course, says Ges., under *gma*, citing this v.; he gives, "he swallows the ground," equivalent says he, to, he runs away with it. He says the same metaphor is of frequent use in Arabic in the verb to swallow up.
12. Ges., under *amn*, citing this v., gives, "does not stand still when

25 As often as trumpet, he says Aha; and from far he smells battle, tumult of leaders, and warlike cry:

26 Whether from insight of thee mounts upward hawk, spreads out wings of him to southern quarter:[1]

27 Whether at mouth[2] of thee flies on high eagle, and that high nest of him:

28 Of rock he dwells, and lodges on tooth of rock[3] and peak:[4]

29 From there he searches out food, to far off eyes of him look:

30 And young of him, they suck in eagerly[5] blood; and wheresoever slain, there he:

CHAPTER XL.

1 And spoke Jehovah with Job and said:

2 Whether *who* contendeth with Almighty should be reprover; reprover of God, let him answer it:

3 And answered Job Jehovah and said:

4 Lo, I am made light of (or am accounted despicable,)[6] what can I answer thee: hand of me put I to mouth:

---

the sound of trumpet is heard: Am. Bib. Un....With trembling and rage he swallows the ground; he believes not that it is the trumpet's voice: The Ital. is....and not can he believe that *it is* the sound of the trumpet.

1. Poetical for the south wind, says Ges., under *timn:* Am. Bib Un... toward the south.

2. The Heb. word is *phi*, mouth, equivalent to *ruh*—breath, spirit, for mouth can't speak without breath: Am. Bib. Un...."at thy command."

3. i. e., says Ges., a sharp rock, from the resemblance to a tooth, citing this v., under *shn*—tooth.

4. " Of mountain," says Ges., under *mtsure*, citing this v.: The Am. Bib. Un. of the v. is: The rock he inhabits; and abides on the tooth of the rock and the stronghold.

5. So Ges., under *olo*, citing this v.

6. So Ges. under *gle:* Ital....Behold I am undervalued, or, vilified: E. V....Behold, I am vile: Am. Bib. Un....the same. (Wholly opposed to Job's language all through the book.)

5 One¹ have spoken I, and not will I reply, and two *times*, and not will I add:

6 And answered Jehovah Job out of storm and said:

7 Gird now like *a* man loins of thee; I will inquire of thee, and thou mayst cause me to know:

8 Whether even wilt thou bring to nothing right² of me; wilt thou declare unrighteous me in order that thou mayest be righteous:

9 And whether arm like God to thee, and in voice like him canst thou thunder:

10 Adorn thyself, I pray thee, of majesty and magnificence; and of splendour and honour clothe thyself:

11 Pour out outpourings of nostril of thee, and behold every arrogant and make low him:

12 Look on every lifted up and bring low him, and trample³ wicked downwards of them:

13 Hide⁴ them in dust together; faces⁵ of them shut up in darkness:

[See note at the end of the chapter.]

14 Then indeed I will celebrate⁶ thee, that can cause deliverance to thee, right hand of thee:

---

1. One, ellipsis, says Ges., one *time*, once.

2. The Heb. is *mshphth i*, for which Ges. under *phrr*, citing this v., gives, "right of me:" Douay....my judgment: E. V....my judgment: Am. Bib. Un....wilt thou annul my right.

3. So Ges., under *edk*, and *tht*, citing this v.

4. "Specially under the earth, bury," says Ges., under *thmn*, citing Exod. 2:12, etc.

5. Face is often used in Scripture, by synecdoche, for the whole person, as is *nphsh*—breath, and *bshr*—flesh: Ges., under *hbsh*, citing this v., renders, "shut up their faces in darkness." The Douay of the v. is: Hide them in the dust together, and plunge their faces into the pit: Am. Bib. Un....Hide them in the dust together; bind up their faces in darkness. [Darkness is used in Scripture for the grave.]

6. Am. Bib. Un....Then I too will praise thee, that thy right hand can save thee.

15 Behold, I pray thee, hippopotamus,[1] which have created I equally with thee; grass like cattle he eats:

16 Behold, I pray thee, strength of him in loins of him, and power of him in firm parts[2] of belly of him:

17 He bends tail of him like *a* cedar; nerves of privy parts of him are woven together:[3]

18 Bones of him tubes of brass; bones of him like hammered bar of iron:

19 He chief of ways of God; who made him can draw near sword of him: Ital....*only* he who made him can.

20 *Behold*, that *the* produce of mountains is borne for him; and all beasts of field sport there:

21 Under shades he lies down; in covert of cane and marsh:

22 Cover him shady trees with shadow of them; cover him willows of stream:

23 If be proud[4] river, not will he make haste; and he trusteth that might break forth Jordan at mouth of him:

24 With eyes of him he receives it;[6] upon snares he bores nose:

---

1. The Heb. is *bemut*—plural of *beme*—beast, "used here in the plural of majesty, great beast, hippopotamus," says Ges., under *beme*, citing this v.: The Douay gives *behemoth*, (the way it writes the Heb. *bemut:*) Ital....elephant: E.V....behemoth: Am. Bib. Un....river-ox: Noyes ....river-horse.

2. i. e., says Ges., the nerves, ligaments, muscles, citing this v., under *shrir:* Douay....in the navel of his belly: Ital....the same: E. V.... the same: Am. Bib. Un....in the sinews of his belly.

3. Douay....the sinews of his testicles are wrapped together: Ital. and E. V....the same: Am. Bib Un....the sinews of his thighs are knit together.

4. Metaphor., of a river overflowing its banks, says Ges., under *oshq*, citing this v.

5. Ges., under *bthn*, citing this v. renders, "he fears nothing, although Jordan should break forth at his mouth."

6. i. e., says Ges., under *lqh*, he perceives: E. V....He taketh it with his eyes: his nose pierceth through snares: Am. Bib. Un....Before his

eyes do they take him, pierce through the nose with snares : Noyes....
Can one take him before his eyes, or pierce his nose with a ring.

NOTE TO V. 13.

I give here what should have been added to note 5, (to Job 17 : 15, 16,) page 71. The Douay, v. 15, is: Where is now then my expectation, and who considereth my patience? v. 16, All that I have shall go down into the deepest pit: [This is another place where the Douay fails to give *hell* for *shaul*, the Heb. word used here:] thinkest thou that there at least I shall have rest? The Ital. is: v. 15, And where is now my hope? Yes, my hope, who can see it? [The Heb. is *e*—it, in v. 15, and *e*—it, in v. 16.] The Ital. v. 16, is: (*My hopes*, inserted) *scenderanno*—[plural ; the Heb. verb is in the singular]—shall go down into the bottom of the sepulchre ; since, or because, the rest (*of all*, inserted) equally *is* in the dust : [The Douay and the Italian Romish versions evade this scripture: correctly rendered it is conclusive against the dogma of the Papacy—" the immortal soul." What ! Job's hope to go down with him into the grave ! How could the Douay and the Ital. say so, when the Papacy teaches that his hope was immediately realized at death ?] The E. V. is, v. 15, And where is now my hope ? as for my hope, who shall see it ? v. 16, They shall go down to the bars of the pit, when *our* rest *is* in the dust. [The word *They*, in v. 16, renders the E. V. unintelligible : substituting the true word, *It* for *They*, the E. V. would be better than the " Amer. Bib. Union" of the verse. The Am. Bib. Un. is, v. 15, And where then is my hope? yea, my hope, who shall see it; v. 16, It will go down to the bars of the under-world, so soon as there is rest in the dust. Noyes renders thus : v. 15, Where then are my hopes? yea, my hopes, who shall see them ? v. 16, They must go down to the bars of the under-world: Yea, we shall descend together into the dust. [Noyes took *tqut* to be the plural of *tque*, a feminine noun, and so took *tquti* to be, hopes of me, which he renders " my hopes ; " and so gives *them* in v. 15, and *They* and we in v. 16, whereas the Heb. is in the singular all through both verses. Noyes failed to observe that, in the Hebrew, feminine nouns ending in *e* change *e* into *t* before *i*—of me, and so, instead of *tquei*, the Heb. is written *tquti* —hope of me—for ease of pronunciation, or euphony. Professor Chs. Wilson, page 109 of his Heb. Grammar, gives the rule : " Feminine nouns ending in *e* change *e* into *t* before the affixes." The affix here is *i* —of me. The Heb. word in v. 16 is *shaul*—the grave. Professor Wilson, page 229 of his Heb. grammar, writes it *shaul*, and gives *id shaul*—hand of grave, and renders *id shaul*, " the hand of the grave—the power of the grave."

We give here two passages where these two words *id shaul* occur in the Hebrew. Ps. 49 : 16, E. V. v. 15, Heb. But *aleim*—God—will set free *nphshi*—breath 'of me (poetical 'for me) from *id shaul*—hand of grave. The Douay is Ps. 48 : 16, and is : But God will redeem my soul from the hand of hell : Ital....my *anima* from the sepulchre : E. V....my soul from the power of the grave. Hosea 13 : 14 : Heb....From *id shaul*—hand of grave—I will set free them ; from death I will redeem them. I will be death of thee, death (so Ges., under *dbr*, citing this v. ;) 1 will be cutting off of thee, *shaul*—grave ; repentance is hid from eyes of me. (For " cutting off," in the v. see Ges., under *qthb*.) The Douay of this v. is....I will redeem thee out of the hand of death, (for the Heb. *shaul*—grave,) I will redeem thee from death ; O death, I will be thy death, O hell, (for the Heb. *shaul*) I will be thy bite: comfort is hidden from my eyes. For *shaul* twice in the v., the Ital. gives *sepolcro*—sepulchre —and the E. V. gives, grave twice.

CHAPTER XLI.

1 Canst thou draw out leviathan¹ with hook, and with cord canst thou sink down tongue of him:²

2 Canst thou put a rope of rushes in nose of him, and for ring canst thou bore jaw bone of him:³

3 Whether will he multiply to thee prayers: whether will he speak to thee soft words:⁴

4 Whether will he cut covenant with thee: canst thou take him for servant for ever:⁵

5 Whether wilt thou sport with him as *with* small birds; and wilt thou bind him for girls of thee:⁶

6 Do the companions⁷ lay snares for him ; do they divide him among the merchants:⁸

---

1. Crocodile, says Ges., under *luitn*.
2. i. e., says Ges., under *shqo*, citing this v., canst thou tame him by putting a cord or bridle in his mouth ?
3. So Ges., under *huh*—a ring, and *lhi*—jaw bone, citing this v. Am. Bib. Un....or bore through his jaw with a hook ?
4. So Ges., under *rk*, citing this v.
5. i. e., says Ges., " as long as he lives," poetically used of a beast, says he, citing this v. under *oulm*.
6. So Ges., under *qshr*.
7. i. e., says Ges., the company of fishermen.
8. Ges. says, this is a much discussed passage : Am. Bib Un....Will partners dig a pit for him, divide him among the merchants ?

7 Whether wilt thou fill with goads hide of him, and with tinkling *instruments* [1] head of him.

8 Put thou upon him hand of thee, think thou on fortune of war; not shalt thou do more:[2]

9 (Heb. 41 : 1.) Lo, hope of him is proved deceitful;[3] whether even not at sight of him *one* is cast down:

10 Not *a* bold[4] so that to anger him; and who he to face can stand firm:[5]

11 Who has come before[6] me, that I should requite: under all these heavens to me it:

12 As to him[7] I will keep silence of members[8] of him, and of report of mighty deeds,[9] and beauty of structure of him:[10]

13 Who has uncovered face of garment of him; into doubling of jaws of him[11] who will come:

---

1. Specially a fish spear, says Ges., citing this v. under *tsltsl:* The Douay is....Wilt thou fill nets with his skin, and the cabins of fishes with his head.

2. So Ges. under *isph*, citing this v. : Ital....thou shalt not remember once the war: Am. Bib. Un....of battle thou shalt think no more.

3. So Ges., under *kzb* citing this v.: Ital....Lo, the hope of *to* catch him is deceitful.

4. So Ges. under *akzr*, citing this v.

5. So Ges., under *itsb*, citing this v. as Job. 41 : 2.

6. So Ges., under *qdm*, citing this v. as Job. 41 : 3. The Ital. word is *prevenuto:* E. V....Who has prevented me, that I should repay *him.* (The same word prevent, for come before, anticipate, is used in 1 Thes. 4 : 15; read verses 15, 16, 17.) The Am. Bib. Un. in Job 41 : 11 is.... Who has first given me, that I should repay?

7. My copy of the Heb. has *la*—not; but Ges., says, in Note 1, under *la*: " By a certain neglect in orthography *la* is sometimes written for *lu*--to him; according to the Masorah, says he, fifteen times, citing the passages, this v. being one of the fifteen.

8. Specially parts of the body, says Ges., citing this v. and Job 18 13:

9. Ges., under *dbr*, citing this v., gives, "I will be silent as to what is said about his strength."

10. So Ges., under *hin*, citing this v. The Ital. of the v. is....I will not conceal the limbs of him, nor that which exists of *his* powers, nor

14 Doors of face of him¹ who has opened; circuits of teeth of him terrible:

15 (Heb. v. 7,) Ornament, strong shields² shut up with seal narrow:³

16 One upon another join they, and air (or wind,)⁴ not can come between them:

17 Man on brother of him (for, one on another) is soldered; they take hold on one another, and not can be put asunder:

18 Sneezings of him are brilliant with light, and eyes of him like eyelids of dawn:⁵

19 Out of mouth of him flames go; sparks of fire go away in haste:⁶

20 (Heb. v. 12,) Out of nostrils of him goeth forth smoke, like pot blown upon⁷ and boiling caldron:⁸

---

the grace of his arrangement: Am. Bib. Un....I will not pass his limbs in silence, and bruited strength, and beauty of his equipment. (It is manifest that *la*—not, is a misprint in this v. for *lu*—*l*—as to, *u*—him; for the account which follows is silent as to the parts of the body, and as to what is reported of his mighty deeds, and beauty of structure.)

11. Ges., under *kphl*, citing this v. renders, "the doubling of his jaws," i. e., says he, his jaw, *that of the crocodile*, armed with a double row of teeth. Am. Bib. Un....his double jaws, who enters in?

1. i. e., the jaws of the crocodile, says Ges., under *dlt*, citing this v.

2. So Ges., under *aphig*, citing this v.

3. So Ges., under *tzr*, citing this v.

4. Heb. *ruh*—breath, air, wind: Douay....*air:* Ital....wind: E. V. ....air: Am. Bib. Un....breath: Noyes....air.

5. Poetical, says Ges., for the rays of the rising sun, citing this v. and Job 3 : 9, under *ophophim*.

6. Poetically used, says Ges., of sparks flying about, citing this v. under *mlth:* Am. Bib. Un....and sparks of fire escape.

7. The Heb. word is *nphuh*, i. e., says Ges. "boiling upon a blown fire:" Neither the Douay, nor the Ital., nor the E. V., nor the Am. Bib. Un., takes any notice of the Heb. word *nphuh* in the v.: It is from the Heb. verb *nphh*—defined to blow, to breathe, an onomatopoietic root, says Ges., (i. e., expressing its meaning by the sounds of it.)

8. So Ges., under *agmn*, citing this v. The Douay in the verse is.... like that of a pot heated and boiling: Ital....like a pot boiling, or a caldron: Am. Bib. Un....like a kettle with kindled reeds.

21 Breath¹ of him live coals blows² and flame from mouth of him goes:

22 In neck of him dwells strength,³ and to face of him dances terror: (The Heb. is, *phni*—face—of him: Am. Bib. Un.....and terror dances before him.)

23 (Heb. v. 15.) Flabby parts of flesh of him cleave; they are pressed upon him, not shake they:

24 Heart of him hard like stone, yea, hard like millstone⁴ lower:

25 At lifting himself up, fear powerful *ones*;⁵ from terrors⁶ they miss the way:⁷

26 If move to him sword, without ability, spear, dart, because of coat of mail

27 He takes for straw, iron, and for wood rotten, brass:

28 Not can put him to flight son of bow,⁸ to chaff are turned, as to him, stones of sling:

---

1. Heb. *nphsh*—breath: Douay....his breath kindleth coals: Ital.... his *alito*—breath: E. V....His breath: Am. Bib. Un....His breath: Noyes....His breath.

2. Ges., under *leth*, gives to "blow, used of the breath," citing this v.: In this v. we have the concurrent testimony of the Douay, the Ital., the E. V., Noyes, and the Am. Bib. Un., that the Heb. *nphsh* (for which the Douay and the E. V. so often give *soul*,) means breath.

3. As if it had its seat there, says Ges.

4. The Heb. has in the verse *phlh*, defined a millstone: The Ital. puts its word for millstone in italics, i. e., as not being in the Hebrew, but supplied: and the E. V. puts the word millstone in italics, as not being in the Heb.: The Douay gives....and as firm as a smith's anvil.

5. i. e., leaders, says Ges., under *aul*.

6. So Ges. under *shbr*, citing this v.

7. Used, says Ges., under *htha*, citing this v., of a man terrified and confounded, and thus in a precipitate flight mistaking the way: The Douay is v. 16, and is....When he shall raise him up, the angels shall fear, and being affrighted shall purify themselves: The Ital. is v. 25, and is....The more strong and brave have fear of him when he raises himself up, *and* purify themselves of their sins for the great *fracasso*—crash—ruin: See E. V.: Am. Bib. Un., v. 25....At his rising up the mighty are afraid; they lose themselves for terror.

8. Poetical for arrow.

29 As straw are accounted club, and he laughs at crashing ¹ of javelin:

30 Lower parts of him sharpnesses of potsherd, he spreads out *a* sharpened upon *the* mud:²

31 He makes bubble up like pot, depths; great river he makes like pot of ointment:

32 Behind him he causes to shine footpath,³ is taken *the* deep for hoary:

33 Not there is upon earth⁴ any thing made like him, which is made without fear:

34 Every thing lofty he views, himself king over all sons of pride:⁵

CHAPTER XLII.

1 And answered Job Jehovah and said:

---

1. Ges., under *rosh*, gives, "noise and crashing which takes place from concussion." Am. Bib. Un....and he laughs at the shaking of the spear.

2. Douay....the beams of the sun shall be under him, and he shall strew gold under him like mire: Ital....*He has* under himself tops pricking, he spreads under himself sharpnesses upon marsh: Am. Bib. Un....Sharp points are under him; he spreads a threshing sledge over the mire. Ges., under *hruts*, citing this v. says: "a sharpened," hence, says he, as a poetical epithet for a threshing wain, an agricultural instrument for rubbing out corn; more fully, says he, a sharpened threshing instrument, citing Isai. 41:15; and hence used without the substantive in the same sense, citing this v. and Isai. 29:27. [The verse in the Heb. is a striking description of the track of the crocodile in the mud.]

3. Heb. *ntib*—footpath—by-way, a poetic word, says Ges., citing this v. and Job 18:10: 27; 7.

4. The Heb. word used here is *ophr*—dust; Ges. gives also for *ol ophr*— "in the earth," "in the world." See E. V.: Am. Bib. Un....On earth there is none that rules him.

5. So Ges., under *shhts*, citing this v. and Job 28:8; i. e., says he, the larger ravenous beasts, as the lion; so called, says he, from the pride of walking.

2 I know that all things thou canst do, and not can be withheld from thee counsel:

3 Who this, hiding counsel without knowledge : so then have uttered I and not have understood ; things wonderful above me and not I know:

4 Hear, I pray thee, and I will speak ; I will ask of of thee, and do thou cause me to know:

5 As to hearing of ear have heard I thee,[1] but now eye of me seeth thee:

6 Therefore I reject[2] and repent me in dust and ashes:

7 And it was after had spoken Jehovah these words to Job, that said Jehovah to Aliphz that Timni, is kindled nostril of me against thee and against *the* two friends of thee, because not have ye spoken as to me that which is fit, like servant of me Job:

8 And now take for yourselves seven young bullocks and seven rams, and go to servant of me Job, and cause them to be offered up burnt offering for yourselves, and Job servant of me will entreat for you ; for lo, face of him[3] I will accept, that not I do with you the folly ;[4] for ye have not spoken as to me that which is fit, like servant of me Job:

9 And went Eliphaz....and Bildad....and Zophar... and did as had spoken to them Jehovah, and accepted Jehovah face of Job:[5]

---

1. Douay....I have heard thee : Ital....have heard *speak* of thee ; Am. Bib. Un....have heard of thee.

2. So Ges., under *mas*, citing this v. : Noyes....Wherefore I abhor myself : Am. Bib. Un....Therefore do I abhor it.

3. Am. Bib. Un....him will I accept.

4. Ges., under *nble*, citing this v., gives "lest I inflict on you the punishment of your folly : " Am. Bib. Un....that I visit not the folly upon you.

5. Am. Bib. Un....accepted Job.

10 And Jehovah turned about captivity of Job on that entreating of him for friends of him; and added Jehovah all which to Job to twofold:

11 And came to him all brothers and all sisters of him, and all knowing him before; and they ate food with him in house of him, and they comforted and pitied him over all that evil which caused to come Jehovah upon him. And they gave to him man[1] *ghsithe*,[2] and man ring of gold[3] one:

12 And Jehovah blessed end of Job more than beginning of him, and there was to him[4] 14,000 small cattle, and 6,000 camels, and *a* thousand pair of oxen, and *a* thousand she asses:

13 And there was to him seven sons and three daughters:

14 And he called name which of first *imime* (anglicised, Jemima,) and name which of second *qtsioe*, (Kezia,) and name which of third *qrn hephuk*, (Keren-happuch:)

15 And not were found women beautiful as daughters of Job in all that land; and gave to them father of them possession among brothers of them:

---

1. Heb. *aish*—man for each: Noyes....every one: Am. Bib Un.... each.

2. Defined by Ges., a certain weight of gold and silver, citing this v. and Gen. 23 : 19 ; Josh. 24 : 32. He says, it may be supposed to contain about four shekels, from the passages, Gen. 33 : 19 ; 23 : 16, compared together. He says, the ancient interpreters almost all understand *a lamb* but for this signification there is no support either in the etymology or in the cognate languages. The Douay gives....And every man gave him one ewe: Ital....a piece of money ; E. V....the same : Am. Bib. Un... a *kesita*, (the way it anglicises the Heb. word.)

3. Not defined in this and other passages, says Ges., whether earring or other kind of ring: Douay....and one earring of gold: Ital....and one necklace of gold : E.V., and every one an earring of gold : Am. Bib. Un....and each a ring of gold.

4. i. e., he had.

16 And lived Job after this, 140 years, and saw sons of him and sons of sons of him four generations:

17 And died Job grown old and satisfied of days.

INDEX.

ABADDON.—Heb. *abdun*, Job 28 : 22, and note 1, p. 117, and note at the end of Chap. 28, and Ps. 88 : 12, E. V. v. 11, in Index under Darkness.

ADVERSARY.—Job 6 : 23, and note 9, p. 33.

AIR.—Job 4 : 15, and notes 3 and 4, p. 25.

ALEIM.—Plural of *ale* and of *al*, rendered in the singular, God: Gesenius says it is the plural of majesty.

    It is used in Job 1 : 5, 6, 8, 9, etc., and in Gen. 1 : 1, etc. And in Gen. 1 : 26 the verb is in the plural, " we will make," agreeing with *aleim*, plural, used in that verse.

ANGEL : Heb. *mlak*, messenger, Job 1 : 14, and note 1, p. 11; Job 4 : 18, and note 1, p. 26; 33 : 23, and note 1, page 136; and note at the end of Chap. 33, p. 136, 7, 8, 9 ; and in a sermon of Rev. Dr. Mendes, at the 44th Street New York Synagogue, p. 26, 27, in note 1.

APOLLYON : meaning of; note at the end of Chap. 28, p. 117.

APOSTASY : Job 6 : 11, and note 2, p. 32 : 16 : 11, and note 1, p. 68.

    And Pope Leo tenth's decree, p. 47, note, and what Luther and Tyndale said of it, p. 48. And Job 21 : 33, and note 3, p. 99; and foot of p. 91 ; and preface, p. 6, 7.

ARTICLE : For our articles, *a* and *the*, see p. 144, the last two paragraphs, and 145, and the last two paragraphs of p. 7 of preface ; and note 4, p. 36. Another rule for rendering Greek into English is, that where the Greek article (i. e. *the*, the only article it has, if, indeed, it be not the demonstrative pronoun), is put before a noun used in an abstract sense, it is not to be rendered in English. It is the same with the Italian and with the French definite article. The effect of improperly omitting our article *a*, and improperly using our article *the*, is often manifest. An instance is found in the Rheims Roman Catholic version of the New Testament in John 20 : 22, where it has " Receive ye the Holy Ghost." The Greek there is, receive *pneuma agion*, (the noun before the adjective, as is usual in the Greek and in the Hebrew): *pneuma* is defined in Liddell and Scott, wind, air, the air we breathe, breath, and *agion* is the neuter of the adjective *agios*, defined holy, pious, pure: so that the Greek is, receive a breath holy, pious, pure; the E. V. follows the Rheims of the verse. The v. proves that *pneuma* means breath. What could be breathed on them but breath.

ATMOSPHERE: Earth's atmosphere is part of the heavens, Job 12: 7, and note 3, p. 53; 35:11, and note 3, p. 141; Gen. 6:7, and Jer. 7:33, in each of which the Heb. is, " winged of these heavens." The Douay has, " the fowls of the air," in each. See E. V. And in Matt. 8:20, the Greek is, " the birds of the heaven." Rheims, " the birds of the air." E. V. the same.

BARNES, Rev. Albert, D. D., what he does by misrendering 2 Tim. 1:10, p. 87, 88.

" BASIS OF REVISION :" Rule prescribed by the American Bible Union for the revision of the Scriptures, p. 92, last clause, and 93. The object of the Union ought to have been to remove the scandal of sects and give unity to the church by resorting to the originals as the common standard and the final appeal.

BLOOD: Heb. *nphsh*, breath, in the blood, Lev. 17:11.

BREATH: There are two Heb. words signifying breath, namely, *nphsh* and *ruh*.

First, *nphsh*: How it should be sounded, see note 4, p. 44. *nphsh* is the word for which the Douay Roman Catholic English version and our authorized version (designated by the letters E. V.) often give the word *soul*.

The Heb. *nphsh* occurs in many passages. The following will show the meaning of the word: The reader will read the notes to them; Job 2:4, 6, p. 13; 6:7, p. 31; 6:11, p. 32; 11:20, p. 51. *nphsh* is used for every breathing thing in 12:10 and note, p. 53; 13:14, p. 57; 14:22, p. 63; 16:4, p. 67; 18:4, p. 72; 23:13, p. 104; 24:12, p. 106; 27:8, p. 112; 30:16, p. 124; 30: 25, p. 126; 31:30, p. 129; 31:39, p. 130; 32:2, p. 132; 33:20, 22, p. 135; see 33:24 and note 2, p. 136; 33:28, p. 136; 33:30, p. 136:36:14, p. 142; 41:21, p. 161. Gesenius defines *nphsh*, " breath, breath of life," hence, says he, " life, vital principle," p. 91; and see there what Luther and Anthon give for *nphsh*, Latin *anima*. For 1 Thess. 5:23. and Hebrews 4:12, see p. 91.

Second: Breath, Hebrew *ruh*, (generally sounded *ruach*). This Hebrew word *ruh* is the word for which the Roman Catholic English version, and our E. V., often give the word *spirit*. It occurs in many passages. In Job 1:19, p. 11; 9:18, p. 41; 10:12, p. 45; 12:10 and note 6, p. 53; 15:13. p. 64; 15:30, p. 66; 16:3, p. 67; 17:1, p. 69; 19:17, p. 75; 20:3, p. 93; 21:4, p. 96; 26:13, p. 111; 27:3, and note 10, p. 111; 27:22, p. 114; 30:15, p. 124; 30:22, p. 125; 32:8, and note 4, p. 132; 32:18, and note 6, p. 132; 33.4, and note 1, p. 135; 34:14, and note 2, p. 139; 37:21, p. 146. And see Ezek. 37:5, 6, 8, 9, 10, 14, and Zech. 6:5, p. 137, 138, in each of which the Heb. is *ruh*.

Gesenius defines the verb *ruh*, "to breathe, to blow," and he defines the noun *ruh*, "spirit, breath," (as synonyms, things equal to the same thing are equal to each other). "Breath of the mouth," citing Ps. 33:6, spoken, says he, of the creative word of God. He cites Isa. 11:4; Job 7:7; Ps. 78:39. He says it is often used of the vital spirit, citing Job 17:1; 19:17; Ps. 135:17; more fully says he, *ruh hiim*, (breath of lives), citing Gen. 6:17; 7:15,22. He also gives "to return *ruh*, to respire," citing Job 9:18. He further says, " *ruh* is equivalent to *nphsh*, Greek *psuche*, Latin *anima*, breath of life, the vital principle, which shows itself in the breathing of the mouth and nostrils, whether of men or of beasts," citing Eccl. 3:21; 8:8; 12:7. Hence, says he, there is said *hii ruhi*, (literally life of breath of me), which he renders, "the life of my spirit," i. e., says he, my life, citing Isa. 38:16; Gen. 45:27; Judges 15:19; and 1 Sam. 30:12; i. e., says he, I revive: (in each of which the Heb. word is *ruh*). He further gives, "there is no spirit, (Heb. *ruh*,) in it," said, says he, of dead and inanimate things, citing Ezek. 37:8; Habak. 2:19. He then says, "sometimes the human spirit is called *ruh* (breath) of God, as being breathed into man by God and returning to him," citing Job 27:3; Gen. 2:7; Eccles. 12:7; Ps. 104:29; compare, says he, Numb. 16:22: the Heb. there is, " God of *ruhut*, (plural of *ruh*), breaths—spirits, in every flesh." Douay, the God of the spirits of all flesh; see E. V. He further defines *ruh*, " breath of the nostrils," citing Job 4:9; Ps. 18:16, E. V. v. 15: " breath of air, air in motion," citing Job 41:8: Jer. 2:24; 10:14; 14:6; " *ruh* of day, breeze of *the* day, for the evening breeze," citing Gen. 3:8. He further defines *ruh*, wind, citing Gen. 8:1; Isa. 7:2; 41:16; " a storm," citing Job 1:19; 30:15; Isa. 27:8; 32:2. He says, " the wind is called *ruh aleim*, (breath of God) the blast of God," citing 1 Kings 18:12; 2 Kings 2:16; Isa. 40:7; 59:19; Ezek. 3:14. See further as to *ruh* under the word *spirit*. See Job 15:30, and note 3, p. 66, an absurd perversion of the Heb., *ruh phiu*, breath of mouth of him.

I have given a very full index in reference to the Heb. word *ruh*, because the word *spirit*, often given for it, is the word now relied on by some for the tenet—inherent immortality; the word *soul* being now given up as not teaching that tenet, as is shown under the word Soul.

In Job 11:20, note 3, p. 51, the Heb. is *mphh nphsh*, breathing out the breath; and in Gen. 35:18, the Heb. is, in going out *nphsh*, breath, of her: the Greek uses *psuche* for *nphsh* in those verses: the E. V. gives *ghost* in those verses. Liddell and Scott's Gr. Lex. under *aphiemi*, gives *aphienai psuchen*, and *aphienai pneuma*, and gives for each, to give up the ghost, citing

Thucydides and other ancient writers. And the Latin gives *supremum spiritum efflare*, the last spirit, i. e., breath, to breathe out, "to give up the ghost" adds Anthon in his Latin and English Dictionary.

BREATHE AFTER: Is used in the Heb. for desire, Job 19:19, p. 75; 36:20, p. 143; 89:9, p. 151. And we have the word *aspire* from the Latin preposition *ad*, for, and the Latin verb *spiro*, to breathe, whence the Latin noun *spiritus*—breath. And we have the words conspire, to breathe together, i. e., to agree; expire, (the Latin verb is exspiro,) to out breathe; inspire; respire; all formed from a Latin particle and the Latin verb spiro, to breathe, whence *spiritus*, breath, which we anglicize by striking off the Latin termination *us*, and writing spirit.

BREATHE OUT: The Heb. verb is *ghuo*, defined, to breathe out, wholly out: its sounds express the thing signified, see Job, p. 18, 19, under the word *ghost*. It is used in reference to every living creature, in Gen. 6:17; and in reference to man in Gen. 25:17; 35:29. It is used in reference to every flesh (i. e., of course, every breathing, and thereby living flesh), in Job 34:15, and in Ps. 104:29. This Heb. verb *ghuo* occurs eight times in Job, namely, Job 3:11; 10:18; 13:19; 14:10; 27:5; 29:18; 34:15; 36:12; and in Job 11:20, and note 3, p. 51, the same thing is expressed by the two appropriate Heb. words *mphh nphsh*—breathing out the breath. See what the E. V. is in the eight verses.

BRIMSTONE: Job 18:15, p. 73.

CALVINISM: In Acts 13:48, the Rheims Roman Catholic version is.... and as many as were ordained to life everlasting believed. The Greek, as does the Hebrew, usually puts the verb before the nominative to it. The Greek in the v. is *episteusan hosoi*, believed as many as, (i. e., as many as believed,) were put in order for *a* life eternal: *episteusan* is in the third person plural and *hosoi* is the nominative plural, and the nominative to *episteusan*: but the Rheims puts the word *believed* last in the sentence, and makes all the rest of the sentence the nominative to it; and the E. V. does the same. The Greek of the sentence is in harmony with every other passage in Scripture concerning faith, whereas the Rheims and E. V. rendering is opposed to every other such passage. We give an example or two: In John 12:46 we have Greek—in order that every who believing in me, in that darkness not may stay; Rheims—that whosoever believeth in me may not remain in darkness: see E. V. And in Prov. 21:16 the Heb. is, man going astray from way of understanding, in congregation of dead will be left, see p. 109, in note; the E. V. is, "Shall remain in the congregation of the dead." And see Job 21:32, and notes 1 and 2, p. 99: E. V.—shall remain in the tomb.

COMMENTARIES: See what Prof. Chas. Wilson says of them, p. 23, top part.
CONSUME: Heb. *abd*, defined, to eat up, devour, consume; Job 1:16, p. 11; 20:26, p. 95; 31:12, p. 127.
COCYTUS: One of the rivers of Hell, Job 21:33, and note 3, p. 99.
COMPLETION: Used for old age, Job 5:26, p. 30. For another sense of the word see Job 30:2, p. 122.
CORRECTIONS: Of the Douay and E. V. of Job 21:19, p. 97; of the E. V. of Ps. 49:11, p. 81: of the E. V. of Job 7:16, note 3, p. 36; of the Rheims and E. V. of Acts 13:48, see Calvinism; of the Douay and E. V. of Job 21:30, p. 98; of the Rheims and E. V. of 1 Cor. 15:29: the Greek there is, *ei olos nekroi ouk egeirontai*, if at all,—wholly, dead not are raised, (i. e., if none of the dead are raised); the Rheims is, "if the dead rise not again at all;" see E. V.

And of 1 Corinth. 15:32; the Greek there is, *ei nekroi ouk egeirontai*,—if dead not are raised; Rheims, "if the dead rise not again;" see E. V.

And in 1 Corinth. 15:22, the Greek is, *osper*—just as, in the or that, Adam all, (i. e., all who are in Adam) die, so also in the, or that, Christ all, (i. e., all who are in that Christ) shall be brought to life, or made alive. And that is the way in which that v. is read in the Theological Seminary at Princeton, as I learned after that verse was so rendered in the "Theology of the Bible."

And see 2 Tim, 1:10, correctly rendered, p. 87, 88, in note.
And see Isa. 53:9, correctly rendered, under Death.
COVERDALE: Who he was, and what he did, p. 92.
CUT OFF: Heb. *abd*, Job 4:7, p. 24; 6:9, p. 32; a metaphor, says Ges., under *btso*, taken from a weaver who cuts off the finished web from the thrum, citing this v. and Isa. 38:12. In Job 14:7, p. 60, the Heb. verb is *krt*, to cut off. In Job 8:14, p. 88, the Heb. is, is cut off hope of him. See note to the E. V. words "cut off" in Job 36:20, and note 8, p. 143, and in the note at the end of Chap. 36, p. 143, 144, 145.
DARKNESS: Used of the grave: Job 10:21, p. 46; 15:22, p. 65; 17:13, p. 71; 40:13, p. 155. See E. V. 1 Sam. 2:9; Psal. 31:17. In John 12:46 we have, Greek,—in order that every who believing in me, in that darkness not may stay; Rheims,—believing in me may not remain in darkness. See E. V. In Ps. 88:11 the Heb. is, whether can be recounted in grave kindness of thee; faithfulness of thee in *abdun*—place of destruction; v. 12, can wonders of thee be known in darkness, and rectitude of thee in land of forgetfulness. The Douay gives "destruction," in v. 11, and the E. V. the same; where the Heb. is *abdun*, place of destruc-

tion; nearly synonymous with *shaul* (the grave,) says Ges., citing Job 26:6; 28:22; Prov. 15:11; in each of which the Heb. word is *abdun*. And in 1 Sam. 2:9, the Heb. is..the wicked in darkness shall be silent; and in Ps. 31:17,..shall be silent in *shaul*. See E. V. of both.

DEATH: Job 3:13, p. 16; 3:16, p. 16; 5:20, p. 29; 7:15, p. 36; 7:21, p. 37; 10:8, p. 45; 10:9, p. 45; 16:16, p. 69; 16:22, p. 69. [In this last verse, "not may I," i. e., I may not. is more suitable to the plain teachings of the Book, than "not shall I," return.] The future is often used in the Hebrew for the subjunctive, because the Hebrew has no subjunctive mood. Job 24:19 to 25, and notes 8, 9, 10, 11, p. 106, 107. In Job 24:24 the Heb. is..and not there is of them; Douay, "and shall not stand;" Ital. "not *are* more;" E. V.,.."but are gone." In Obadiah, v. 16, the Heb. is, and shall be they as if not existed they; the Douay there is..and they shall be as though they were not; E. V..and they shall be as though they had not been. And see Job 27:15, and note 3, p. 113. In Job 27:19, and notes 5 and 6, the Heb. is, rich shall lie down, and not shall be gathered; eyes of him he opens, and not there is of him. Ges., under *ophir*, rich, citing this v. and others, says, "inasmuch as riches are the foundation of pride, and pride is used in Hebrew as equivalent to impiety." See the verse and notes, p. 113.

In Isa. 53:9 the Heb. is, and was given with wicked grave, or, burial of him, and with rich in death of him, *ol*—although not wrong did he, and not deception in mouth of him; for *although* the Douay gives because; the E. V. too has because; the Ital. is, without that. For *ol* Ges. gives "although," citing Job 16:17; Isa. 53:9.

DEATH, PERSONIFIED: Job 28:22, p. 117. The wages, pay, of sin, death; but the gift of God a life eternal through Jesus Christ, Romans 6:23. See that verse again, under Punishment.

DEAD: Those dead, Job 26:5, and note 3, p. 108, 109, 110. Read Job 14:22 and note 6, p. 63, and read the E. V. of it; and what Noyes says of it, p. 86, in note. His remark there in reference to Job 14:22, has a much stronger application to Job 27:19, given above.

DEAD: Heb. *rphaim*, Job 26:5, and note 3, p. 108, 109, 110. In Prov. 21:16 the Heb. is, Man that wandereth out of way of understanding, in congregation *rphaim*—of dead—will remain. E. V.. "shall remain in the congregation of the dead," (i. e., in the grave.) See Job 21:32, and note 2, p. 99, and the E. V. of it. And see Isaiah 26:14, and 26:19, p. 109, in note.

DEAD LANGUAGES: How the languages in which the revealed word was written became dead languages, p. 91, 92.

Devil: Job 16 : 11, and note, p. 68. In 1 Maccabees 1 : 38, the Douay is, And this was a place to lie in wait against the sanctuary, and an evil devil in Israel. The E. V. there is, For it was a place to lie in wait against the sanctuary, and an evil adversary to Israel. And see foot note to the Douay, in note 1, p. 68. In 1 Sam. 16 : 13, the Heb. is..and fell *ruh, a* breath,—spirit—of Jehovah upon David. Douay..and the Spirit (capital S) of the Lord came upon David. E. V. the same ; v. 14, Heb., *u*—and, or, but, *ruh, the* breath,—spirit—of Jehovah ceased from with Saul, and suddenly came upon him *ruh roe*—a breath bad (i. e., a sickness, as is shown by v. 23) from Jehovah. Douay, But the Spirit (capital S) of the Lord departed from Saul, and an evil spirit (small s) from the Lord troubled him. E. V. the same. And in v. 15, the Heb. is *ruh aleim roe*—a breath of (i, e., from) God bad. Douay..an evil spirit (small s) from the Lord troubled him. E. V. the same. In v. 23 the Heb. is, And it was, at being *ruh aleim, the* breath of God—upon Saul, that took David that harp and played with hand of him, and *ruh*—breath—to Saul that good to him, and departed from upon him *ruh é roe*—breath which bad. Douay, So whensoever the evil spirit (small s) from the Lord was upon Saul, David took his harp, and played with his hand, and Saul was refreshed, and was better, for the evil spirit (small s) departed from him. The E. V. is..so Saul was refreshed, and was well, and the evil spirit departed from him. So in the New Testament, evil spirits,—devils (i. e., things *of evil,*) are diseases, sicknesses, bad breaths. These verses from Samuel show us where the evil spirits, unclean spirits, devils, of the Rheims and E. V. New Testament, came from. All sick persons have bad breaths; bad breath was the Heb. idiom for disease,—sickness, and a very apt phrase. For devils see p. 118 of the Book.

Destruction, Place of: Job 26 : 6, p. 110; 28 : 22, p. 117. Heb. *abdun*, (written Abaddon) place of destruction, p. 117, 118, 119, in note. Whether not destruction (Heb. *aid*) to wicked, Job 31 : 3, p. 127. Place of destruction (Heb. *abdun*) Job 31 : 12, p. 127. Destruction (Heb. *aid*) of (i. e., from) God, 31 : 23, p. 128. The Douay and E. V. give " destruction " as well for *abdun* as for *aid;* why this confusion ?

Shaul and *abdun* mean the same, Job 26 : 6, and notes 1 and 2, p. 110.

Die: Job 3 : 11, p. 16; 7 : 8, p. 35; 7 : 9, p. 35; 7 : 21, p. 37; 10 : 18, p. 46; 10 :19, p. 46; 10 : 21, p. 46; 11 : 20, p. 51; 12 : 2, p. 52; 13 : 19, p. 58; 13 : 28, p. 59, the Heb. verb there is, *ble*, defined, is brought to nothing; 14 : 10, p. 60; 14 : 14, and notes 3 and 4, p. 61; 20 : 11, p. 94; 21 : 23, 25, 26, p. 98; 23 : 17, p. 104.

DOCTRINE: The Book with its references to later Scriptures condemns Rome's apostasy, (i. e., departure from the faith,) and restores primitive Christianity—the doctrines and faith of the first Christians, for which the pious and learned men who made the first translations of the Bible from the originals suffered death at the hands of the Apostasy. See Apostasy and Martyrs.

ECLIPSES: Job 3:5, p. 15.

ENCHANTERS: Job 3;8, p. 15.

ENTRAILS: Job 20:14, p. 94. And see note to the E. V. words, "the spirit within me," p. 133, 134.

EVIL: Heb. *ouil*, Job 16:11, p. 68, and note.

EXTINGUISHED: Job 23:17, p. 104.

EYELIDS OF DAWN: Job 3:9, p. 16; 41:18, p. 160.

FAITH: ..The just by faith (i. e., they who shall be accounted just) shall live again, p. 62, in note. Whately's language is, "to embrace by faith the offer of salvation through Christ." "Salvation through Christ" is equivalent to the correct rendering of Rom. 6:23, and 2 Tim. 1:10.

FACE: Job 40:13, p. 155.

FIRE: The devouring, consuming, destroying element: Job 20:26, p. 95; 22:20, p. 101, and note at the end of Chap. 22, p. 102, 3. For the Rheims, and E. V. hell fire, see *gehenna*.

FIRE OF *aleim*—God, i. e., lightning, Job 1:16, p. 11; and see lightning.

FLESH: Used by Synecdoche for every breathing flesh; every flesh has a ghost to give up, Job 34:15, and notes 4 and 5, p. 139, 140. Gen. 6:17, Heb. *ighuo*—shall breathe out; Ital..shall die; E. V. the same.

GATHERED: They are gathered, i. e., says Ges., "to their ancestors," i. e., says he, they are dead, Job 24:24, p. 107.

GEHENNA: See under *shaul*.

GHOST: The Heb. verb *ghuo* is, to breathe wholly out. It is used eight times in Job, and in Gen. 6:17; 25:8, 17; 35:29; Jer. 15:9; Lament. 1:19. See note on the word *ghost* at the end of Chap. 3, p. 18 and following; and see Job 10:18, and note 5, p. 46. ghost, soul, spirit, all mean the same, namely, breath, Job 10:12, and note 4, p. 45. The "American Bible Union" in their Job do not use the word *ghost* at all; see p. 52 in note. The Douay Old Testament does not use the word *ghost* at all, p. 46, note 5.

GIANTS: Job 26:5, p. 108, 109.

GRAVE: Heb. *qbr*, Job 3:22, p. 17; 5:26, p. 30. Job 7:9, p. 35, Heb. *shaul*; Douay hell; Italian, sepulchre; "Am. Bible Union" the under world; Job 11:8, Heb. *shaul*, p. 49; 14:13, *shaul*, p. 61; 17:1, Heb. *qbrim* (plural of *qbr*), graves, p. 69. See Job 21:30, and note 12, p. 98, 99; 21:32, and note 1 and 2, p. 99. In Job

17:13, p. 71, the Heb. is *shaul;* 17:16, p. 71, *shaul;* 21:13, p. 97, *shaul;* 24:19, p. 106, Heb. *shaul*. Job 26:6, Heb. *shaul* and *abdun*, p. 110 notes 1 and 2.

BOTTOMLESS PIT: Rheims and E. V., in Rev. 9:1, 2; see note beginning at foot of p. 117. Upon dust shall lie down, i. e., says Ges., in the grave, Job 20:11, and note 3, p. 94. Grave, hell, and the heart of the earth, all mean the same, Matt. 12:40; Ps. 16:10. The Hebrew Ps. 16:10 is *nphshi in shaul*.

HEAVEN: The Heb. is always in the plural, *shmim*, heavens, Gen. 1:1, Heb., as to origin, created *alcim* these heavens and this earth. Job 9:8, p. 40; 11:8, p. 49; 12:7, p. 53; 20:6, p. 93; 22:12, p. 100; 22:14, p. 100; 26:11, p. 110; 26:13, p. 111; 28:21, p. 116; 28:24, p. 117; 35:11 and note 3, p. 141; 38:29, p. 149; "bottles of heavens," Job 38:37. p. 150; Gen. 6:7, winged of these heavens: Douay, the fowls of the air; E. V. the same; Jer. 7:18, Douay..to make cakes to the queen of heaven; E. V. the same, (i. e., the moon).

HELL: Heb. *shaul*; see Grave, and *shaul*.

Hell fire, see Gehenna under *shaul*.

HOPE: For hope of impious, see Job 8:13, p. 38; 18:5, p. 72; 11:20, p. 51; 14:19, 20, p. 63; 15:22, p. 65; 15:30 and note 3, p. 66; 18:17, p. 73; 27:8, p. 112; 36:6, p. 142. And see under Perish. For Job 14:19, p. 63, Noyes gives, "so thou destroyest the hope of man," i. e., says he in a note, "the hope of living again after death."

HOPE OF JOB: Job 13:15, p. 57; 14:14 and notes 3 and 4, p. 61, 62; 17:15 and 16, and notes 4 and 5, p. 71, and note at the end of Chap. 40, p. 157; and Job 19:25, 26, 27, and the note to these verses at the end of Chap. 19, p. 76.

IMMORTALITY: How Professor Eadie, and the "American Bible Union" would make Job teach inherent immortality, p. 80, 83. And see Romans 2:7, cited p. 89, 2d paragraph; and see how Rev. Albert Barnes, D. D., would derive it from 2 Tim. 1:10, p. 87, 88.

In Wisdom of Solomon, in the so-called Apocrypha, Chap. 3, v. 4, we have in the Greek: For and though in sight of men *kolasthosin* [from *kolazo*] they be cut off, the hope of them, of immortality full: (i. e., they had in life that hope.) Douay, and though in the sight of men they suffered torments, their hope *is* full of immortality. E. V., for though they be punished in the sight of men, yet *is* their hope full of immortality. All the Books called Apocryphal were received as canonical by the Jews, and they agree in doctrine with the other Scriptures.

ITALICS: Words inserted in the Douay, Italian, and E. V., are put in italics.

JUST: The character Job in the drama represents a just man, 17:9, p. 70.

JUSTICE : A word used in the Douay, and in the E. V., is in the Hebrew and the Greek, justness, Job 19 : 7 and note 3, p. 74.

LAID DOWN WITH FATHERS OF HIM : Job 3 : 13 and note 2, p. 16. In 24 : 24, p. 107, the Heb. is " they are gathered," i. e., says Ges., note 3, " to their ancestors," i. e., says he, " they are dead." Gen. 15 : 15 is, " and thou shalt go to thy fathers in peace; thou shalt be buried in old age good." A marginal note to this v. in the Brown Bible by the Patersons says, " this phrase, ' thou shalt go to thy fathers,' seems plainly to intimate the existence of souls after death ! "

LIGHTNING : Heb., sons of lightning, Job 5 : 7, p. 28. Lightnings, " they go and say to thee, behold us," Job 38 : 35, p. 150.

LOCKE, JOHN, views of : See SLEEP OF DEATH.

LOST : Job 4 : 7, p. 24.

LUCIFER : p. 50 and 51, note 4; and p. 68, note 1.

LUTHER : What he says of Pope Leo tenth's decree of the dogma of the Papacy,—inherent immortality, p. 48. The decree is p. 47, in note.

MARTYRS : p. 92, 93 in note.

MILTON, JOHN : Views of, p. 78, 79.

PERISH : In Job 3 : 3, p. 15; 4 : 7, p. 24; 4 : 11, p. 25; 4 : 20, p. 26, " to eternity they perish ; " 6 : 18, p. 33; 8 : 13, p. 38; 11 : 20, p. 51; 12 : 23, p. 55 ; 14 : 19, p. 63; 18 : 17, p. 73; 30 : 7, p. 93, " as dung of him to eternity he shall perish ;" eleven passages ; the Heb. verb used is *abd*, defined, " to be lost, to perish, to be destroyed," citing many passages; among them, Jer. 10 : 11, where the Heb. is .. gods that heavens and earth not have made *iabdu*, (from *abd*), shall perish, from earth and from under heavens these; the Douay there is, The gods that have not made heaven and earth, let them perish from the earth, and from among those places that are under heaven. See E. V. And see Job 24 20, p. 106 ; 24 : 24, p. 107 ; 30 : 2, p. 122. Redeeming breath of him from to perish in pit, Job 33 : 28, p. 136, and v. 30; and Job 36 : 12 and notes 5 and 6, p. 142.

PIT : Equivalent to *shaul*, grave, Job 17 : 14, p. 71, notes 3 and 4 ; 33 : 24 and note 2, p. 136 ; Job 9 : 31 and note 7, p. 43; and Job 33 : 30 p. 136.

PUNISHMENT : The word used in the Rheims, and E. V. of Matt. 25 : 46; see Job 36 : 20 and note 8, p. 143, and the remarks on the words " cut off," p. 143, 144, 145, at the end of Chap. 36.

The *opsonia*—wages, pay, of sin, death, Rom. 6 : 23. Orthodoxy says, death is a figure of speech for eternal life in misery. And the entire system of orthodoxy rests on this perversion. I have the pleasure of an acquaintance with a lady known to fame as " one of the finest poets in all New England," (the land of poets), and as the author of a beautiful volume of exquisite poems, entitled "Gold Thread," who, having seen in the "Theology of the Bible," the language of the late Archbishop Whately, of the English Church, (the ablest ecclesiastic of the century), that the church " does not make it a point of Christian faith to interpret figuratively and not literally the death and destruction spoken of in Scripture as the doom of the condemned, and to insist on the belief that they are to be kept alive forever," wrote a very polite and earnest letter to several of the most distinguished clergymen, one of them a Gamaliel, asking each whether he read the word "death" in Rom. 6 : 23 figuratively. They all put their hands to their mouths,—failed to answer, except one who had kicked out of the traces, and was therefor muzzled by the sect to which he belonged. He gracefully answered, that he read the word literally.

In 2 Thess. 1 : 9 we have Greek, These (see v. 8) penalty shall pay, *olethron (olethros* is defined in Liddell and Scott "destruction, death,") *aionion*—destruction, death, eternal, from face of the Lord, Master, and from the glory of the power of him : v. 10, When he shall come to be glorified *en*—in or through the holies of him, and to be wondered at *en* all them that believe in that day. The Rheims is, v. 9, Who shall suffer eternal punishment in destruction, from the face of the Lord and from the glory of his power; v. 10, When he shall come to be glorified in his saints, &c. See E. V.

REDEEMER : Meaning of the word in Job 19 : 25, p. 81, and p. 85 last half; and Job 33 : 28, 30, p. 136. And in Ps. 49: 16, E. V. v. 15, we have Heb., But God will redeem *nphsh* of me from *id shaul*,—hand of grave, see E. V. And in Hosea 13 : 14 we have, Heb. from *id shaul*—hand of grave—I will redeem them, from death I will redeem them ; I will be destruction, or death, of thee, death ; I will be cutting off of thee, *shaul*. The Douay is, I will deliver them out of the hand of death. I will redeem them from death : O death, I will be thy death, O hell, I will be thy bite. See E. V. Prof. Charles Wilson, of the University of St. Andrews, Scotland, p. 229 of his Heb. Grammar, writes "*id shaul*," hand of grave, and renders "the hand of the grave;" see p. 157, near foot, and 158. Where *he* for *I*, in Job 19 : 25, came from, see p. 88, foot, and p. 89. And *he* is used for *I* in Job 13 : 28 and note 2, p. 59. For the Septuagint rendering of the three verses, Job 19 : 25, 26, 27, see p. 89, and what is said of the Greek rendering at the foot of that page.

RESURRECTION : Job 7 ; 9 and note 6, p. 35 ; 8 : 19, p. 39, and the remark at the foot of that page; 14:14 and notes 3 and 4, p. 61, 62; 19 : 25, p. 76, and note at the end of Chap. 19, and p. 88, 89, in note ;

20:7 and note 3, p. 93; 21:30 and note 12, p. 98, 99; 21:32 and notes 1 and 2, p. 99; 24:19 and notes 8, 9, 10, 11, p. 106, 107; 27:8 and note 5, p. 112; 27:15 and note 3, p. 113; 27:19 and notes 5 and 6, p. 113; Ps. 16:10, Heb..that not wilt thou leave *nphshi*, poetical for *me*, in *shaul*; Douay..my soul in hell; Ital.. my *anima* in the sepulchre; E. V..my soul in hell; Ps. 49;12, E. V., v. 11, p. 81, last half. Some copies of the Heb. have *qrb* inwards, entrails, by mistake for *qbr* grave, and my copy has *qrb*. The Septuagint gives grave, a conclusive proof that the Hebrew from which the Septuagint was translated had the right word; and the Latin and the Douay follow the Septuagint. Ps. 49;15, like sheep in *shaul* they place them; see p. 81. Prov. 21:16, see E. V. Isa. 26:14, see E. V. Prov. 26:19, see E. V. Luke 20:35, 36, *Gr.* they who shall be accounted worthy of that *aion*, life, age, (so defined) are children of God, being children of the resurrection. John 12:46, *Gr..* that every who believing in me, in that darkness not may stay. Acts 4:2, *Gr..* and proclaimed, through Jesus the resurrection from among dead. (They did not proclaim through Jesus, but they proclaimed the resurrection through Jesus). The Rheims is.. and preached in Jesus the resurrection from the dead. And see under Calvinism, how Prof. Eadie, would make Job teach the resurrection of all the dead, p. 81. In Rom. 6:5, the Greek is..also of the resurrection we shall be. Ital..*in the likeness of his* resurrection; see E. V., there is no *gr.* for the words inserted, they are wrong. His resurrection was without undergoing corruption. And for Resurrection, see under *Corrections*, and under *Darkness*, and under *Death*, and under *Hope*, and under *Sleep of Death*.

In the persecution of the Jews by Antiochus, The Douay (my copy of the Hebrew has not the Apocrypha) of 2 Maccabees 7: 14, (the Chapter headed "The glorious martyrdom of the seven brethren and their mother,") is: And when he (the fourth) was ready to die, he spoke thus: It is better, being put to death by men, to look for hope from God, to be raised up again by him; for as to thee (the King) thou shalt have no resurrection unto life; the E. V. of the v. is: It is good, being put to death by men, to look for hope from God to be raised up again by him; as for thee (the King) thou shalt have no resurrection to life.

I asked a Bishop of the Episcopal Church whether there would be a resurrection of any one if Christ had not died and been raised from the dead. He promptly answered, "Certainly not." I replied, "that covers the whole ground." If they who shall be accounted just cannot be raised without raising the wicked to an eternity of woe, it would be better on orthodox views, that there should be no resurrection.

RIGHT: That which is just; Job 19:7, p. 74; 19:29, p. 76: 22:4, p. 100; 23:7, p. 103; 27:2, p. 111; 31:13, p. 128; 36:17, p. 143; 40:8, . p. 155.

ROGERS, JOHN: Who he was, and what he did, for which he suffered martyrdom at the hands of the Apostasy, p. 92.

SATAN: Job 1:6; Preface p. 4, last paragraph; sermon of Rev. Doct. Mendes, of the 44th Street New York Synagogue, p. 26, 27, in note. How Noah Webster gets Satan, Job 11:17 and note 4, p. 50, 51, in note 4.

SHADES: Job 26 : 5 and note 3, p. 108, 109, 110; Job 10 : 21 and note 9, p. 46, 47.

SHAUL: Noyes's rendering of *shaul*, p. 87. *Shaul* is used eight times in Job, namely, 7 : 9, p. 35; 11 : 8, p. 49; 14 : 13, p. 61; 17 : 13 and 16, p. 71; 21 : 13, page 97; 24 : 19, p. 106; 26 : 6, p. 110. *Shaul* is used seven times in the Pentateuch—the five books of Moses, called the law : They are given in note 2, p. 61, with the different renderings of the word in those verses.

Gehenna. The Rheims New Testament uses the word hell seven times in Matt., three times in Mark, once in Luke, and once in James. In two places it uses the words "hell fire," namely, Matt. 5 : 22, and 18 : 9; and in Mark 9 : 46, "the fire of hell;" the E. V. is v. 47, "hell fire." In all these twelve places the Greek word is *geenna;* the Italian, *geenna;* the Latin, *gahenna.* The Greek word *geenna* is formed from the two Hebrew words for the valley of Hinnom, mentioned in the old Testament. In Jer. 7 : 31 it is called, the valley of the son of Hinnom. It was a valley near Jerusalem in which the filth of that city was burned up—consumed. The Greek, the Italian, and the Latin, use *geenna* for the two Heb. words. They who made the Rheims New Testament thought it better to give for *geenna*, the word *hell.* Hence we have "hell fire;" better suited to the notions of the Papacy.

Fire is the consuming element, as well as the purifying element. And Christ used the fire of that valley as a figure for utter destruction. But some, particularly preachers who say, "give them more hell," would have it to be a figure for the eternal conscious existence in misery of what they call the souls of the wicked. The mere statement of the pretension shows its absurdity. The E. V. follows the Rheims, and gives the same amount of "hell fire" and of "hell."

Christ was buried, 1 Cor. 15 : 4. He went to the dead, for God raised him from the dead. Rom. 4 : 24. The Apostle's creed is, "he descended into hell." The Nicene creed is, "he was buried." Having learned that *hell* means the grave, we learn that both creeds mean the same thing, and mean just what

Paul says: "he was buried." So simple is truth when it is found.

The Jews buried in gardens, 2 Kings 21 : 18, 26. Jesus was buried in garden. Our word *paradise* is an untranslated word, "a word of Persian origin, found also in other Eastern tongues, and means a garden."—*Eadie*. The Heb. word in the Old Testament for which the Greek gives *paradeisos* is *gn*—garden. In Luke 23 : 43, Jesus says to the penitent thief on the cross.... Thou wilt be with me in *paradeiso*—in garden, i. e. in burial : Ital....in *paradiso :* Rheims....in paradise : E. V....in paradise. To be with Christ in burial, is, to be in a grave from which there will be a resurrection. And see 2 Cor. 12 : 2 and 4, for Paul's ecstasy : "caught up to the third heaven,","into *paradise*," i. e. garden of delight. In Ezek. 36 : 35 the Heb. is, *gn oden*—garden of delight : Douay, garden of pleasure : Ital., garden of Eden : E. V., the same.

See a plain proposition at the end of this index.

SLEEP OF DEATH : Job 3 : 13, p. 16.

The great John Locke, in his Treatise entitled "Reasonableness of Christianity," citing Gen. 2 : 17....in the day....thou shalt surely die, says : "Ecclesiastics read the last *thou, thy body* shall surely die." "So that the reading of the ecclesiastics would be, in the day thy body eateth thereof thy body shall die." He proceeds to say : "A law requires the plainest and directest words ; yet some insist that death means eternal life in misery." Locke further says : "By *death* I understand nothing but a ceasing to be ; under which death they should have lain for ever, had it not been for the redemption by Jesus Christ." He says further : "Loss of immortality is the portion of sinners ; " i. e. non-acquisition of immortality from the grave ; for he has before said : "Death is a ceasing to be"....as above. And he further says : "That living torment is worse than no being at all every one's sense determines, against vain philosophy and foolish metaphysics."

SOUL : Heb. *nphsh*, see Breath.

The Papal dogma—inherent immortality, condemned by the Reformers, p. 47, 48.

What John Eadie, D. D., LL. D., Professor of Biblical Literature and Exegesis to the United Presbyterian Church, in his "Biblical Cyclopædia," says of the word "soul, p. 78. And see what John Milton says of it, p. 78 79. How Noyes thinks the "separate existence of the soul seems to be implied," see p. 86, 87.

Every breathing thing is called in the Hebrew an *nphsh*—a breath, by synecdoche, a figure of speech which puts an essential part for the whole. So in the Hebrew, every flesh is, by the same figure, put for every breathing flesh. The Heb. generally puts the noun before the adjective, and before the participle; and so does the Greek. The Heb. gives *nphsh hie*—breath living, and the Greek *psuche zosa*, breath living, where the Douay and E. V. have "living soul." These two Heb. words *nphsh hie*, and their Greek equivalents are used together fourteen times in the Heb. and Greek Scriptures, and in thirteen of these places, all but Gen. 2:7, they are used of the lower orders of animals: see p. 82. No wonder Prof. Eadie could not find anything immortal in the word soul. In Ezek. 47:9 the Heb. has the two words *nphsh hie*,—breath,—soul—living: the Douay there gives "every living creature," and the E. V. every thing that liveth, see p. 82, 83. Why did not the Douay give "living creature" for the same two words in Gen. 2:7.

uphsh, breath, soul—in entrails, see note, p. 133, 134.

SPIRIT: Heb, *ruh*: see under Breath: the Latin word used for *ruh* is *spiritus*: see under Breathe after. Our word *expire* should be written exspire: it is the Latin verb *exspiro*, to out-breathe,—breathe entirely out; we don't put the letter s in it; the sound of the s is included in the sound of the x. For the meaning of the word *spirit*, both in Scripture and in the Latin writers, see Job 12:10 and note 6, p. 53, 54; Job 30:15, p. 124; 30:22 and notes 2 and 3, p. 125. Spirit, soul, ghost, all mean the same, Job 10:12 and note 4, p. 45 For where the Douay and E. V. *soul* and *spirit* are in man, see Job 27:3 p. 111; 32:18 and note 6, p. 132, and note to the Douay and E. V. words, "the spirit within me," p. 133, 134. Every living thing has spirit, Numb. 16:22. Heb.. God of the *ruht*—breaths—spirits—in every flesh; Douay.. God of the spirits of all flesh; E. V.. the same. In 1 Cor. 15:39, Paul gives the four kinds of flesh.

What Prof. Eadie would make of the word *spirit*, see p. 78, the paragraph beginning Under "soul," and p. 79, the last two paragraphs; and see Job 33:23, p. 136, and the note at the end of Chap. 36, p. 137, 8, 9.

For what John Milton understood by the word *spirit* see p. 78.

How Prof. Eadie would "infer" immortal spirit from 1 Thess. 5:23, and Hebrews 4:12, see p. 90, 91, 92, 93; and see what Milton says of those verses, p. 78, 79.

For "Holy Spirit," "Holy Ghost," see Prof. Eadie's citation of the phrases, p. 79, last paragraph. The Greek, as usual, puts the noun first, and the two Greek words are *pneuma agion; pneuma* is defined in Liddell and Scott's Greek Lexicon, wind, air, the air we breathe, breath; *agion* is the neuter of the Greek *agios*, agreeing in gender with *pneuma*; *agios* is defined in the same

Lex., holy, pious, pure. We give but a single example, "Holy Ghost" and "Holy Spirit," meaning the same. In Acts 5:3 the Greek is..why has filled that *satanas* thy heart to belie the *pneuma* the *agion*—the breath (or spirit) the holy; we have only to give the equivalent definition and render, the breath the pious, to show plainly the meaning of the words. The Rheims is..that thou shouldst lie to the Holy Ghost, (a sheer perversion): the E. V. follows the Rheims. In Ps. 104:4 E. V., the Douay is: Who makest thy angels spirits.

SPIRITISM: (wrongly called spiritualism): see p. 54 in note; and in Heb. 1:7 the Rheims is: He that maketh his angels spirits. See the E. V. of these verses: the correct rendering of them is, he maketh his messengers the winds; see note at the end of Chap. 33, p. 137, 8, 9; and p. 125 note 3; and p. 28, 2d paragraph; and p. 86, Noyes' "disembodied spirit," man's language.

Another passage in which "spirits," plural, is used, is 1 Peter 3:19. The Ital. is, In the which also he went *formerly*, and preached to the *spiriti*—breaths—that *are* in prison: see E. V. Archbishop Whately says: "This passage has been supposed to allude to a conscious state of departed spirits, but this seems to me (him) a very unlikely interpretation." And he then gives three interpretations of the passage, one by Bishop Hall, one by Archbishop Secker, and one by Bishop Pearson. These interpretations all say, that the preaching was to the living antediluvians; and that it was not Christ that preached to them, but Noah. The Greek is..heralded to those *pneumasi*—(plural of *pneuma*)—breaths,—spirits—in guard, (i. e., that are now in guard, i. e., in the grave, see Job 21:32 and note 2; 11:10 and note 7; 12:14 and note 1), We thus see that the living antediluvians were called breaths,—spirits; the Gr. *pneuma* breath,—spirit—being equivalent to the Gr. *psuche*—breath—soul, often used for the living person, as the Heb. *ruh* (for which the Gr. uses *pneuma*) is used as equivalent to the Heb. *nphsh*. Bishop Pearson says: the preaching was to the antediluvians "by the ministry of a prophet, by the sending of Noah, a preacher of righteousness," see 2 Pet. 2:5. It is plain that it was by means of the *pneuma* proceeding from God, the same *pneuma* with which v. 18 ends, and by which the Christ was made alive again, that Noah preached to the antediluvians. The Gr. *poreutheis* in v. 19, for which the Ital. and the E. V. give "he went," is, being sent. Bishop Pearson gives "by the sending." Noah was the messenger, the one sent.

In Rom. 1:4 we have, Gr. *pneuma agiosunes*—breath of holiness: Rheims..spirit of sanctification: E. V., spirit of holiness. 1 Thess. 3:13, Gr..blameless in holiness: Rheims and E. V. the same. 1 Thess. 4:7, Rheims, God hath called us unto sanctification: E. V., unto holiness, v. 8, God, who hath given *the pneuma the agion*—the breath—the holy—of him in us: Rheims, his holy spirit in us: E. V., his holy spirit unto us.

TRANSLATORS: The first translators of the Bible from the originals into English, and what became of them and their translations, p. 92, 93.

TYNDALE: Who he was, and what he did, and what was his end, p. 92.

WICKED, Hope of: See under Hope; and see Job 21:30 and notes 11 and 12, p. 98. The Douay and the E. V. there are wrong. And see Job 40:13, and notes 4 and 5, p. 155. And see under *Perish*.

WIND: See under Breath, *ruh;* and under Angel. And see Job 30:22 and note 2, p. 125.

WITCH OF ENDOR: p. 87.

WORM: Man a worm; Job 25:6, p. 108.

A PLAIN PROPOSITION.

The Old Testament writings were the only Scriptures the Messiah and his Apostles had, and the Scriptures men were told to search. The proposition is: If in the Old Testament death is eternal nothingness to the wicked, it can't mean eternal life in misery in the New Testament. And if in the Old Testament, hell means the grave, it can't mean the Papacy's hell in the New Testament. And if the Old Testament teaches the resurrection of the just only, (i. e. of them who shall be accounted just), the New Testament cannot teach the resurrection of the wicked. It is worse than idle to say, or imagine, that Christ, or his Apostles, added, or could add, any new feature to the system taught in their Scriptures. The New Testament could not contradict the Old; and correctly translated it does not, but agrees with it in every feature. And as to faith, faith under the Old Testament was faith in a Messiah to come. Under the New Testament, Christian faith is faith in the Messiah come.

And now I affirm with entire confidence, that whoever reads this book, with willingness to learn, will become satisfied that the system which the Papacy imposed on Christendom, centuries before the Reformation, and which, after the Reformation, it reimposed, in its essential features, by almost incredible persecutions, (see pages 91, 92, 93,) is wholly unscriptural. And whoever will so read this book will also have gained what it is said, Sir Walter Raleigh longed for, namely, the peace of an assured faith.

www.ingramcontent.com/pod-product-compliance
Lightning Source LLC
Chambersburg PA
CBHW031440160426
43195CB00010BB/800